Basic Fundamentals of Marketing

Basic Fundamentals of Marketing

Anshuman Sharma

RANDOM

RANDOM PUBLICATIONS

NEW DELHI (INDIA)

Basic Fundamentals of Marketing

ISBN 978-93-5111-343-0

Published in 2014 in India by

Reprint 2020

RANDOM PUBLICATIONS
4376-A/4B, Gali Murari Lal, Ansari Road
New Delhi-110 002
Phone : +91-11-43580356, +91-11-23289044
e-mail: randomexports@gmail.com, sales@randompublications.com,
info@randompublications.com

Type Setting by : Keystoneprintads, Delhi-110051
Printed at : Mehra Printers, Delhi-110 092

Preface

Marketing staff will work together to develop a more customer and market-driven approach. They will understand how an integrated marketing approach will benefit the organisation in terms of efficient and effective performance in the marketplace.

The key principles learnt on the workshop can be directly applied in the workplace. Marketing Management is a business discipline which is focused on the practical application of marketing techniques and the management of a firm's marketing resources and activities. Rapidly emerging forces of globalization have compelled firms to market beyond the borders of their home country making International marketing highly significant and an integral part of a firm's marketing strategy.

Marketing managers are often responsible for influencing the level, timing, and composition of customer demand accepted definition of the term. In part, this is because the role of a marketing manager can vary significantly based on a business' size, corporate culture, and industry context.

Organisations are increasingly recognising the importance of marketing's role and contribution in achieving sustainable growth and profitability. Marketing is critical in delivering high quality and differentiated products and services that deliver value to targeted intermediaries and end users.

Any factor that could be considered important to the understanding of a particular business. Fundamentals are usually considered outside the context of the market as a whole. Some examples of fundamentals include a company's growth, revenues, earnings, management, and capital structure. The use of fundamentals as an investment strategy is called fundamental analysis in marketing.

Marketing is used to identify the customer, to keep the customer, and to satisfy the customer. With the customer as the focus of its activities, it can be concluded that marketing management is one of the major components of business management.

The evolution of marketing was caused due to mature markets and overcapacities in the last 2-3 centuries. Companies then shifted the focus from production to the customer in order to stay profitable. This book focuses on the key concepts and functions that are common to most marketing situations.

I thank all associates of my group who have helped in the preparation of the book. My individual thanks go to "Random Publications" who have in print the book.

— *Anshuman Sharma*

Contents

Preface ... *v-vi*

1. Introduction ... 1

Scope of Marketing ... 3
Concept of Marketing ... 4
Functions of Marketing ... 8
Social Responsibility in Marketing ... 17
Ethics in Marketing ... 20
Futures Markets ... 25

2. Marketing Management ... 31

Introduction ... 31
Capital Requireds in Marketing Management ... 35
Direct Marketing Management ... 44
Managing Product Movement ... 54
Modern Marketing Management ... 59

3. Marketing Environment ... 65

Elements of the Marketing Environment ... 65
Marketing Term of Marketing Environment ... 68
Indian Marketing Environment ... 71
Economic Impacts on Specific Stakeholder Groups ... 73
Governmental Environment in Marketing ... 79
Performance Management and Appraisal ... 85
Global Marketing Environment ... 93

4. Marketing Planning and Strategy ... 96

Introduction ... 96
Marketing Plan ... 100
Importance of Marketing Planning ... 102
Components of Strategic Planning ... 110
Models of Strategic Planning ... 113
The Five-Factor Model ... 115
Basics of Strategic Planning ... 122

5. **Industrial Marketing** **156**

Introduction 156
Characteristics of the Industrial Marketing 156
Scope of the Industrial Market 161
Industry Analysis 164
Development and Growth in Derivative Products 174

6. **Marketing Research Management** **183**

Introduction 183
Importance of Marketing Research 184
Marketing Research Process 186
Role of Marketing Research 190
Classification of Marketing Research 191

7. **Consumer Marketing and Behaviour** **206**

An Overview 206
Customer Value 208
Consumer Buying Behaviour 210
Continuous Consumer Panels 210
Types of Consumer Purchase Decisions 213

8. **Brand Management** **254**

Introduction 254
Brand Architecture 255
Trademark 261
Corporate Branding 262
Importance of Brand Awareness 263
Branding Decisions 267

Index **288**

1

Introduction

Marketing is the process by which companies determine what products or services may be of interest to customers, and the strategy to use in sales, communications and business development. It is an integrated process through which companies create value for customers and build strong customer relationships in order to capture value from customers in return.

Marketing is used to identify the customer, to keep the customer, and to satisfy the customer. With the customer as the focus of its activities, it can be concluded that *marketing management* is one of the major components of business management. The evolution of marketing was caused due to mature markets and overcapacities in the last 2-3 centuries. Companies then shifted the focus from production to the customer in order to stay profitable.

The term *marketing concept* holds that achieving organizational goals depends on knowing the needs and wants of target markets and delivering the desired satisfactions. It proposes that in order to satisfy its organizational objectives, an organization should anticipate the needs and wants of consumers and satisfy these more effectively than competitors.

Marketing: Several definitions have been proposed for the term marketing. Each tends to emphasize different issues. Memorizing a definition is unlikely to be useful; ultimately, it makes more sense to thinking of ways to benefit from creating customer value in the most effective way, subject to ethical and other constraints that one may have. The 2006 and 2007 definitions offered by the American Marketing Association are relatively similar, with the 2007 appearing a bit more concise.

Note that the definitions make several points:

- A main objective of marketing is to create customer value.
- Marketing usually involves an exchange between buyers and sellers or between other parties.
- Marketing has an impact on the firm, its suppliers, its customers, and others affected by the firm's choices.
- Marketing frequently involves enduring relationships between buyers, sellers, and other parties.

- Processes involved include "creating, communicating, delivering, and exchanging offerings."

Delivering customer value. The central idea behind marketing is the idea that a firm or other entity will create something of value to one or more customers who, in turn, are willing to pay enough to make the venture worthwhile considering opportunity costs. Value can be created in a number of different ways. Some firms manufacture basic products but provide relatively little value above that. Other firms make products whose tangible value is supplemented by services.

It is not necessary for a firm to physically handle a product to add value—e.g., online airline reservation systems add value by:

- Compiling information about available flight connections and fares,
- Allowing the customer to buy a ticket,
- Forwarding billing information to the airline, and
- Forwarding reservation information to the customer.

It should be noted that value must be examined from the point of view of the customer. Some customer segments value certain product attributes more than others. A very expensive product—relative to others in the category—may, in fact, represent great value to a particular customer segment because the benefits received are seen as even greater than the sacrifice made. Some segments have very unique and specific desires, and may value what—to some individuals—may seem a "lower quality" item—very highly.

SOME FORMS OF CUSTOMER VALUE

The marketing process involves ways that value can be created for the customer. *Form utility* involves the idea that the product is made available to the consumer in some form that is more useful than any commodities that are used to create it. A customer buys a chair, for example, rather than the wood and other components used to create the chair. Thus, the customer benefits from the specialization that allows the manufacturer to more efficiently create a chair than the customer could do himself or herself. *Place utility* refers to the idea that a product made available to the customer at a preferred location is worth more than one at the place of manufacture.

It is much more convenient for the customer to be able to buy food items in a supermarket in his or her neighbourhood than it is to pick up these from the farmer. *Time utility* involves the idea of having the product made available when needed by the customer. The customer may buy a turkey a few days before Thanksgiving without having to plan to have it available. Intermediaries take care of the logistics to have the turkeys—which are easily perishable and bulky to store in a freezer—available when customers demand them. *Possession utility* involves the idea that the consumer can go to one store and obtain a large assortment of goods from different manufacturers during one shopping occasion. Supermarkets combine food and other household items from a number of different suppliers in one place. Certain "superstores" such as the European *hypermarkets* and the Wal-Mart "super centres" combine even more items into one setting.

MARKETING VS. THE SELLING CONCEPT

Two approaches to marketing exist. The traditional *selling* concept emphasizes selling existing products. The philosophy here is that if a product is not selling, more aggressive measures must be taken to sell it—e.g., cutting price, advertising more, or hiring more aggressive sales-people. When the railroads started to lose business due to the advent of more effective trucks that could deliver goods right to the customer's door, the railroads cut prices instead of recognizing that the customers ultimately wanted *transportation* of goods, *not* necessarily *railroad* transportation. Smith Corona, a manufacturer of typewriters, was too slow to realise that consumers wanted the ability to process documents and *not* typewriters per se. The *marketing* concept, in contrast, focuses on getting consumers what they seek, *regardless of whether this entails coming up with entirely new products.*

The 4 *Ps*—*product, place, promotion,* and *price*—represent the variables that are within the control of the firm. In contrast, the firm is faced with uncertainty from the environment.

SCOPE OF MARKETING

Marketing people are involved in marketing 10 types of entities: Goods, services, experiences, events, persons, places, properties, organizations, information, and ideas.

Goods: Physical goods constitute the bulk of most countries' production and marketing effort. The United States produces and markets billions of physical goods, from eggs to steel to hair dryers. In developing nations, goods—particularly food, commodities, clothing, and housing—are the mainstay of the economy.

Services: As economies advance, a growing proportion of their activities are focused on the production of services. The U.S. economy today consists of a 70–30 services-to-goods mix. Services include airlines, hotels, and maintenance and repair people, as well as professionals such as accountants, lawyers, engineers, and doctors. Many market offerings consist of a variable mix of goods and services.

Experiences: By orchestrating several services and goods, one can create, stage, and market experiences. Walt Disney World's Magic Kingdom is an experience; so is the Hard Rock Cafe.

Events: Marketers promote time-based events, such as the Olympics, trade shows, sports events, and artistic performances.

Persons: Celebrity marketing has become a major business. Artists, musicians, CEOs, physicians, high-profile lawyers and financiers, and other professionals draw help from celebrity marketers.

Places: Cities, states, regions, and nations compete to attract tourists, factories, company headquarters, and new residents. Place marketers include economic development specialists, real estate agents, commercial banks, local business associations, and advertising and public relations agencies.

Properties: Properties are intangible rights of ownership of either real property or financial property. Properties are bought and sold, and this occasions a marketing effort by real estate agents and investment companies and banks.

Organizations: Organizations actively work to build a strong, favourable image in the mind of their publics. Philips, the Dutch electronics company, advertises with the tag line, "Let's Make Things Better." The Body Shop and Ben and Jerry's also gain attention by promoting social causes. Universities, museums, and performing arts organizations boost their public images to compete more successfully for audiences and funds.

Information: The production, packaging, and distribution of information is one of society's major industries. Among the marketers of information are schools and universities; publishers of encyclopedias, and specialized magazines; makers of CDs; and Internet Web sites.

Ideas: Every market offering has a basic idea at its core. In essence, products and services are platforms for delivering some idea or benefit to satisfy a core need.

CONCEPT OF MARKETING

Since the later part of the 19th century, marketing has gradually evolved through various marketing orientations. These stages in marketing evolution present a generalised picture and a sufficiently significant number of companies have adopted the most modern marketing concept or philosophy.

CONCEPT OF SELLING

Sales concept seems to be based on a lurking apprehension that customers will not buy the product in sufficient quantities unless aggressively pressurised. The selling concept was the major means of increasing sales and profits during 1920s to 1950s in the developed countries of that period. Companies believed that the most important marketing activities were personal selling, advertising, and distribution. Selling concept is geared towards converting existing product(s) into cash rather than first finding and then satisfying customer needs.

Sales concept is often observed in practice when companies show heavy reliance on their promotional capabilities based on "hard sell" approach. It is obvious that if a company's products do not match the changing tastes and requirements of customers, with many alternative choices available, managers might be inclined to go for aggressive promotional efforts to sell enough quantities. In his book, The End of Marketing as We Know It, Sergio Zyman writes that the purpose of marketing is to sell more stuff to more people more often for more money in order to make more profit. Of late, this has been happening in case of some Credit Cards in our country. Generally, "hard sell" is often seen in case of products or services that people buy without giving much thought to the matter, such as non-essential goods, and tend to postpone such purchases. With ever intensifying competition, products becoming more standardised without any meaningful differentiation *i.e.*, commoditization, heavy promotional efforts in all possible manners are bound to remain the practice, in order to grab more share of the customers' purse. The consequences of "hard sell" might harm the customer base to the extent that, in some cases, they might even bad-mouth the product if the product fails to match up to their expectations.

CONCEPT OF PRODUCTION

This concept, viewed as one of the oldest of managerial orientations, typically aimed at achieving as high an output as possible. This philosophy assumed that customers would be more interested in acquiring conveniently available, reasonably priced, and well-made products. Keeping in view the market behaviour prevailing in times when customers did not have much choice, it was a sound approach. The focus of managers, generally having backgrounds in manufacturing and engineering, was to concentrate on achieving increasingly higher efficiency in production, lower production costs, and more intensive distribution. Even today, this approach seems to be quite sensible in relatively underdeveloped and developing economies because customers are more interested in owning a product and not overly concerned about finer features and aesthetic appeal.

In general, one important condition seems to be favourable to adopt production orientation: when the masses look for a cheaper product and demand far exceeds production. In India, The National Textile Corporation (NTC) and all its subsidiaries are sticking to this philosophy while producing textiles for the huge, poverty-stricken population in this country. Their philosophy and positioning is reflected in their ad, "Clothiers of the nation with affordable prices." In the global scenario, for nearly three decades Intel Corporation focused on achieving increasingly high production output of its successive generations of processors so as to bring down the prices of each improved version. The production concept is unlikely to get discarded for a very long time to come, because there would always be products and populations of such a nature that some companies would feel comfortable with this philosophy.

PROPOSES OF MARKETING CONCEPT ERA

Thus, the marketing concept era began. Marketing concept proposes that an organisation should focus on customer needs and wants, coordinate its efforts, and endeavour to accomplish organisational goals. Geraldine E Williams reported that the CEO of Nike said, "For years we thought of ourselves as a production-oriented company, meaning we put all our emphasis on designing and manufacturing the product. But now we understand that the most important thing we do is market the product." The major focus of all sets of organisational activities should be satisfying customer needs. This requires carefully listening to customers as a student listens to a teacher. Stanley F Slater and John C Narver reported that there is positive relationship between market orientation and performance. Sometimes, philosophies that sound quite reasonable and appear attractive on paper, are difficult to put into practice.

To embrace the marketing concept as the guiding philosophy, the concerned firm must accept certain general conditions and manage some problems. Alan Grant and Leonard Schlesinger are of the view that market-orientation requires organisation-wide generation of market intelligence across departments, and organization wide responsiveness to it.

It means establishing a reliable information system to learn about real needs of customers and design the right need satisfying solutions. Setting up an information system can usually be an expensive proposition and requires committing money and time to its development and maintenance. Company-wide coordination may require restructuring the internal operations and overall objectives in case of one or more departments.

Appreciating the critical role of marketing, the head of marketing has to be part of the top management team. Acceptance and implementation of marketing concept demands support of top management and other managers and staff. To inculcate a customer-orientation culture, it is necessary that employees at all levels in the organisation should understand the value of the customer and the importance of the customer satisfaction. Obviously, the internal customers (company employees at all levels) themselves should be satisfied and motivated to promote an organisation-wide culture that puts high value on creating a satisfied customer.

For this, the company has to ensure an appropriate work environment and take care of their legitimate needs. Benson P. Shapiro is of the opinion that a company is customer focused if the answers are "yes" to the four critical questions:

- Are we easy for customers to do business with?
- Do we keep our promises?
- Do we meet the standards we set?
- Are we responsive to customer needs?
- The marketing concept emphasises three main principles.

Achieve Organizational Goals: The reward of doing the job well will bring in sales and profits because without profits, the firm cannot survive, neither would it be in a position to improve its offers. Marketing concept is significantly different from production concept and selling concept. Not long ago, Indian auto companies, Hindustan Motors, Premier Automobiles, and

Bajaj Auto hardly showed any consideration for customers, producing obsolete models in large numbers (demand exceeded the supply). Though the prices kept on increasing, little was done to improve the models. Bajaj was the only manufacturer of scooters preferred by customers and to own one, customers had to deposit money in advance and wait for five to ten years before they could become proud owners. It is only after the entry of Maruti cars, with Japanese collaboration, that things started changing. Premier Auto, and Hindustan Motors experienced major setbacks, sales declined and ultimately there were hardly any willing buyers. In the beginning, Maruti found it difficult to meet the demand and buyers willingly booked the car and waited for delivery.

Bajaj Auto faced a similar situation as customers had many choices of two-wheelers. The position now appears as if almost every auto manufacturer is desperately trying to please customers. Customers have strong preferences for certain features and price ranges. Maruti has even started selling second-hand, reconditioned, and reliable cars from its outlets to customers looking for such deals, is order to expand its hold on the market.

In line with the marketing concept, it is imperative that the typical pyramid depicting an organisation needs to be inverted to pursue marketing concept. In an inverted position, the customer will occupy the highest pedestal and top management will be at the bottom position. The communication flow will start from the customer, and the employees and executives will look up to learn what the customer wants and then respond to the inputs. This is the way to offer desired value, deliver more satisfaction, and help retain the customer.

Marketing concept is sometimes interpreted as a philosophy of attempting to satisfy all customers' needs with no concern for the cost. This would seem to be a sure way to financial disaster. The marketing concept is consistent with the idea of taking into consideration only those customer segments that the company can satisfy both effectively and profitably. The firm has to earn profits to survive, offer new and better products and services, and be a meaningful member of society. A company might therefore choose to offer less costly products and services to unprofitable customer segments, or even avoid them altogether. Being market-oriented pays dividends and has a significant effect on company performance.

Organisational Activities: Mainly product planning, pricing, distribution, and promotion should be combined in a sensible and consistent manner, and the head of marketing should be a part of top-level management.

Planning and Implementations: It should be the sole aim of all employees, irrespective of their department or functional area, to satisfy customers' needs. It would require carefully segmenting the market on the basis of the right criteria, targeting suitable segment(s), learning about customer needs and wants, analysing and spotting the right opportunities and matching them with the company's strengths.

FUNCTIONS OF MARKETING

One of the best ways to obtain an appreciation of the nature and extent of the marketing task is through an understanding of the basic functions which are the essence of the marketing process.

MARKETING FUNCTIONS DEFINED AND LISTED

A marketing function may be defined as a major economic activity which is inherent in the marketing process, pervades it, and which, through a continuous division of labour, tends to become specialized. In this sense a marketing function is not a technique, a tool, or a special activity that may be properly considered as but a part or phase of some more basic function. Specialization may be intra organizational or inter organizational—the former is illustrated by the existence of salesmen or buyers in a marketing company and the latter by companies that specialize in the performance of a particular function or aspect of a function. The major functions which are recognized when marketing is viewed as a social process may be quite different from specific marketing activities which are performed by individual companies. Some writers have listed numerous detailed marketing activities of manufacturers or middlemen, and have proceeded to call them marketing functions, thus confusing the activities of selected individual enterprises with marketing functions, even though some of the activities are not universal in their application or inevitable, and despite the fact that marketing functions are also being performed daily by farmers and consumers.

Others have set down the numerous *activities* involved in marketing a given commodity and have labeled them marketing functions. This method, too, is subject to the objection that many of the activities in connection with a specific commodity are but part of a major marketing function or are not universally applicable. For the sake of simplicity and clarity, the authors have confined their statement of functions to those *major activities that must be performed in the marketing of all products*. These functions are:

- Buying
- Selling
- Transportation
- Storage
- Standardization and grading
- Financing
- Risk bearing
- Marketing information.

The first two of these functions are known as the *functions of exchange*, for they are directly concerned with the change in ownership. They are complementary in the sense that both are involved in every transaction. For every sale there is a purchase and for every purchase there must be a sale.

Transportation and storage are the *functions of supply,* frequently referred to as *physical distribution,* both having to do with the actual, physical handling of goods incident to their movement from places of plenty to places of relative scarcity or to their storage from times of plenty to times of scarcity, or with the provision of services at times and at places as needed. The remaining functions, namely, standardization, financing, risk bearing, and the collection and dissemination of marketing information, are *facilitating functions,* inasmuch as each of them aids in the performance of all of the other marketing functions.

To some critics it may appear that certain activities are not covered by these eight functions. The so-called function of *assembling* goods in large quantities for economical shipment and handling or from different sources for the purpose of providing an assortment of merchandise may, upon closer analysis, well be considered but a part of the buying function. Similarly, the so-called function of *dividing* large quantities into the smaller amounts required by customers is but a small part of the selling function; while *packaging,* which is sometimes named as a separate marketing function, is often but coincidental to the function of grading and standardization and may at times even be regarded as a manufacturing rather than marketing operation. It is therefore believed that practically all activities of those engaged in marketing are embraced in the functions herein outlined.

Universality of Marketing Functions

The significance of the functional concept lies in the universality of the major activities that are recognized as functions. Buying involves on the part of the purchaser a determination of the kind, quality, and quantity of products to be bought, and the choice of sellers from whom they are to be procured. From the stand point of the businessman, it may require a concentration of a quantity of like goods or the assembling of a number of different items from hundreds of sources of supply for the convenience of customers.

Selling includes the seeking out of markets, influencing of demand through advertising and sales promotional effort, actual sales through salesmen and other means, and the servicing of the sales after they have been effected. Selling is especially important in a competitive society where, driven by a desire for profits, vendors take the initiative in promoting and satisfying the wants of customers. That customers also benefit from these efforts by sellers.

Transportation is a marketing function which has greatly increased in relative importance in modern times. Even in the case of the simplest marketing mechanism, where the consumer buys directly from a local farm or factory, transportation is involved and must be performed either by buyer or seller. Such direct relationships are, however, not common. For example, the citrus fruit growers of Florida and California find their markets all over the United States and in Europe. Hardware manufacturers of the eastern states find good markets on the Pacific Coast, and the wheat of our Northwest has a world market.

The consumer is reluctant to anticipate his future needs and cannot or will not provide storage for goods in quantity. He demands that supplies be made accessible for satisfying his current wants. To meet these requirements marketing agencies must, in some way, provide for storage. One of the important services which the retailer performs is that of assembling and storing goods for the convenience of the consumer. Wholesalers find in the storage function one of the principal reasons for their existence. Back of the manufacturer, who also carries a stock of raw materials, goods in process, and finished goods, lies a marketing mechanism with many responsibilities in the storage of raw materials. Some storage is taken care of by the original producer on farms or at mines; further storage occurs at country points and in the cars in which the goods move to a central market.

Consumers generally prefer to purchase certain types of articles of a known size and quality. Manufacturers, like consumers, have need for special grades of materials. The manufacturer of cotton yarn must have raw cotton of certain grades or qualities, depending upon the kind of yarn to be manufactured. On the other hand, no grower can produce oranges of a single size and quality. Oranges as they come from the grove vary in any one season, and variable climatic factors may produce sharp differences between seasons. Hence, standardization and grading become an essential marketing activity.

The consumer is accustomed to receive financial assistance in connection with his purchases. He may ask the seller to extend credit, and the assistance or service may take other forms. The retailer, even when the consumer pays cash, assumes the financial function through investments in stocks of goods.

If the retailer receives credit extensions from the wholesaler, the latter assists in financing the retailer's operations. Wholesalers in their turn receive certain financial assistance from manufacturers. Finally, the capital of merchants and manufacturers is augmented by assistance received from financial institutions such as commercial banks.

The owner of goods always assumes the risks of price changes. Other contingencies, too, may bring losses. Fires and floods may destroy goods, or they may be stolen. Customers may fail to pay for their merchandise and cause bad debt losses to sellers. Crop failures and recessions may curtail demand. Certain of these contingencies can be insured against, as, for example, in the case of the losses due to fire, flood, and theft. However, the premiums paid add to the costs of operation, and the indemnity paid by the insurer rarely compensates for all losses.

In a few trades businessmen may minimize losses due to price changes in raw materials by hedging. In spite of hedging and modern insurance developments, many market risks must be borne by merchants and manufacturers, and the losses can be minimized only through the exercise of good business judgment.

The collection and dissemination of marketing information involves not merely the passive receipt or acceptance of information offered by sellers but active efforts to collect data from other sources, such as governmental institutions and trade associations. Moreover, the collection of information would be of little value unless it is interpreted and disseminated with skill and intelligence. No small part of business success is attributed to the skill with which specialized marketing research departments and companies collect, analyse, and distribute factual information that serves as the basis for marketing decisions.

Also, some marketing institutions such as brokers and resident buyers owe their existence, in large part, to their skill in obtaining, analyzing, and distributing information concerning sources of supply, prices and price trends, and other market conditions. From the foregoing it is apparent that *marketing functions are indispensable and universal, regardless of the institution that may choose to perform them or the commodity or service in connection with which they may be performed.* They pervade the entire marketing process and are inescapable.

A certain institution, like the retailer or wholesaler, may be eliminated in the distribution of a given product; but the marketing functions remain nevertheless, and someone else will be forced to undertake their performance. The result of such a change may be to raise the costs of marketing or to lower them, depending upon the effectiveness and efficiency of the new agency that has assumed the functions. Be the cycle of distribution long or short, complex or simple, the functions of marketing essentially remain unaltered and inevitable.

CHANNELS OF DISTRIBUTION

Still another method of judging the magnitude and complexity of the marketing task is by giving consideration to the multiplicity of channels through which products move from origin to destination.

Channel of Distribution Defined

The course taken in the transfer of title to a product constitutes its channel of distribution. The title may be transferred directly, as when the product is bought or sold outright, or indirectly, as when the transaction is negotiated through a functional middleman such as an agent or broker who does not himself actually take title to it. It is the *route taken by the title to a product in its passage from its first owner,* the agricultural producer or manufacturer as the case may be, *to the last owner,* the ultimate consumer or the business user. The links in the channel or chain of distribution of necessity include both such owners inasmuch as they always participate to some extent in the marketing process.

Vertical Aspects

Normally, the channel of distribution is viewed vertically, that is, from the standpoint of the various *types* of links of which it is composed. It is concerned with the number of levels through which the title to goods is passed in the flow from source to final destination. For example, a manufacturer may sell direct to consumers, or he may utilize different types of middlemen who perform a variety of functions at different stages in the flow of title transfer. The most common vertical variations in channels for consumer and industrial goods, respectively.

The simplest channel is obviously that where manufacturers sell direct to consumers. This is sometimes accomplished by those who make a wide line of related merchandise, the sales of which can support the operation of company-owned retail establishments. Stores operated by some manufacturers of paint or of men's clothing are illustrative. The direct channel is also used by manufacturers of articles that have qualities sufficiently distinctive to make possible mail-order sales. A third method of direct sale is through house-to-house salesmen.

A number of situations account for the manufacturer-retailer-consumer channel. Many manufacturers of men's and women's clothing sell direct to retailers, because the retailers handling such goods ordinarily purchase in fairly large quantities. This may be true because the stores are large. Vertical aspects of channels of distribution, illustrating channels commonly used by manufacturers of consumer and industrial goods, respectively.

The channel is also used by some manufacturers of perishable commodities. The meat packing industry is illustrative; here, sale to retailers through company-owned branches is common because of the financial strength of large producers and because of the special storage and handling requirements of the commodity. A less direct channel is to use agents or brokers to contact the retail trade. Such a channel is usually favoured by small or specialized manufacturers who cannot afford to maintain their own sales organizations. Sales may be made more economically through agents or brokers because their costs of distribution are spread over the product lines of several manufacturers. This channel is generally used in contacting large retailing organizations, such as chain stores, department stores, and larger specialty stores.

The manufacturer-wholesaler-retailer-consumer channel is most common in the distribution of convenience goods to independent retail stores. Most manufacturers of tobacco, hardware, drugs, groceries, and other convenience goods have only a few products in their line of merchandise and cannot economically contact the thousands of retail stores needed for adequate distribution. Consequently, they call upon wholesalers who stock merchandise and cultivate the entire retail market, even in the remotest regions. Then there are numerous companies whose potential sales volume is so small or whose business is of such a seasonal nature that they cannot develop a sales organization to contact even wholesalers. This accounts in large measure for the use of agents and brokers who serve as substitutes for a manufacturer's own selling organization. In the canned fruit and vegetable industry, for example, many small manufacturers market through food brokers, who render a comparable service to other grocery product companies, including many flour millers and beet sugar refining companies.

In marketing business or industrial goods, direct manufacturer-user relationships are more common. Industrial installations usually involve sales of high unit value and require factory-trained sales engineers for effective sale and service. Semi-manufactured goods, such as sheet steel and parts, like motors for washing machines, are usually sold in large individual contracts. Consequently, many manufacturers of such items are able to sell direct. Producers of standardized equipment and tools of the type used in numerous factories often find it more economical to distribute through industrial wholesalers. Operating in a manner similar to the consumer goods wholesaler, but selling to industrial users rather than to retail stores, these organizations are to be found in all principal cities and are known by such terms as *industrial distributors, mill supply houses, equipment distributors,* and so on. Short-line manufacturers of industrial goods often use agents and brokers for the same reason that these functional middlemen are used in consumer goods marketing.

Marketing Establishments of Integrated Firms

An important vertical phase of channels—namely, the position of marketing establishments that are owned and operated by integrated companies. Examples are manufacturer-owned retail stores, manufacturer-owned wholesale branches, warehouses, or petroleum bulk tank distributing stations, and retailer-owned wholesale warehouses.

According to a strict interpretation of the definition of the term *channel of distribution,* one may question the inclusion of such establishments in a discussion of channels. Actually, there is no *legal* transfer of title between factory and manufacturer-owned sales branch or retail store, nor is there any between the chain store warehouse and retail units in the same organization. Since, however, the census is taken on the basis of establishments and the information must be published for individual industries and lines of trade and by states and local areas, it is necessary that each reporting *unit* of a multiple-unit organization report as though it were operated as an independent establishment.

That procedure is followed by the Bureau of the Census, even when goods are transferred from one plant of a manufacturing company to another for further processing; and while they are designated as *interplant transfers,* they are viewed as in the nature of sales or shipments. Furthermore, manufacturers' wholesale branches and chain store warehouses operate similar to independent wholesale establishments of the same character, and manufacturers' own retail stores operate similar to independent or chain retail stores of the same type and character. *Functionally,* therefore, such establishments operating on the same level are fairly identical irrespective of differences in ownership. Failure to consider them as links in the chain of distribution would lead to confusion when comparing one channel with another or in comparing costs of distributing through alternative channels. From a practical standpoint, therefore, transfers of goods to different kinds of establishments within an integrated company must be considered in the nature of sales.

Horizontal Aspects

Many manufacturers also have important alternatives to consider with regard to the *horizontal* aspects of different levels in the channel. On any given level (wholesale or retail) there are many different kinds of establishments when classified by line of goods handled or by method of operation.

Although the situation varies considerably from one line of goods to another, the character of the problem may be illustrated with an example. Prepared baby foods were originally marketed as specialty goods and were sold chiefly through drugstores, because they were purchased by mothers upon the advice of pediatricians or general medical practitioners who prescribed feeding programmes for babies. When the first mass producer of such goods began to sell them through the grocery trade, a different channel was used even though it may have comprised the same types of links. More recently, this was illustrated by the change made by another manufacturer of such items who primarily produced drug merchandise and hence found it natural to sell also the few baby food items through such line of business.

This manufacturer originally distributed these products through wholesale drug firms who, in turn, sold them to the retail drug trade. As such products became more widespread in use, they were purchased by the housewife as convenience goods and mostly in retail grocery outlets. Because wholesale druggists did not have contact with retail grocery outlets, many wholesale grocers purchased the products from wholesale druggists and in this unnatural manner the items eventually found their way to the retail grocer.

The marketing pattern changed to such an extent that about 85 per cent of total consumer purchases of these baby foods was being made from grocery stores. When this was recognized by the manufacturer, a decision was made to simplify the channel of distribution by making the product directly available to wholesale grocery organizations. This change was fraught with real significance. National distribution was formerly accomplished by direct dealings at the most with only about 300 wholesale drug firms. Wholesale grocers, however, are much more numerous. It would be essential to contact at least about 3,000 such firms to provide dense nation-wide coverage among retail grocery outlets.

This called for basic marketing changes. Since it was not feasible for the manufacturer to expand his own sales organization to the extent necessary to handle such a large number of channel contacts, food brokers were employed to sell from the manufacturer to wholesale grocery organizations.

Thus, a decision to modify the channel horizontally on the wholesale level, by shifting from drug wholesalers to grocery wholesalers, was a channel problem of very great importance. Even in the absence of the introduction of brokers, the shift from drug to grocery wholesale outlets was of sufficient significance to constitute a change in the channel of distribution. Horizontal modifications of channels have become increasingly important. In former decades, it was rather common to find that there was a single natural channel for many kinds of commodities. Especially since the middle 1940's, however, there has been considerable diversification of merchandise lines by many kinds of stores. Many drug items, toilet goods, and housewares are now sold in food stores, especially of the supermarket type.

The modern large drugstore sells many items of general merchandise not formerly part of drugstore retailing. Many automobile accessory stores have become rather complete hard-line stores, handling all kinds of household appliances, hardware, lawn and garden supplies, and housewares. Such changes, sometimes popularly described as "scrambled merchandising," have increased the complexity of horizontal aspects of many manufacturers' distribution efforts.

Other Channel Variations

There are additional reasons which complicate the channel question. Many manufacturers find it necessary or desirable to use more than one kind of channel (in the vertical or horizontal sense) for the same product. The vertical aspect is particularly true of commodities which have a double market. Automotive tires are an important example. That portion of the industry's output which is sold for original equipment on new cars is distributed direct from tire factories to automobile manufacturers. Tires for replacement equipment on cars on the road are sold principally through manufacturers' branches to retailers, or through regular wholesalers to retailers.

Some manufacturers have different products that require separate distribution channels. Illustrative is the meat packing industry. In addition to meat sales to retail stores, the industry is confronted with the problems of selling numerous types of by-products to different classes of customers, each of which poses a special channel-selection problem. Finally, some manufacturers find it feasible to use different channels in different parts of the country. Many manufacturers of factory machinery and store equipment sell direct to industrial consumers in regions where customers are highly concentrated but rely on manufacturers' agents for effecting sales in those areas where potential customers are widely scattered.

The foregoing discussion has been concerned with the distribution of manufactured goods. Channels for agricultural commodities involve a greater multiplicity of types of middlemen. Distribution of such goods is more complicated because they come from large numbers of small producers. In local growers' markets, various types of assembling middlemen are found. These include independent cash buyers of farm products, trucker-buyers, and the assembling agencies of cooperative marketing associations. Then there are also unique types of concentrating agencies in the major city wholesale markets. Of particular importance are the fruit and vegetable auctions found in a number of our leading cities.

Selection of Channels

It must not be assumed that every manufacturer has a wide range of alternatives to consider in selecting channels. Many middlemen, particularly wholesalers and retailers who handle a wide range of merchandise items, regard themselves as purchasing agents for a group of customers rather than as distributing organizations for manufacturers. At any given time, they are likely to be stocking what they consider to be the maximum feasible number of items in a particular classification. Thus, a manufacturer often finds it difficult to obtain distribution among new outlets. The point is that the channel of distribution may be determined as much by the middleman, acting as a buyer, as it is by the manufacturer, acting as a seller.

Another factor which limits freedom in selection consists of changes in consumer buying habits. The trend toward consumer buying of baby food items in food stores forced a drug firm to market its baby food items through such outlets, even though from a standpoint of operating convenience and utilization of an existing sales organization, it would have preferred to continue distribution through the drug trade. No manufacturer of a highly competitive product can maintain his historic share of market by confining his distribution to types of outlets which are of decreasing relative importance for a class of products. In the last analysis, the relative importance of different channels for consumer and industrial goods items is determined by the buying decisions of ultimate consumers and business purchasers, respectively.

Moreover, in some cases a variety of types of middlemen is not available. In certain lines, such as high-fashion apparel, wholesalers are of such limited significance that they do not constitute a practical alternative. In other cases, such as elaborate industrial machinery, the requirements of each potential customer are so unique that a direct manufacturer-to-user channel is dictated by unalterable circumstances.

Nevertheless, many manufacturing sellers have considerable freedom in channel selection. Whether to sell direct or to utilize the services of one or a number of types of middlemen is often a perplexing question of marketing strategy. The manufacturer may also be faced with determining whether one channel will suffice, or whether two or more different channels are required because of differences in the products made or markets served. Finally, he may have to decide upon the kinds of business or lines of trade through which his goods should move, which will, in turn, determine not only the types of links to be used but the number of links. Cases abound where such decisions have been reached in a haphazard manner. To approach this problem scientifically, it is essential to know how various products are distributed and what factors govern the choice of given channels.

Policies of different vendors in the choice of trade channels vary widely. The authors have deemed it best to analyse and discuss such policies in connection with the treatment of each important marketing institution. This approach tends to make the presentation of marketing institutions more complete and rounded, it emphasizes the strategic role of customers in the determination of channels which is in line with modern concepts of marketing orientation, and it gives the study of trade channels a more realistic setting.

SOCIAL RESPONSIBILITY IN MARKETING

ETHICAL RESPONSIBILITIES AND CONSTRAINTS

Businesses and people face some constraints on what can ethically be done to make money or to pursue other goals. Fraud and deception are not only morally wrong but also inhibit the efficient functioning of the economy. There are also behaviours that, even if they are not strictly illegal in a given jurisdiction, cannot be undertaken with a good conscience. There are a number of areas where an individual must consider his or her conscience to decide if a venture is acceptable. Some "paycheck advance" loan operators charge very high interest rates on small loans made in anticipation of a consumer's next paycheck. Depending on state laws, effective interest rates may exceed 20% per month. In some cases, borrowers put up their automobiles as security, with many losing their only source of transportation through default. Although some consider this practice unconscionable, others assert that such loans may be the only way that a family can obtain cash to fill an immediate need. Because of costs of administration are high, these costs, when spread over a small amount, will amount to a large percentage. Further, because the customer groups in question tend to have poor credit ratings with high anticipated rates of default, rates must be high enough to cover this.

SUSTAINABILITY

Sustainability is a notion that proposes that socially responsible firms will somehow financially outperform other less responsible firms in the long run. This might result from customer loyalty, better employee morale, or public policy favouring ethical conduct. Empirical results testing this hypothesis are mixed, neither suggesting that more responsible firms, on the average, have a clear financial advantage nor a large burden.

Thus, a useful approach may be to determine:

- Specific circumstances under which a firm may actually find the more responsible approach to be more profitable,
- Under which circumstances responsible behaviour can be pursued without an overall significant downside, and
- The ethical responsibilities that a firm faces when a more responsible approach may be more costly.

INDIVIDUAL, FIRM, AND SOCIETY

Different individuals vary in their ethical convictions. Some are willing to work for the tobacco industry, for example, while others are not. Some are willing to mislead potential customers while others will normally not do this. There are, however, also broader societal and companywide values that may influence the individual business decision maker. Some religions, including Islam, disfavour the charging of interest. Although different groups differ somewhat in their interpretations of this issue, the Koran at the very least prohibits usury-charging excessive interest rates.

There is some disagreement as to whether more modest, fair interest rates are acceptable. In cultures where the stricter interpretation applies, a firm may be unwilling to set up an interest-based financing plan for customers who cannot pay cash. The firm might, instead, charge a higher price, with no additional charge for interest. Some firms also have their own ethical stands, either implicitly or explicitly. For example, Google has the motto"Do no evil." Other firms, on the other hand, may actively encourage lies, deception, and other reprehensible behaviour. Some firms elect to sell in less developed countries products that have been banned as unsafe in their own countries.

MAKING IT PROFITABLE FOR THE TOBACCO INDUSTRY TO"HARVEST"

Many see the tobacco industry as the"enemy" and may not want to do anything that can benefit the industry. However, in principle, it may actually be possible to make it profitable for the tobacco industry to"harvest"-to spend less money on brand building and gradually reduce the quantities sold. The tobacco industry is heavily concentrated, with three firms controlling most of the market. Some other industries are exempt from many antitrust law provisions. If the tobacco companies were allowed to collude and set prices, the equilibrium market price would probably go up, and the quantity of tobacco demanded would then go down. It is been found that among teenagers, smoking rates are especially likely to decrease when prices increase. The tobacco companies could also be given some immediate tax breaks in return for giving up their trademarks some thirty years in the future. This would reduce the incentive to advertise, again leading to decreased demand in the future. The tax benefits needed might have to be very high, thus making the idea infeasible unless the nation is willing to trade off better health for such large revenue losses.

"WIN-WIN" MARKETING

In some cases, it may actually be profitable for companies to do good deeds. This may be the case, for example, when a firm receives a large amount of favourable publicity for its contributions, resulting in customer goodwill and an enhanced brand value. A pharmacy chain, for example, might pay for charitable good to develop information about treating diabetes. The chain could then make this information on its web site, paying for bandwidth and other hosting expenses that may be considerably less than the value of the positive publicity received.

"SPONSORED FUNDRAISING"

Non-profit groups often spend a large proportion of the money they take in on fundraising. This is problematic both because of the inefficiency of the process and the loss of potential proceeds that result and because potential donors who learn about or suspect high fundraising expenses may be less likely to donor. This is an especially critical issue now that information on fundraising overhead for different organizations is readily available on the Internet.

An alternative approach to fundraising that does not currently appear to be much in use is the idea of"sponsored" fundraising. The idea here is that some firm might volunteer to send out fundraising appeals on behalf of the organization. For example, Microsoft might volunteer to send out letters asking people to donate to the American Red Cross. This may be a very cost effective method of promotion for the firm since the sponsor would benefit from both the positive publicity for its involvement and from the greater attention that would likely be given a fundraising appeal for a group of special interest than would be given to an ordinary advertisement or direct mail piece advertising the sponsor in a traditional way.

One issue that comes up is the potential match between the sponsor and sponsee organization. This may or may not be a critical issue since respondents are selected for the solicitation based on their predicted interest in the organization. Microsoft-directly or indirectly through the Bill and Melinda Gates Foundation-has been credited with a large number of charitable ventures and has the Congressional Black Caucus as one of its greatest supporters. In many cases, firms might volunteer for this fundraising effort in large part because of the spear heading efforts of high level executives whose families are affected by autism.

COMMERCIAL COMEDY

Another win-win deal potential between industry and non-profit groups involves the idea of commercial comedy. Many non-profit groups are interested in finding low cost, high quality entertainment for fundraising events. After all, money spent on buying entertainment reduces the net proceeds available for the organization's prigramme. Firms, on the other hand, have difficulty getting current and potential customers to give attention to advertising in traditional media. If firms were able to create some high quality entertainment involving their mascotss-e.g., the Energizer Bunny, the Pillsbury Doughboy, and the AFLAC Duck-the audience at a fundraising event would give attention for an extended period of time. Good will would also be generated, and it is likely that the performance would receive considerable media coverage.

ETHICS IN MARKETING

Ethics are a collection of principles of right conduct that shape the decisions people or organizations make. Practicing ethics in marketing means deliberately applying standards of fairness, or moral rights and wrongs, to marketing decision making, behaviour, and practice in the organization.

In a market economy, a business may be expected to act in what it believes to be its own best interest. The purpose of marketing is to create a competitive advantage. An organization achieves an advantage when it does a better job than its competitors at satisfying the product and service requirements of its target markets. Those organizations that develop a competitive advantage are able to satisfy the needs of both customers and the organization.

As our economic system has become more successful at providing for needs and wants, there has been greater focus on organizations' adhering to ethical values rather than simply providing products. This focus has come about for two reasons. First, when an organization behaves ethically, customers develop more positive attitudes about the firm, its products, and its services. When marketing practices depart from standards that society considers acceptable, the market process becomes less efficient—sometimes it is even interrupted. Not employing ethical marketing practices may lead to dissatisfied customers, bad publicity, a lack of trust, lost business, or, sometimes, legal action. Thus, most organizations are very sensitive to the needs and opinions of their customers and look for ways to protect their long-term interests.

Second, ethical abuses frequently lead to pressure for institutions to assume greater responsibility for their actions. Since abuses do occur, some people believe that questionable business practices abound. As a result, consumer interest groups, professional associations, and self-regulatory groups exert considerable influence on marketing. Calls for social responsibility have also subjected marketing practices to a wide range of federal and state regulations designed to either protect consumer rights or to stimulate trade.

The Federal Trade Commission and other federal and state government agencies are charged both with enforcing the laws and creating policies to limit unfair marketing practices. Because regulation cannot be developed to cover every possible abuse, organizations and industry groups often develop codes of ethical conduct or rules for behaviour to serve as a guide in decision making. The American Marketing Association, for example, has developed a code of ethics. Self-regulation not only helps a firm avoid extensive government intervention; it also permits it to better respond to changes in market conditions. An organization's long-term success and profitability depends on this ability to respond.

UNFAIR OR DECEPTIVE MARKETING PRACTICES

Marketing practices are deceptive if customers believe they will get more value from a product or service than they actually receive. Deception, which can take the form of a misrepresentation, omission, or misleading practice, can occur when working with any element of the marketing mix.

Because consumers are exposed to great quantities of information about products and firms, they often become skeptical of marketing claims and selling messages and act to protect themselves from being deceived. Thus, when a product or service does not provide expected value, customers will often seek a different source.

Deceptive pricing practices cause customers to believe that the price they pay for some unit of value in a product or service is lower than it really is. The deception might take the form of making false price comparisons, providing misleading suggested selling prices, omitting important conditions of the sale, or making very low price offers available only when other items are purchased as well. Promotion practices are deceptive when the seller intentionally misstates how a product is constructed or performs, fails to disclose information regarding pyramid sales or employs bait-and-switch selling techniques.

False or greatly exaggerated product or service claims are also deceptive. When packages are intentionally mislabeled as to contents, size, weight, or use information, that constitutes deceptive packaging. Selling hazardous or defective products without disclosing the dangers, failing to perform promised services, and not honouring warranty obligations are also considered deception.

OFFENSIVE MATERIALS AND OBJECTIONABLE MARKETING PRACTICES

Marketers control what they say to customers as well as and how and where they say it. When events, television or radio programming, or publications sponsored by a marketer, in addition to products or promotional materials, are perceived as offensive, they often create strong negative reactions. For example, some people find advertising for all products promoting sexual potency to be offensive. Others may be offended when a promotion employs stereotypical images or uses sex as an appeal. This is particularly true when a product is being marketed in other countries, where words and images may carry different meanings than they do in the host country.

When people feel that products or appeals are offensive, they may pressure vendors to stop carrying the product. Thus, all promotional messages must be carefully screened and tested, and communication media, programming, and editorial content selected to match the tastes and interests of targeted customers. Beyond the target audience, however, marketers should understand that there are others who are not customers who might receive their appeals and see their images and be offended.

Direct marketing is also undergoing closer examination. Objectionable practices range from minor irritants, such as the timing and frequency of sales letters or commercials, to those that are offensive or even illegal. Among examples of practices that may raise ethical questions are persistent and high-pressure selling, annoying telemarketing calls, and television commercials that are too long or run too frequently. Marketing appeals created to take advantage of young or inexperienced consumers or senior citizens— including advertisements, sales appeals disguised as contests, junk mail and the use and exchange of mailing lists—may also pose ethical questions. In addition to being subject to consumer-protection laws and regulations, the Direct Marketing Association provides a list of voluntary ethical guidelines for companies engaged in direct marketing.

ETHICAL PRODUCT AND DISTRIBUTION PRACTICES

Several product-related issues raise questions about ethics in marketing, most often concerning the quality of products and services provided. Among the most frequently voiced complaints are ones about products that are unsafe, that are of poor quality in construction or content, that do not contain what is promoted, or that go out of style or become obsolete before they actually need replacing. An organization that markets poor-quality or unsafe products is taking the chance that it will develop a reputation for poor products or service. In addition, it may be putting itself in jeopardy for product claims or legal action. Sometimes, however, frequent changes in product features or performance, such as those that often occur in the computer industry, make previous models of products obsolete. Such changes can be misinterpreted as planned obsolescence.

Ethical questions may also arise in the distribution process. Because sales performance is the most common way in which marketing representatives and sales personnel are evaluated, performance pressures exist that may lead to ethical dilemmas. For example, pressuring vendors to buy more than they need and pushing items that will result in higher commissions are temptations. Exerting influence to cause vendors to reduce display space for competitors' products, promising shipment when knowing delivery is not possible by the promised date, or paying vendors to carry a firm's product rather than one of its competitors are also unethical.

Research is another area in which ethical is sues may arise. Information gathered from research can be important to the successful marketing of products or services. Consumers, however, may view organizations' efforts to gather data from them as invading their privacy. They are resistant to give out personal information that might cause them to become a marketing target or to receive product or sales information. When data about products or consumers are exaggerated to make a selling point, or research questions are written to obtain a specific result, consumers are misled. Without self-imposed ethical standards in the research process, management will likely make decisions based on inaccurate information.

DOES MARKETING OVERFOCUS ON MATERIALISM?

Consumers develop an identity in the market place that is shaped both by who they are and by what they see themselves as becoming. There is evidence that the way consumers view themselves influences their purchasing behaviour. This identity is often reflected in the brands or products they consume or the way in which they lead their lives.

The proliferation of information about products and services complicates decision making. Sometimes consumer desires to achieve or maintain a certain lifestyle or image results in their purchasing more than they need or can afford. Does marketing create these wants? Clearly, appeals exist that are designed to cause people to purchase more than they need or can afford. Unsolicited offers of credit cards with high limits or high interest rates, advertising appeals touting the psychological benefits of conspicuous consumption, and promotions that seek to stimulate unrecognized needs are often cited as examples of these excesses.

SPECIAL ETHICAL ISSUES IN MARKETING TO CHILDREN

Children are an important marketing target for certain products. Because their knowledge about products, the media, and selling strategies is usually not as well developed as that of adults, children are likely to be more vulnerable to psychological appeals and strong images. Thus, ethical questions sometimes arise when they are exposed to questionable marketing tactics and messages. For example, studies linking relationships between tobacco and alcohol marketing with youth consumption resulted in increased public pressure directly leading to the regulation of marketing for those products.

The proliferation of direct marketing and use of the Internet to market to children also raises ethical issues. Sometimes a few unscrupulous marketers design sites so that children are able to bypass adult supervision or control;

sometimes they present objectionable materials to underage consumers or pressure them to buy items or provide credit card numbers. When this happens, it is likely that social pressure and subsequent regulation will result. Likewise, programming for children and youth in the mass media has been under scrutiny for many years.

In the United States, marketing to children is closely controlled. Federal regulations place limits on the types of marketing that can be directed to children, and marketing activities are monitored by the Better Business Bureau, the Federal Trade Commission, consumer and parental groups, and the broadcast networks. These guidelines provide clear direction to marketers.

ETHICAL ISSUES IN MARKETING TO MINORITIES

The United States is a society of ever-increasing diversity. Markets are broken into segments in which people share some similar characteristics. Ethical issues arise when marketing tactics are designed specifically to exploit or manipulate a minority market segment. Offensive practices may take the form of negative or stereotypical representations of minorities, associating the consumption of harmful or questionable products with a particular minority segment, and demeaning portrayals of a race or group. Ethical questions may also arise when high-pressure selling is directed at a group, when higher prices are charged for products sold to minorities, or even when stores provide poorer service in neighbourhoods with a high population of minority customers. Such practices will likely result in a bad public image and lost sales for the marketer.

Unlike the legal protections in place to protect children from harmful practices, there have been few efforts to protect minority customers. When targeting minorities, firms must evaluate whether the targeted population is susceptible to appeals because of their minority status. The firm must assess marketing efforts to determine whether ethical behaviour would cause them to change their marketing practices.

ETHICAL ISSUES SURROUNDING THE PORTRAYAL OF WOMEN IN MARKETING EFFORTS

As society changes, so do the images of and roles assumed by people, regardless of race, sex, or occupation. Women have been portrayed in a variety of ways over the years. When marketers present those images as overly conventional, formulaic, or oversimplified, people may view them as stereotypical and offensive. Examples of demeaning stereotypes include those in which women are presented as less intelligent, submissive to or obsessed with men, unable to assume leadership roles or make decisions, or skimpily dressed in order to appeal to the sexual interests of males. Harmful stereotypes include those portraying women as obsessed with their appearance or conforming to some ideal of size, weight, or beauty. When images are considered demeaning or harmful, they will work to the detriment of the organization. Advertisements, in particular, should be evaluated to be sure that the images projected are not offensive.

FUTURES MARKETS

In the late 1970s and early 1980s, radical changes in the international currency system and in the way the Federal Reserve managed the U.S. MONEY SUPPLY produced unprecedented volatility in INTEREST RATES and currency exchange rates. As market forces shook the foundations of global financial stability, businesses wrestled with heretofore unimagined challenges. Between 1980 and 1985, Caterpillar, the Peoria-based maker of heavy equipment, saw exchange-rate shifts give its main Japanese competitor a 40 percent price advantage. Meanwhile, even the soundest business borrowers faced soaring double-digit interest rates. Investors clamored for dollars as commodity prices collapsed, taking whole nations down into insolvency and ushering in the Third World debt crisis.

Stymied financial managers turned to Chicago, where the traditional agricultural futures markets had only recently invented techniques to cope with financial uncertainty. In 1972, the Chicago Mercantile Exchange established the International Monetary Market to trade the world's first futures contracts for currency. The world's first interest-rate futures contract was introduced shortly afterward, at the Chicago Board of Trade, in 1975. In 1982, futures contracts on the Standard and Poor's 500 index began to trade at the Chicago Mercantile Exchange. These radically new tools helped businesses manage in a volatile and unpredictable new world order. How? Futures are standardized contracts that commit parties to buy or sell goods of a specific quality at a specific price, for delivery at a specific point in the future. The concept of buying and selling for future delivery is not in itself new. In thirteenth-and fourteenth-century Europe, buyers contracted for wool purchases one to several years forward. Cistercian monasteries that produced the wool sold forward more than their own production, expecting to buy the remainder on the market (presumably at a lower price) to satisfy their obligation. In seventeenth-century JAPAN, merchants bought and sold rice for future delivery. And banks have long offered their customers the opportunity to buy and sell currencies forward, with both the bank and the customer contracting today and settling their obligation in the future. But the complex legal and financial arrangements that make the modern futures market possible are thoroughly modern.

In the nineteenth century, Chicago's trading pits offered an organized venue in which farmers and other suppliers of agricultural commodities, such as warehouse owners and brokers, could remove the risk of price fluctuations from their business plans. The futures exchanges were private, member-owned organizations. Members bought "seats" on the exchange and enjoyed various trading rights. It may seem strange that markets originally established to trade agricultural commodity futures in the nineteenth century should become centers of trade for financial contracts in the twentieth. But the key to success as a trader is to understand the market; traders therefore consider themselves experts on market movements rather than authorities on minerals and crops. This is why financial futures were relatively easy to introduce to markets originally designed for agricultural commodity futures: one thing interest rates and corn have in common is a fast-changing market.

Although the underlying risks have changed, some important futures markets still operate much as they always have, with traders standing in a ring or a pit shouting buy and sell orders at each other, competing for each fraction of a cent. But electronic trading is rapidly changing how traders trade. Computer terminals linked to each other through electronic trading systems let traders access a virtual trading floor from anywhere in the world. The need to raise capital to build these systems has led several big exchanges to go public, issuing stock to investors and operating as any public corporation providing a service—the service of a market. Exchanges compete with each other to attract traders by doing a better job of providing the benefits that traders expect from a fair market.

Take futures contracts, for example. They are not contracts directly between buyers and sellers of goods. The farmer who sells a futures contract and commits to deliver corn in six months does not make his commitment to a specific corn buyer, but rather, through a broker, to the clearinghouse of the futures exchange. The clearinghouse, another modern institution, stands between buyers and sellers and, in effect, guarantees that both buyers and sellers will receive what they have contracted for.

Thanks to the clearinghouse, the farmer does not have to be concerned about the financial stability of the buyer of the futures contract, nor does the buyer need to be concerned about the progress of any particular farmer's crop. New information about changes in supply and DEMAND causes the prices of futures contracts to fluctuate, sometimes moving them up and down many times in a trading day. For example, news of drought or blight that may reduce the corn harvest, cutting future supplies, causes corn futures contracts to rise in price. Similarly, news of a rise in interest rates or a presidential illness can cause stock-index futures prices to fall as investors react to the prospect of difficult or uncertain times ahead. Every day, the clearinghouse tallies up and matches all contracts bought or sold during the trading session. Parties holding contracts that have fallen in price during the trading session must pay the clearinghouse a sort of security deposit called "margin." When the contracts are closed out, it is the clearinghouse that pays the parties whose contracts have gained in value. Futures trading is what economists call a zero-sum game, meaning that for every winner there is someone who loses an equal amount.

But in a fundamental economic sense, futures trading is positive sum. Both sides expect to gain, or they would not trade. Another way of saying this is that the loser may be perfectly happy to lose. That is because many businesses use futures markets as a form of INSURANCE. A candy maker, for example, might buy sugar and cocoa futures contracts to lock in a price for some portion of its requirement for these important ingredients. The contracts are as good as physically buying the commodities and storing them. If prices rise, the futures contracts will also be more valuable. The company can choose to sell the contracts and pocket the cash, then buy the commodities from its usual suppliers at market prices, or else accept delivery of the ingredients from the seller of the contract and buy less on the market.

Either way, its cost of raw materials is lower than if it had not bought the contracts. The company has cushioned itself against a price risk and does not have to worry that its production and marketing strategy will be disrupted by a sudden price increase. But what if prices fall? In that case the company loses some money on its futures contracts. But the same price decrease that causes that loss also caused something good: the company pays less for its ingredients. Remember, the purpose of buying the futures contract was to protect against something bad happening—a price rise. The bad thing did not happen; prices fell instead. The loss on the futures contract is the cost of insurance, and the company is no worse off than a person who purchases fire insurance and then does not have a fire.

The biggest users of the futures markets rely on them for risk management. That is surely one reason why defaults are rare. But there is an additional security measure between the individual trader and the clearinghouse. Buyers and sellers of futures must do business through intermediaries who are exchange members. Instead of standing between two individual traders, therefore, the clearinghouse stands between two exchange member firms. Each firm monitors its own customers and makes a "margin call" when the customer's losses make additional margin necessary. If the customer cannot pay the margin, the firm closes the account, sells off the positions, and may have to take a small loss. While firms pay attention to the credit of their customers, the clearinghouse pays attention to the credit of the firms. The clearinghouse needs to make good on a trade only if losses are so great that the exchange member firm itself fails. This happens occasionally when firms badly mismanage their risks or when a major financial crisis occurs.

Because futures contracts offer assurance of future prices and availability of goods, they provide stability in an unstable business environment. Futures have long been associated with agricultural commodities, especially grain and pork bellies, but they are now more likely to be used by bankers, airlines, and computer makers than by farmers—at least in North America and Europe. By the early 2000s, although commodities remained the mainstay of futures markets in Asia, in the developed countries of the West financial futures contracts had almost totally eclipsed commodities. The Chicago Mercantile Exchange claimed in 2004 that financial futures accounted for 99 percent of its business, and financial futures also accounted for the lion's share of business at the Chicago Board of Trade and at Euronext.liffe. In Japan, by contrast, commodity futures trading dwarfed financial futures. This does not mean that commodities were more important than finance in the Japanese economy, of course. Financial futures got a slow start in Japan because Japanese regulations discouraged them. Traders who wanted to trade such futures had to—and did—trade them elsewhere. Thus, the first futures on Japan's Nikkei stock index traded in Singapore, and the first yen futures traded in Chicago.

Obviously, the idea of hedging against an unstable financial environment has great appeal. Companies like Caterpillar, Microsoft, or Citibank can now protect themselves against currency shifts by buying and selling futures contracts or similar instruments. Investors use contracts on interest rates, BONDS, and stock indexes to protect against a decline in the value of their INVESTMENTS, just as farmers have long used futures to protect against a drop in the price of corn or beans.

Farmers who planted corn in the spring had no way of knowing what the price of their crop would be when they harvested in the fall. But a farmer who planted in the spring and sold a futures contract committed to deliver his grain in the fall for a definite price. Not only did he receive cash in the spring in return for his commitment, but he also received the contract price for his crop even if the market price subsequently fell because of an unexpected glut of corn. In exchange the farmer gave up the chance to get a higher price in the event of a drought or blight; he received the same fixed price for which he had contracted. In the latter case, the farmer would have netted more if he had not sold the future; however, most farmers prefer not to gamble on the corn market. Farming is risky enough, thanks to uneven rainfalls and unpredictable pests, without adding the risk of changes in market prices.

Farmers thus seek to lock in a value on their crop and are willing to pay a price for certainty. They give up the chance of very high prices in return for protection against abysmally low prices. This practice of removing risk from business plans is called hedging. As a rule of thumb, about half of the participants in the futures markets are hedgers who come to market to remove or reduce their risk.

For the market to function, however, it cannot consist only of hedgers seeking to lay off risk. There must be someone who comes to market in order to take on risk. These are the "speculators." Speculators come to market to take risk, and to make money doing it. Some speculators, against all odds, have become phenomenally wealthy by trading futures. Interestingly, even the wealthiest speculators often report having gone broke one or more times in their career. Because speculation offers the promise of astounding riches with little apparent effort, or the threat of devastating losses despite even the best efforts, it is often compared to casino gambling.

The difference between speculation in futures and casino gambling is that futures market speculation provides an important social good, namely liquidity. If it were not for the presence of speculators in the market, farmers, bankers, and business executives would have no easy and economical way to eliminate the risk of volatile prices, interest rates, and exchange rates from their business plans.

Speculators, however, provide a ready and liquid market for these risks—at a price. Speculators who are willing to assume risks for a price make it possible for others to reduce their risks. COMPETITION among speculators also makes hedging less expensive and ensures that the effect of all available information is swiftly calculated into the market price. Weather reports, actions of central banks, political developments, and anything else that can affect supply or demand in the future affect futures prices almost immediately. This is how the futures market performs its function of "price discovery."

There seems to be no limit to the potential applications of futures market technology. The New York Mercantile Exchange (NYMEX) began to trade heating oil futures in 1978. The exchange later introduced crude oil, gasoline, and natural gas futures. Airlines, shipping companies, public transportation authorities, home-heating-oil delivery services, and major multinational oil and gas companies have all sought to hedge their price risk using these futures contracts. In 1990 the NYMEX traded more than thirty-five million ENERGY futures and option contracts.

Meanwhile, international STOCK MARKET investors have discovered that stock-index futures, besides being useful for hedging, also are an attractive alternative to actually buying stocks. Because a stock-index future moves in tandem with the prices of the underlying stocks, it gives the same return as owning stocks. Yet the stock-index future is cheaper to buy and may be exempt from certain taxes and charges to which stock ownership is subject. Some large institutional investors prefer to buy German stock-index futures rather than German stocks for this very reason.

Because stock-index futures are easier to trade than actual stocks, the futures prices often change before the underlying stock prices do. In the October 1987 crash, for example, prices of stock-index futures in Chicago fell before prices on the New York Stock Exchange collapsed, leading some observers to conclude that futures trading had somehow caused the stock market crash that year. In fact, investors who wanted to sell stocks could not sell quickly and efficiently on the New York Stock Exchange and therefore sold futures instead. The futures market performed its function of price discovery more rapidly than the stock market did.

Futures contracts have even been enlisted in the fight against air pollution and the effort to curb runaway HEALTH INSURANCE costs. When the Environmental Protection Agency decided to allow a market for sulfur dioxide emission allowances under the 1990 amendments to the Clean Air Act, the Chicago Board of Trade developed a futures contract for trading what might be called air pollution futures. The reason? If futures markets provide price discovery and liquidity to the market in emission allowances, companies can decide on the basis of straightforward economics whether it makes sense to reduce their own emissions of sulfur dioxide and sell their emission allowance to others, or instead to sustain their current emission levels and purchase emission allowances from others.

Without a futures market it would be difficult to know whether a price offered or demanded for emissions allowances is high or low. But hedgers and speculators bidding in an open futures market will cause quick discovery of the true price, the equilibrium point at which buyers and sellers are both equally willing to transact. Similar reasoning has led to some decidedly unconventional applications of futures technology. The Iowa Electronic Market introduced political futures in 1988, and this market has generally beaten the pollsters at predicting not only the winner of the White House but also the winning margin. This makes sense because people are much more careful with information when they are betting money on it than when they are talking to a pollster. Economist Richard Roll showed that the orange juice futures market is a slightly better predictor of Florida temperatures than the National Weather Service.

2

Marketing Management

INTRODUCTION

Marketing Management is a business discipline which is focused on the practical application of marketing techniques and the management of a firm's marketing resources and activities. Rapidly emerging forces of globalization have compelled firms to market beyond the borders of their home country making International marketing highly significant and an integral part of a firm's marketing strategy. Marketing managers are often responsible for influencing the level, timing, and composition of customer demand accepted definition of the term. In part, this is because the role of a marketing manager can vary significantly based on a business' size, corporate culture, and industry context.

For example, in a large consumer products company, the marketing manager may performance as the overall general manager of his or her assigned product To create an effective, cost-efficient Marketing management strategy, firms must possess a detailed, objective understanding of their own business and the market in which they operate. In analyzing these issues, the discipline of marketing management often overlaps with the related discipline of strategic planning.

STRUCTURE

Traditionally, marketing analysis was structured into three areas: Customer analysis, Company analysis, and Competitor analysis. More recently, it has become fashionable in some marketing circles to divide these further into certain five "Cs": Customer analysis, Company analysis, Collaborator analysis, Competitor analysis, and analysis of the industry Context.

Department analysis is to develop a schematic diagram for market segmentation, breaking down the market into various constituent groups of customers, which are called customer segments or market segmentations. Marketing managers work to develop detailed profiles of each segment, focusing on any number of variables that may differ among the segments: demographic, psychographic, geographic, behavioural, needs-benefit, and other factors may all be examined. Marketers also attempt to track these segments' perceptions of the various products in the market using tools such as perceptual mapping.

In company analysis, marketers focus on understanding the company's cost structure and cost position relative to competitors, as well as working to identify a firm's core competencies and other competitively distinct company resources. Marketing managers may also work with the accounting department to analyse the profits the firm is generating from various product lines and customer accounts. The company may also conduct periodic brand audits to assess the strength of its brands and sources of brand equity.

The firm's collaborators may also be profiled, which may include various suppliers, distributors and other channel partners, joint venture partners, and others. An analysis of complementary products may also be performed if such products exist.

Marketing management employs various tools from economics and competitive strategy to analyse the industry context in which the firm operates. These include Porter's five forces, analysis of strategic groups of competitors, value chain analysis and others. Depending on the industry, the regulatory context may also be important to examine in detail.

In competitor analysis, marketers build detailed profiles of each competitor in the market, focusing especially on their relative competitive strengths and weaknesses using SWOT analysis. Marketing managers will examine each competitor's cost structure, sources of profits, resources and competencies, competitive positioning and product differentiation, degree of vertical integration, historical responses to industry developments, and other factors.

Marketing management often finds it necessary to invest in research to collect the data required to perform accurate marketing analysis. As such, they often conduct market research to obtain this information.

Marketers employ a variety of techniques to conduct market research, but some of the more common include:

- Qualitative marketing research, such as focus groups
- Quantitative marketing research, such as statistical surveys
- Experimental techniques such as test markets
- Observational techniques such as ethnographic observation

Marketing managers may also design and oversee various environmental scanning and competitive intelligence processes to help identify trends and inform the company's marketing analysis.

Marketing Strategy

If the company has obtained an adequate understanding of the customer base and its own competitive position in the industry, marketing managers are able to make their own key strategic decisions and develop a marketing strategy designed to maximize the revenues and profits of the firm. The selected strategy may aim for any of a variety of specific objectives, including optimizing short-term unit margins, revenue growth, market share, long-term profitability, or other goals.

To achieve the desired objectives, marketers typically identify one or more target customer segments which they intend to pursue. Customer segments are often selected as targets because they score highly on two dimensions: 1) The segment is attractive to serve because it is large, growing, makes frequent purchases, is not price sensitive, or other factors; and 2) The company has the resources and capabilities to compete for the segment's business, can meet their needs better than the competition, and can do so profitably. In fact, a commonly cited definition of marketing is simply"meeting needs profitably."

The implication of selecting target segments is that the business will subsequently allocate more resources to acquire and retain customers in the target segment(s) than it will for other, non-targeted customers. In some cases, the firm may go so far as to turn away customers who are not in its target segment.The doorman at a swanky nightclub, for example, may deny entry to unfashionably dressed individuals because the business has made a strategic decision to target the"high fashion" segment of nightclub patrons.

In conjunction with targeting decisions, marketing managers will identify the desired positioning they want the company, product, or brand to occupy in the target customer's mind. This positioning is often an encapsulation of a key benefit the company's product or service offers that is differentiated and superior to the benefits offered by competitive products. For example, Volvo has traditionally positioned its products in the automobile market in North America in order to be perceived as the leader in"safety", whereas BMW has traditionally positioned its brand to be perceived as the leader in"performance."

Ideally, a firm's positioning can be maintained over a long period of time because the company possesses, or can develop, some form of sustainable competitive advantage. The positioning should also be sufficiently relevant to the target segment such that it will drive the purchasing behaviour of target customers.

Implementation Planning

After the firm's strategic objectives have been identified, the target market selected, and the desired positioning for the company, product or brand has been determined, marketing managers focus on how to best implement the chosen strategy. Traditionally, this has involved implementation planning across the "4Ps" of marketing: Product management, Pricing, Place and Promotion. Taken together, the company's implementation choices across the 4Ps are often described as the marketing mix, meaning the mix of elements the business will employ to "go to market" and execute the marketing strategy. The overall goal for the marketing mix is to consistently deliver a compelling value proposition that reinforces the firm's chosen positioning, builds customer loyalty and brand equity among target customers, and achieves the firm's marketing and financial objectives.

In many cases, marketing management will develop a marketing plan to specify how the company will execute the chosen strategy and achieve the business' objectives.

The content of marketing plans varies from firm to firm, but commonly includes:

- An executive summary
- Situation analysis to summarize facts and insights gained from market research and marketing analysis
- The company's mission statement or long-term strategic vision
- A statement of the company's key objectives, often subdivided into marketing objectives and financial objectives
- The marketing strategy the business has chosen, specifying the target segments to be pursued and the competitive positioning to be achieved
- Implementation choices for each element of the marketing mix

Project, Process, and Vendor Management

Once the key implementation initiatives have been identified, marketing managers work to oversee the execution of the marketing plan. Marketing executives may therefore manage any number of specific projects, such as sales force management initiatives, product development efforts, channel marketing prigrammes and the execution of public relations and advertising campaigns. Marketers use a variety of project management techniques to ensure projects achieve their objectives while keeping to established schedules and budgets.

More broadly, marketing managers work to design and improve the effectiveness of core marketing processes, such as new product development, brand management, marketing communications, and pricing. Marketers may employ the tools of business process reengineering to ensure these processes are properly designed, and use a variety of process management techniques to keep them operating smoothly.

Effective execution may require management of both internal resources and a variety of external vendors and service providers, such as the firm's advertising agency. Marketers may therefore coordinate with the company's Purchasing department on the procurement of these services.

Organizational Management and Leadership

Marketing management may spend a fair amount of time building or maintaining a marketing orientation for the business. Achieving a market orientation, also known as "customer focus" or the "marketing concept", requires building consensus at the senior management level and then driving customer focus down into the organization. Cultural barriers may exist in a given business unit or functional area that the marketing manager must address in order to achieve this goal. Additionally, marketing executives often performance as a "brand champion" and work to enforce corporate identity standards across the enterprise.

In larger organizations, especially those with multiple business units, top marketing managers may need to coordinate across several marketing departments and also resources from finance, research and development, engineering, operations, manufacturing, or other functional areas to implement the marketing plan. In order to effectively manage these resources, marketing executives may need to spend much of their time focused on political issues and inte-departmental negotiations.

The effectiveness of a marketing manager may therefore depend on his or her ability to make the internal "sale" of various marketing prigrammes equally as much as the external customer's reaction to such prigrammes.

Reporting, Measurement, Feedback and Control Systems

Marketing management employs a variety of metrics to measure progress against objectives. It is the responsibility of marketing managers–in the marketing department or elsewhere–to ensure that the execution of marketing prigrammes achieves the desired objectives and does so in a cost-efficient manner.

Marketing management therefore often makes use of various organizational control systems, such as sales forecasts, sales force and reseller incentive prigrammes, sales force management systems, and customer relationship management tools. Recently, some software vendors have begun using the term "marketing operations management" or "marketing resource management" to describe systems that facilitate an integrated approach for controlling marketing resources. In some cases, these efforts may be linked to various supply chain management systems, such as enterprise resource planning, material requirements planning, efficient consumer response, and inventory management systems.

Measuring the return on investment of and marketing effectiveness various marketing initiatives is a significant problem for marketing management. Various market research, accounting and financial tools are used to help estimate the ROI of marketing investments. Brand valuation, for example, attempts to identify the percentage of a company's market value that is generated by the company's brands, and thereby estimate the financial value of specific investments in brand equity. Another technique, integrated marketing communications, is a CRM database-driven approach that attempts to estimate the value of marketing mix executions based on the changes in customer behaviour these executions generate.

CAPITAL REQUIREDS IN MARKETING MANAGEMENT

To carry on the necessary marketing activities, an enterprise needs at least two major types of funds, one for permanent investment and the other for temporary or short-term financial requirements.

PERMANENT CAPITAL

Permanent or long-term capital must be supplied for the purchase and acquisition of fixed assets such as land, buildings, delivery equipment, furniture and fixtures, warehousing equipment, and other assets of a more or less permanent nature. A sufficient amount must also be provided in this manner for normal working capital. This may be termed permanent working capital; it constitutes that portion of the funds of a business enterprise which is required from week to week and from month to month. It is the sum needed to carry normal or at least minimum inventories of merchandise and supplies, to provide for the carrying of a normal or minimum investment in accounts and notes receivable, and to insure that there will be adequate funds on hand to meet payrolls and provide for other operating expense disbursements such as advertising, rental payments, insurance premiums, etc.

The funds required for long-term investment purposes may be secured through investment by the parties engaged in the marketing operations or through long-term borrowing. Unincorporated enterprises, including the sole proprietorships and the partnerships, make provision for at least a major portion of the long-term capital investment out of their own personal funds. Corporations, on the other hand, raise equity capital by the sale of stock. Both corporations and unincorporated enterprises resort to the use of investment credit, namely, they secure loans for purely investment purposes through the issue of relatively long-term obligations. These obligations take the form of bonds, real estate mortgages, chattel mortgages, and long-term promissory notes. These are all promises to pay definite sums of principal either in a lump amount of at certain intervals.

While it is *desirable* for a firm to obtain all of its permanent capital requirements from equity or long-term sources, this is a *practical* impossibility for most of them, especially small business enterprises. Consequently, it is rather common to provide for a substantial portion of the permanent capital needed for inventories, accounts receivable, and other assets through reliance upon financial institutions or trade creditors.

Temporary Financial Requirements

Every merchandising enterprise requires temporary additions to its long-term needs and for a variety of circumstances. One of the most important is *seasonal fluctuations* in marketing activity. Purchases of goods for resale are seldom distributed evenly throughout the year, nor do seasons of heavy buying necessarily coincide with those of peak sales.

Seasonal conditions of form-utility production or of consumption require large advance expenditures for stock. Wholesale grocers, for example, often purchase a full year's supply of canned goods during the canning season. Retailers of ready-to-wear apparel must concentrate stocks of all fall merchandise in the summer in order to show it in advance of the peak autumn selling season. Pronounced seasonal peaks in sales volume place a heavy financial burden upon merchandising firms, since they are followed by proportionately heavy increases in accounts receivable. The seasonal aspect in marketing is sometimes accentuated as a result of unusually slow transitions. When a season is "slow," goods do not sell in quantity until late, thereby tying up some capital in excessive premature inventories. There is also much "frozen credit," because under these conditions purchasers fail to pay their bills promptly, and it is exceedingly difficult to realise on many receivables outstanding.

All marketing organizations are affected by *cyclical fluctuations* business conditions. Periods of prosperity or recession may be characterized, respectively, by upward or downward price movements. Purchases are always heavier in anticipation of rising prices and correspondingly light when prices take a downward trend. Similarly, buyers hold off the market during periods of price uncertainty. Even when prices are stable and remain at a given level for any length of time, the needs for current financing will vary with the condition of the times.

There are other situations that may require varying amounts of temporary capital. Exceptionally favorable opportunities to purchase goods in larger than usual quantities may present themselves, or it may become advisable to take advantage of cash discounts by paying merchandise creditors before the bills become due.

SOURCES OF CURRENT MARKETING CAPITAL

Most of the temporary capital requirements and varying proportions of the long-term capital needed for investment in current assets are obtained by business firms through the use of relatively short-term credit. This credit may be obtained from commercial banks, other specialized financial agencies, or trade credit sources.

Commercial Banks

Commercial bank credit may be defined as the power that enables commercial banking institutions to attract funds of depositors, to create obligations through the issue of paper money, and to make loans.

Uses

One of the purposes of bank credit is to make loans to individuals or firms for relatively short periods of time. Sellers borrow from banks in order to help them carry their accounts and notes receivable, while purchasers of merchandise resort to bank loans as a means of securing funds for the payment of bills upon the insistence of creditors or for the purpose of taking advantage of cash discounts. Such loans may be unsecured when the basis for granting them is the general credit standing of the borrower, or they may be secured by assignment of accounts receivable, warehouse receipts, or other collateral. Another use of bank credit is financing purchases of machinery and equipment through instalment loans to business. Such loans are usually secured by a chattel mortgage and are amortized by regular instalment payments, ordinarily over a period of 24 to 36 months or, in the case of very expensive machinery or equipment with a long life expectancy, over periods ranging up to 60 monthly payments.

Limitations

An important limitation that often prevents businessmen from relying heavily upon bank credit is the length of the credit period. Except for the instalment loans just noted, this usually varies from 30 to 90 days. The 90-day limitation is rather common because only those notes that mature within such time can be rediscounted by member banks at the Federal Reserve Banks.

This limitation applies to all types of commercial paper arising out of the domestic production or trade in manufactured goods. Notes based upon loans for agricultural purposes or those that arise out of foreign trade transactions may be rediscounted through the Federal Reserve banking system even if for longer periods of time. An even more significant reason for the short term of bank credit lies in the reason for its existence.

A commercial bank has the function of helping businesses to carry the peak of the load at the time they are paying for their purchases and waiting for remittance from their own customers. It does not aim to supply permanent working capital, although it is not uncommon for banks to extend loans to acceptable risks for periods much longer than 90 days, usually by the process of renewal. Since banks, however, desire their customers to clear their accounts at certain intervals, most businesses cannot place too much reliance upon this source for permanent working capital.

Factors

Among the oldest of the special types of financial institutions used in connection with the marketing process are factors. They have given continuous financial support to the textile industry and apparel trades for over a century and a half and have, in recent decades, spread their services to such other lines of trade as paper, glassware, shoes, petroleum, cosmetics, chemicals, furniture, and furs.

Services

The principal service of the factor is that of financing accounts receivable. After sales are made, the factor functions by buying or discounting sales invoices. A seller, in this manner, obtains immediate cash for current operations and does not suffer from delay in receipt of payment for goods. Factors usually make outright purchases of accounts receivables (*i.e.*, purchase without recourse) and thus assume all collection risks and responsibilities.

Clients of the factor usually notify their customers that the account has been "factored" and instruct them to make payment to the factoring company.

This is normally done by stamping payment instructions on the customer's invoice. In some cases, factoring is handled on a nonnotification basis. This variation is for the benefit of clients who do not want their customers to know that the account has been sold to a factor. In this case, the client's customers pay their accounts to him, and he in turn forwards such payments to the factor immediately upon receipt.

For this type of financing service, the factor receives income in two ways. The first is an interest charge based on all advances, usually at the rate of 6 per cent per annum. The second part is a charge or commission that is made for the services of advising clients on the selection of risks and for collecting the accounts when they become due. This service charge, as distinct from the interest rate charged for the use of money, varies from a fraction of 1 per cent to 3 per cent of the face amount of the invoice. Because the money invested in receivables is usually turned over several times a year, the effective rate implicit in the service charge often runs into a considerable percentage figure.

For example, if a 2 per cent service charge is made upon an advance that matures within 60 days, the effective annual rate is 12 per cent since there are six 60-day periods in a year. When this rate is added to the first part of the factor's compensation, say an interest rate of 6 per cent per annum, the factor may be able to earn a gross return of approximately 18 per cent upon the capital used in his business. The rates for the service charge are not highly standardized, however, but are a matter of individual negotiation based upon the type of customers, whether the factor assumes the risk of noncollection, amounts of money advances, length of the credit period, and the number and kind of other services rendered.

Conditions Relating to Use

The factor's financial service is often regarded by his clients as superior to that of the commercial bank, for he advances a larger percentage of the value of the accounts receivable from customers, assumes the risk of credit losses, and takes over much of the routine bookkeeping work associated with a credit department. Wide knowledge of particular lines of business makes it possible for him to do this, also to serve as a valuable and skilled adviser to his clients. Furthermore, his risks are widely distributed, thereby warranting him to assume hazards that might spell ruin to a single manufacturer with only a few customers, each of which required large amounts of goods on credit. In addition, the credit department of the factor prevents frauds and impositions by buyers, who fear to impair their credit standing with this specialized type of banker known to control the credits of a number of possible sources of supply.

Sellers of goods must meet certain qualifications, however, before the factor can be called upon for financial assistance. The client must have a generally good reputation for reliable merchandise, prompt shipment, and a good class of customers. The client's customers must be well established and not seriously affected by changes in business conditions.

Open Accounts Receivable Financing

Factoring, as described above, is to be distinguished from open accounts receivable financing as carried on by banks and other financial institutions. In open account financing, accounts are assigned without notification and with recourse, so that the seller retains responsibility for credit-granting, collection, and the risk of credit losses. Another form of such financing consists of promissory notes which are secured by accounts pledged as collateral.

Sales Finance Companies

Sales finance companies such as the General Motors Acceptance Corporation, the Universal CIT Credit Corporation, the Commercial Credit Company, and hundreds of other smaller and less well-known similar organizations are important principally for their activities in financing instalment purchases of automobiles and other durable goods by ultimate consumers. In this connection, their services are discussed in a following major section which deals with consumer credit.

Many of the sales finance companies also engage in business financing. Some of them acquire open accounts receivable, in a manner similar to factors. Another service consists of instalment lien obligations in connection with the purchase, by merchants and manufacturers, of items of machinery, fixtures, or equipment that are used in the conduct of business.

One of the principal business financing services of sales finance companies is what is generally known as floor planning. This is a method of financing inventories of automobiles and other types of high unit value durable goods, especially major household appliances and certain types of industrial equipment sold through distributors. The practice may be illustrated with reference to the automobile industry. Automobile manufacturers normally expect cash payment upon delivery of cars to the dealer. Few dealers have the capital necessary to stock a large assortment of automobiles.

The commercial bank's standards of credit and maturity length of loans have been too strict to be of great value to the average dealer, who has therefore turned to the sales finance company for aid in carrying adequate inventories. Under the floor plan method, the dealer acquires new cars, stores or displays them, and executes a trust receipt for the benefit of the finance company. In this manner, the dealer has physical possession of the merchandise and can display and attempt to sell it, but he does not have legal title to it. Title to the automobiles is vested in the finance company, the dealer merely holding the goods in trust. In some companies, chattel mortgages are used to secure the loans upon cars in storage rather than a trust receipt.

When a sale is made, the proceeds must be immediately turned over to the finance company before the car can be moved from the dealer's premises. In many instances, this is largely in the nature of a bookkeeping transaction rather than a transfer of cash funds, for the same sales finance company often finances the major part of the ultimate consumer's purchase price. The amount loaned to dealers under the floor plan method usually does not exceed 90 per cent of the cost of the article from the manufacturer.

Financing Through Warehouse Receipts

Every public warehouse issues to depositors receipts for goods placed in storage, and these warehouse receipts are used as a basis for securing advances on the stored goods from commercial banks and, to some extent, also from finance companies. The owner may receive a *negotiable* warehouse receipt executed in his name and which he may endorse to the order of his bank or other lending institution, or he may obtain a *nonnegotiable* receipt issued originally in the name of the lender. Either type of receipt is regarded as sound collateral. Loans amounting to 60 or 70 per cent of the market value of the merchandise are often made on the basis of such security. Until the loan is repaid, the borrower cannot regain possession of the merchandise. If the loan is defaulted, the bank can claim the merchandise and have it sold to satisfy the obligation. When the borrower wishes to make a partial withdrawal of the merchandise which is so pledged, arrangements can easily be made to repay part of the loan or to pledge additional security of an equally satisfactory character.

Field Warehousing

A natural development of the principle of using warehouse receipts as a basis for outside financing is field warehousing. The idea is simply that warehouse receipts normally issued on goods stored in a public warehouse shall be made available for financing the storage of merchandise on the premises of the manufacturer or whoever owns the goods. The warehouse is in effect moved to the owner's plant or warehouse. The owner of the goods actually leases a portion of his storage facilities to a licensed warehouseman who places a representative in charge, posts signs stating that a designated portion of the warehouse is in charge of the outside organization, and adds to or takes from stock as directed by the banker who has the stock as collateral.

The field warehouse representative may actually be a regular employee of the owner of the pledged inventory, but must be covered by a fidelity bond commensurate with the degree of financial responsibility involved. Under this arrangement, such a representative can continue with the performance of his normal responsibilities, so that there is very small personnel expense connected with the warehousing. Field warehousing is thus, in reality, more of a credit arrangement than a strictly storage operation. Experience has shown that collateral so warehoused is just as secure as when it is placed in a public warehouse.

Typical illustrations of the plan in use are manifold. A paint manufacturer found himself with an overstock. Three options existed. He could cut the price, take a large loss, and perhaps move it into the market. He could deposit the merchandise in a public warehouse and borrow on it, but that was too expensive. The third plan, that of assigning a part of the stock to a field warehouseman, was adopted with success and economy. Manufacturers of tin cans store them in canners' warehouses until they are needed by the canner, when he makes the required payment before they are released by the manufacturer.

He thus reduces the time for his loans to a few days, for as soon as they are filled they become the basis of another loan, as they can be at once turned over to the same field warehouseman who had them while they were empty. A steel pipe manufacturer has used the plan for carrying reserve stocks in three widely scattered cities. Farm implement manufacturers find it equally useful in connection with the accumulation of inventory for seasonal selling peaks. In fact, any manufacturer or middleman with substantial stocks of standardized goods which are in ready demand can use the plan for addtional financing.

The advantages of field warehousing are several. First, it is economical, since it is unnecessary to move the stock to a public warehouse for deposit. Liquids can be left in their natural containers, cans of food need not be cased or labeled until their buyer is determined and is ready to pay for them, and in some cases goods to be further processed can be left adjacent to their next step of production, thus eliminating the two-way trip to a public warehouse. Second, banks arc ready to quote a lower rate of interest on loans so secured than on loans based on an open line of credit, for the notes can be rediscounted with a reserve bank. Third, if the manufacturer cannot be supplied with funds locally, paper secured by field warehouse receipts can be more readily sold in a nation-wide commercial paper market.

The principal limitation is the cost of arranging for field warehousing services. Service fees must be charged to cover the cost of segregating the warehouse area involved, providing locks and signs, bonding a warehouse representative, and making periodic audits of goods held in storage. Such charges are relatively small when inventories of large value are involved but are prohibitive in connection with very small-scale financing. The minimum loan which is considered economically practical for a field warehousing company to handle is about $10,000.

Mercantile Credit

Mercantile credit is the credit one businessman extends to another when selling goods on time for resale or for commercial use. It includes all postponements of payment involved in the purchase of goods throughout the process of distribution, from the time they are in the state of raw materials until they reach the hands of the retailer or business user. Its purpose is to facilitate the marketing of goods through channels of trade.

Terms of Sale

The terms of sale in mercantile credit commonly comprise two distinct elements—the net credit period and the cash discount. The length of time for which credit is extended is called the *net credit period.* Wholesalers and manufacturers adjust their credit periods to different lines of business, but great differences are sometimes observed in the same line and even within individual establishments when granting credit to different customers. In general, the length of the credit period tends to conform roughly to the receipt of income, on the part of buyers, from the sale of goods and services. The rate of turnover of the purchaser's stock of goods is the most fundamental and determining factor as to the amount of time involved. In the wholesale tobacco trade, where the typical customer's rate of stock turnover is very high, wholesalers' terms to retailers are usually 7 to 10 days, but in the jewelry trade, where retail stock turnover is ordinarily very slow, terms ranging from 60 to 120 days, or even longer, are usual.

While the rate of stock turnover is the fundamental consideration, other factors modify this relationship and sometimes obscure it completely. Longer periods are common when customers are located at a considerable distance from the seller, and when goods must be in transit for extended periods. In some instances, the credit period offered to particular buyers is governed by the length of the credit period granted by preceding sellers. If customers of the purchaser receive income seasonably, as in farming areas, the retailers' credit requirements are magnified and longer periods are common. *Cash discounts* are generally granted in the mercantile field whenever goods are sold on credit, as a means of stimulating advance payment of bills.

Cash discounts are premiums for advance payment, at a rate which is considerably higher than the prevailing rate of interest, because of advantages that accrue to the seller from such a procedure. An illustration of this may be afforded by the following terms which are more or less common in certain lines of trade. Assume that a bill of goods is purchased on terms of 2/10, net 30 days. This means that if the purchaser pays for the goods within 10 days from date of the shipment or date of the invoice (which are usually synonymous), he will receive a 2 per cent discount to be deducted from the amount billed on the invoice. If, on the other hand, he waits the full 30 days and pays his bill at expiration of the net credit period, he must pay the full amount of the bill. Thus, by deferring payment for 20 days beyond the 10-day period, the purchaser sacrifices 2 per cent of the full amount involved. Receiving a 2 per cent discount for a period of 20 days is the equivalent of earning interest on the amount involved in the transaction at the rate of 36 per cent per annum. This is true because the discount is paid for a period of time which is approximately one-eighteenth of a year.

The seller justifies this discount policy on the ground that it gives him quicker possession of the money, which can be turned over again, and also reduces the credit and moral risks. Immediate possession of the money from the sale of goods tends to increase the rate of working capital turnover, furnishes adequate funds to operate the business, obviates the necessity for elaborate credit and collection machinery, reduces losses from bad debts, and tends to promote a spirit of good will between seller and customer through the elimination of some occasions for friction.

While the cash discount is generally regarded as a premium for payment in advance of due date, it is very often difficult to distinguish it from trade discounts or deductions from list prices quoted to the trade.

The same procedure may be used in order to ascertain the effective rate of interest involved in any cash discount, provided the length of the credit period is known. This may be generalized as follows:

- Subtract the number of days in the cash discount period from the number of days in the credit period. The result is the length of the period for which the discount is granted.
- Divide 360 days (the number of days assumed to represent an interest year) by the answer to 1, above. This shows the number of comparable periods in a year.
- Multiply the answer to 2, above, by the cash discount percentage.

Limitations

Most sellers establish quantitative credit limits which state the maximum amount of credit that may be allowed to be outstanding on each individual customer's account. Such limits are approximate ceilings that reflect the considered judgment of the selling company as to the amount of credit that may be extended safely to a given purchaser. It is an amount which a careful analysis of the character, capacity, capital, and conditions surrounding the business of the purchaser reveals to be in proper proportion to other aspects of the subject's business. There are other limitations to the use of mercantile credit. Some customers, because of their poor credit standing, may not be able to secure any credit accommodations whatever from their sources of supply, or may be granted exceedingly small amounts and for limited periods of time. Some types of suppliers sell only on a cash basis. Finally, when relatively large cash discounts are available, failure to take advantage of them makes mercantile credit an expensive form of outside financing. This causes many buyers to seek other sources of capital, in order to take cash discounts, and thereby to avoid undue dependence upon trade credit.

DIRECT MARKETING MANAGEMENT

Direct marketing is a form of advertising that reaches its audience without using traditional formal channels of advertising, such as TV, newspapers or radio. Businesses communicate straight to the consumer with advertising techniques such as fliers, catalogue distribution, promotional letters, and street advertising.

Direct Advertising is a sub-discipline and type of marketing. There are two main definitional characteristics which distinguish it from other types of marketing. The first is that it sends its message directly to consumers, without the use of intervening commercial communication media. The second characteristic is the core principle of successful Advertising driving a specific "call to action." This aspect of direct marketing involves an emphasis on trackable, measurable, positive responses from consumers regardless of medium.

If the advertisement asks the prospect to take a specific action, for instance call a free phone number or visit a Web site, then the effort is considered to be direct response advertising.

Direct marketing is predominantly used by small to medium-size enterprises with limited advertising budgets that do not have a well-recognized brand message. A well-executed direct advertising campaign can offer a positive return on investment as the message is not hidden with overcomplicated branding. Instead, direct advertising is straight to the point; offers a product, service, or event; and explains how to get the offered product, service, or event.

The term direct marketing is believed to have been first used in 1967 in a speech by Lester Wunderman, who pioneered direct marketing techniques with brands such as American Express and Columbia Records. The term junk mail, referring to unsolicited commercial ads delivered via post office or directly deposited in consumers' mail boxes, can be traced back to 1954. The term spam, meaning "unsolicited commercial e-mail," can be traced back to March 31, 1993, although in its first few months it merely referred to inadvertently posting a message so many times on UseNet that the repetitions effectively drowned out the normal flow of conversation.

Although Wunderman may have been the first to use the term direct marketing, the practice of mail order selling essentially began in the U.S. upon invention of the typewriter in 1867.

The first modern mail-order catalog was produced by Aaron Montgomery Ward in 1872. The Direct Mail Advertising Association, predecessor of the present-day Direct Marketing Association, was first established in 1917. Third class bulk mail postage rates were established in 1928.

Direct marketing's history in Europe can be traced to the 15th century. Upon Gutenberg's invention of movable type, the first trade catalogs from printer-publishers appeared sometime around 1450.

Benefits and Drawbacks

Direct marketing is attractive to many marketers, because in many cases its positive effect can be measured directly. For example, if a marketer sends out 1,000 solicitations by mail, and 100 respond to the promotion, the marketer can say with confidence that campaign led directly to 10% direct responses. The number of recipients who are offended by junk mail/spam, however, is not easily measured. By contrast, measurement of other media must often be indirect, since there is no direct response from a consumer. Measurement of results, a fundamental element in successful direct marketing.

The Internet has made it easier for marketing managers to measure the results of a campaign. This is often achieved by using a specific Web site landing page directly relating to the promotional material, a call to action will ask the consumer to visit the landing page, and the effectiveness of the campaign can be measured by taking the number of promotional messages distributed and dividing it by the number of responses.

Another way to measure the results is to compare the projected sales for a given term with the actual sales after a direct advertising campaign. While many marketers recognize the financial benefits of increasing targeted awareness, some direct marketing efforts using particular media have been criticized for generating unwanted solicitations, not due to the method of communication but because of poorly compiled demographic databases, advertisers do not wish to waste money on communicating with consumers not interested in their products. For example, direct mail that is irrelevant to the recipient is considered "junk mail," and unwanted e-mail messages are considered "spam."

Some consumers are demanding an end to direct marketing for privacy and environmental reasons, which direct marketers are able to do to some extent by using "opt-out" lists, variable printing, and more-targeted mailing lists.

In response to consumer demand and increasing business pressure to increase the effectiveness of reaching the right consumer with direct marketing, companies such as Ireland Advertising specialize in targeted direct advertising to great effect, reducing advertising budget waste and increasing the effectiveness of delivering a marketing message with better geodemography information, delivering the advertising message to only the consumers interested in the product, service, or event on offer.

Channels

Direct Mail

The most common form of direct marketing is direct mail, sometimes called junk mail, used by advertisers who send document mail to all postal customers in an area or to all customers on a list.

Any low-budget medium that can be used to deliver a communication to a customer can be employed in direct marketing. Probably the most commonly used medium for direct marketing is mail, in which marketing communications are sent to customers using the postal service.

The term direct mail is used in the direct marketing industry to refer to communication deliveries by the Post Office, which may also be referred to as "junk mail" or "admail" or "crap mail" and may involve bulk mail.

Junk mail includes advertising circulars, catalogs, free trial CDs, pre-approved credit card applications, and other unsolicited merchandising invitations delivered by mail or to homes and businesses, or delivered to consumers' mailboxes by delivery services other than the Post Office. Bulk mailings are a particularly popular method of promotion for businesses operating in the financial services, home computer, and travel and tourism industries.

In many developed countries, direct mail represents such a significant amount of the total volume of mail that special rate classes have been established. In the United States and United Kingdom, for example, there are bulk mail rates that enable marketers to send mail at rates that are substantially lower than regular first-class rates. In order to qualify for these rates, marketers must format and sort the mail in particular ways – which reduces the handling required by the postal service. Advertisers often refine direct mail practices into targeted mailing, in which mail is sent out following database analysis to select recipients considered most likely to respond positively. For example a person who has demonstrated an interest in golf may receive direct mail for golf related products or perhaps for goods and services that are appropriate for golfers. This use of database analysis is a type of database marketing. The United States Postal Service calls this form of mail "advertising mail".

Telemarketing

Another common form of direct marketing is telemarketing, in which marketers contact consumers by phone. The unpopularity of cold call telemarketing has led some US states and the US federal government to create "no-call lists" and legislation including heavy fines. This process may be outsourced to specialist call centres.

In the US, a national do-not-call list went into effect on October 1, 2003. Under the law, it is illegal for telemarketers to call anyone who has registered themselves on the list. After the list had operated for one year, over 62 million people had signed up. The telemarketing industry opposed the creation of the list, but most telemarketers have complied with the law and refrained from calling people who are on the list. Canada has passed legislation to create a similar Do Not Call List. In other countries it is voluntary, such as the New Zealand Name Removal Service.

E-mail Marketing

E-mail Marketing is a third type of direct marketing. A major concern is spam. As a result of the proliferation of mass spamming, ISPs and e-mail service providers have developed increasingly effective E-Mail Filtering programmes. These filters can interfere with the delivery of e-mail marketing campaigns, even if the person has subscribed to receive them, as legitimate e-mail marketing can possess the same hallmarks as spam. There are a range of e-mail service providers that provide services for legitimate opt-in e-mailers to avoid being classified as spam.

Door-to-Door Leaflet Marketing

Leaflet distribution services are used extensively by the fast food industries, and many other business focussing on a local catchment Business to consumer business model, similar to direct mail marketing, this method is targeted purely by area, and costs a fraction of the amount of a mailshot due to not having to purchase stamps, envelopes or having to buy address lists and the names of home occupants.

Broadcast Faxing

A fourth type of direct marketing, broadcast faxing, is now less common than the other forms. This is partly due to laws in the United States and elsewhere which make it illegal.

Voicemail Marketing

A fifth type of direct marketing has emerged out of the market prevalence of personal voice mailboxes, and business voicemail systems. Due to the ubiquity of e-mail marketing, and the expense of direct mail and telemarketing, voicemail marketing presented a cost effective means by which to reach people directly, by voice.

Abuse of consumer marketing applications of voicemail marketing resulted in an abundance of "voice-spam", and prompted many jurisdictions to pass laws regulating consumer voicemail marketing.

More recently, businesses have utilized guided voicemail to accomplish personalized business-to-business marketing formerly reserved for telemarketing. Because guided voicemail is used to contact only businesses, it is exempt from Do Not Call regulations in place for other forms of voicemail marketing.

Couponing

Couponing is used in print media to elicit a response from the reader. An example is a coupon which the reader cuts out and presents to a super-store check-out counter to avail of a discount. Coupons in newspapers and magazines cannot be considered direct marketing, since the marketer incurs the cost of supporting a third-party medium; direct marketing aims to circumvent that balance, paring the costs down to solely delivering their unsolicited sales message to the consumer, without supporting the newspaper that the consumer seeks and welcomes.

Direct-response Television Marketing

Direct marketing on TV has two basic forms: long form and short form, which refers to typical 30-second or 60-second commercials that ask viewers for an immediate response.

TV-response marketing—i.e. infomercials—can be considered a form of direct marketing, since responses are in the form of calls to telephone numbers given on-air. This both allows marketers to reasonably conclude that the calls are due to a particular campaign, and allows the marketers to obtain customers' phone numbers as targets for telemarketing. Under the Federal Do-Not-Call List rules in the US, if the caller buys anything, the marketer would be exempt from Do-Not-Call List restrictions for a period of time due to having a prior business relationship with the caller. Firms such as QVC, Thane Direct, and Interwood Marketing Group then cross-sell and up-sell to these respondents.

One of the most famous DRTV commercials was for Ginsu Knives by Ginsu Products, Inc. of RI. Several aspects of ad, such as its use of adding items to the offer and the guarantee of satisfaction were much copied and came to be considered part of the formula for success with short-form direct-response TV ads

Direct Selling

Direct selling is the sale of products by face-to-face contact with the customer, either by having salespeople approach potential customers in person, or through indirect means such as Tupperware parties.

Popularity of Direct Advertising

A report produced by the Direct Marketing Association found that 57% of the campaigns studied were employing integrated strategies. Of those, almost half launched with a direct mail campaign, typically followed by e-mail and then telemarketing.

SALES

A sale is the pinnacle activity involved in the selling products or services in return for money or other compensation. It is an act of completion of a commercial activity.

The seller - the provider of the goods or services - completes a sale in response to an acquisition or to an appropriation or to a request. There follows the passing of title in the item, and the application and due settlement of a price, the obligation for which arises due to the seller's requirement to pass ownership. Ideally, a seller agrees upon a price at which he willingly parts with ownership of or any claim upon the item. The purchaser, though a party to the sale, does not execute the sale, only the seller does that. To be precise the sale completes prior to the payment and gives rise to the obligation of payment. If the seller completes the first two stages of the sale prior to settlement of the price, the sale remains valid and gives rise to an obligation to pay.

Sales Techniques

A sale can take place through:

- Direct sales, involving person to person contact
- Pro forma sales
- Agency-based
  - Sales agents
  - Sales outsourcing through direct branded representation
  - Transaction sales
  - Consultative sales
  - Complex sales
  - Consignment
  - Telemarketing or telesales
  - Retail or consumer
- Traveling salesman
  - Door-to-door methods
  - Hawking
- *Request for proposal*: An invitation for suppliers, through a bidding process, to submit a proposal on a specific product or service. An RFP usually represents part of a complex sales process, also known as "enterprise sales".
- *Business-to-business*: Business-to-business sales are much more relationship-based owing to the lack of emotional attachment to the products in question. Industrial/professional sales involves selling from one business to another
- Electronic
  - *Web*: Business-to-business and business-to-consumer
  - *Electronic Data Interchange*: A set of standard for structuring information to be electronically exchanged between and within businesses
- Indirect, human-mediated but with indirect contact
  - Mail-order
  - Vending machine
- Sales methods:
  - Selling technique
  - IMPACT Selling
  - SPIN Selling
  - Consultative selling
  - Sales enablement

- Solution selling
- Conceptual Selling
- Strategic Selling
- Transactional Selling
- Sales Negotiation
- Reverse Selling
- Paint-the-Picture
- The take away

Sales Agents

Agents in the sales process can represent either of two parties in the sales process; for example:

1. *Sales broker or Seller agency or seller agent*: This is a traditional role where the salesman represents a person or company on the selling end of a deal
2. *Buyers broker or Buyer brokerage*: This is where the salesman represents the consumer making the purchase. This is most often applied in large transactions.
3. *Disclosed dual agent*: This is where the salesman represents both parties in the sale and acts as a mediator for the transaction. The role of the salesman here is to oversee that both parties receive an honest and fair deal, and is responsible to both.
4. *Transaction broker*: This is where the salesperson doesn't represent either party, but handles the transaction only. The seller owes no responsibility to either party getting a fair or honest deal, just that all of the documents are handled properly.
5. Sales outsourcing involves direct branded representation where the sales reps are recruited, hired, and managed by an external entity but hold quotas, represent themselves as the brand of the client, and report all activities back to the client. It is akin to a virtual extension of a sales force.
6. *Sales managers*: Qualified and talented sales managers aim to implement various sales strategies and management techniques in order to facilitate improved profits and increased sales volume. They are also responsible for coordinating the sales and marketing department as well as oversight concerning the fair and honest execution of the sales process by their agents.
7. *Salesmen*: The primary function of professional sales is to generate and close leads, educate prospects, fill needs and satisfy wants of consumers appropriately, and therefore turn prospective customers into actual ones. Questioning - to understand a customer's goal

and requirements relevant to the product - and the creation of a valuable solution by communicating the necessary information that encourages a buyer to achieve their goal at an economic cost comprise the functions of the salesperson or of the sales engine. A good salesman should never mis-sell or over-evaluate the customer's requirements.

Inside Sales vs. Outside Sales

Since the advent of the telephone a distinction has been made between "inside sales" and "outside sales", although it is generally agreed that these terms do not have hard-and-fast definitions. In the United States, the Fair Labour Standards Act defines outside sales representatives as "employees sell their employer's products, services, or facilities to customers away from their employer's place(s) of business, in general, either at the customer's place of business or by selling door-to-door at the customer's home" while defining those who work "from the employer's location" as inside sales. Inside sales generally involves attempting to close business primarily over the phone via cold calling or telemarketing, while outside sales will usually involve initial phone work to book sales calls at the potential buyer's location to attempt to close the deal in person. Some companies have an inside sales department that works with outside representatives and book their appointments for them. Inside sales sometimes refers to upselling to existing customers.

The Relationships between Sales and Marketing

Marketing and sales differ greatly, but have the same goal. Marketing improves the selling environment and plays a very important role in sales. If the marketing department generates a list of potential customers, that can benefit sales. A marketing department in an organization has the goal increasing the number of interactions between potential customers and the organization.

Achieving this goal may involve the sales team using promotional techniques such as advertising, sales promotion, publicity, and public relations, creating new sales channels, or creating new products, among other things. It can also include bringing the potential customer to visit the organization's website(s) for more information, or to contact the organization for more information, or to interact with the organization via social media such as Twitter, Facebook and blogs.

The relatively new field of sales process engineering views "sales" as the output of a larger system, not just as the output of one department. The larger system includes many functional areas within an organization. From this perspective, "sales" and "marketing" label for a number of processes whose inputs and outputs supply one another to varying degrees. In this context, improving an "output" involves studying and improving the broader sales process, as in any system, since the component functional areas interact and are interdependent.

Most large corporations structure their marketing departments in a similar fashion to sales departments and the managers of these teams must coordinate efforts in order to drive profits and business success. For example, an "inbound" focused campaign seeks to drive more customers "through the door", giving the sales department a better chance of selling their product to the consumer. A good marketing programme would address any potential downsides as well.

The sales department would aim to improve the interaction between the customer and the sales facility or mechanism and/or salesperson. Sales management would break down the selling process and then increase the effectiveness of the discrete processes as well as the interaction between processes. For example, in many out-bound sales environments, the typical process includes out-bound calling, the sales pitch, handling objections, opportunity identification, and the close. Each step of the process has sales-related issues, skills, and training needs, as well as marketing solutions to improve each discrete step, as well as the whole process.

One further common complication of marketing involves the inability to measure results for a great deal of marketing initiatives. In essence, many marketing and advertising executives often lose sight of the objective of sales/revenue/profit, as they focus on establishing a creative/innovative programme, without concern for the top or bottom lines - a fundamental pitfall of marketing for marketing's sake.

Many companies find it challenging to get marketing and sales on the same page. The two departments, although different in nature, handle very similar concepts and have to work together for sales to be successful. Building a good relationship between the two that encourages communication can be the key to success - even in a down economy.

Marketing Potentially Negates the Need for Sales

Some sales authors and consultants contend that an expertly planned and executed marketing strategy may negate the need for outside sales entirely. They suggest that by effectively bringing more customers"through the door" and enticing them into contact, sales organizations can dramatically improve their results, efficiency, profitability, and allow salespeople to provide a drastically higher level of customer service and satisfaction, instead of spending the majority of their working hours searching for someone to sell to.

Industrial Marketing

The idea that marketing can potentially eliminate the need for sales people depends entirely on context. For example, this may be possible in some B2C situations; however, for many B2B transactions this is mostly impossible. Another dimension is the value of the goods being sold. Fast-moving consumer-goods require no sales people at the point of sale to get them to jump off the supermarket shelf and into the customer's trolley. However, the purchase of large mining equipment worth millions of dollars will require a sales person to manage the sales process - particularly in the face of competitors.

Sales and Marketing Alignment and Integration

Another area of discussion involves the need for alignment and integration between corporate sales and marketing functions. According to a report from the Chief Marketing Officer Council, only 40 per cent of companies have formal programmes, systems or processes in place to align and integrate the two critical functions. Traditionally, these two functions have operated separately, left in siloed areas of tactical responsibility. Glen Petersen; The Profit Maximization Paradox sees the changes in the competitive landscape between the 1950s and the time of writing as so dramatic that the complexity of choice, price and opportunities for the customer forced this seemingly simple and integrated relationship between sales and marketing to change forever.

Petersen goes on to highlight that salespeople spend approximately 40 per cent of their time preparing customer-facing deliverables while leveraging less than 50 per cent of the materials created by marketing, adding to perceptions that marketing is out of touch with the customer and that sales is resistant to messaging and strategy. Internet applications, commonly referred to as Sales 2.0 tools, have also increasingly been created to help align the goals and responsibilities of marketing and sales departments.

MANAGING PRODUCT MOVEMENT

In addition to enlisting the assistance of retailers and wholesalers to make products available to customers, marketers also face additional concerns when trying to meet their distribution objectives. We examine the tasks that must be carried out in order to physically move products to customers. In some cases the marketer will take on the responsibility of carrying out some functions, while other tasks may be assigned to distribution service providers. Whether handled by the marketer or contracted to others, these functions are crucial to having a cost-effective and efficient distribution system.

We explore the movement of product by first examining how physical distribution decisions often involve analysing the trade-off between the service level the marketer offers to customers versus the costs associated with providing these services.

Next we provide an in-depth examination of three major tasks that the marketer or distribution service providers may need to carryout in order to ship products to customers. These tasks include:

- Ordering and Inventory Management
- Product Storage
- Transportation

It is worth noting that while most physical distribution is concerned with moving tangible products, some of the issues covered here are also applicable to intangible products, such as services and to digital products.

TRADE-OFF ANALYSIS: SERVICE-LEVEL VS. COST

The distribution activities we discuss in this part of the Principles of Marketing tutorial are important elements in the marketer's overall customer service package. Marketers strive to deliver an optimal level of service to their customers. However, "optimal" does not always translate into providing the "best" service options to customers. The service-level marketers' offer for their distribution activities, like the service-level offered by other company-related activities that impact customers (e.g., customer help desk), is determined using trade-off analysis.

With service-level trade-off analysis, the marketer compares the number and quality of distribution features (e.g., speed of delivery, ease of placing orders, order tracking, etc.) they would like to offer versus the cost of providing the features. For instance, when it comes to transportation options (e.g., truck, railroad, air, etc.), trade-off analysis may show that choosing the fastest method for delivery may not make economic sense since options for fast delivery often are very expensive compared to slower methods. While the customer may appreciate having their order arrive quickly, the marketer may find fast delivery to be an expensive proposition that significantly reduces their profit margin.

Since most distribution activities are non-revenue producing (i.e., are used to support the selling of a product but do not actually create a sale) and, thus, represent a cost to the marketer, it should be understood that the marketer's distribution system choice may not be the overall best available in terms of getting the product into customer's hand as fast as possible. Rather, the marketer's choice for what is optimal will be determined by analysing distribution features and costs and evaluating how these fit within the marketer's overall objectives (e.g., financial objectives, product positioning, etc.).

ORDERING AND INVENTORY MANAGEMENT

Having products available when customers want to make purchases may seem like a relatively straightforward process. All a seller needs to do is make sure there is product (i.e., inventory) in their possession and ready for the customer to purchase. Unfortunately, being prepared for customer purchasing is not always easy.

Having the right product available when the customer is ready to buy requires a highly coordinated effort involving order entry and processing systems, forecasting techniques, customer knowledge, strong channel relationships and efficiency at physically handling products.

Order Entry and Processing System

The marketer must have a system allowing customers to easily place orders. This system can be as simple as a consumer walking to the counter of small food stand to purchase a few vegetables or as complicated as automated computer systems where an electronic order is triggered from a retailer to a manufacturer each time a consumer purchases a product at the retailer's store. In either case, the order processing system must be able to meet the purchasing needs of the customer. In some cases, an efficient ordering system can be turned into a competitive advantage. Firms such as Amazon.com, turned their order handing system into a product feature with the patented "1-click" ordering option that streamlines online ordering by reducing the number of clicks needed to make purchases.

Forecasting

Inventory management is often an exercise in predicting how customers will respond in the future. By predicting purchase behaviour the marketer can respond by making sure the right amount of product is available. For most large-scale resellers effective inventory forecasting requires the use of sophisticated statistical tools that look at many variables, such as past purchase history, amount of promotional effort that triggers an increase in customer ordering, and other market criteria to determine how much of the product will be needed to meet customer demand.

Customer Knowledge

Inventory management can be fine-tuned to respond to customer's needs. As a marketer learns more about a customer they begin to observe trends in how and when purchases are made. Combining customer knowledge with forecasting techniques allows the marketer to better estimate product demand and inventory requirements. The key to understanding customers is to have in place a customer relationship management (CRM) system that tracks all customer activity and allows for data mining activities that analyse customer information in order to identify patterns in customer activity.

Channel Relationships

While the marketer who uses channel members to sell consumer products has access to information for their immediate customers (e.g., resellers) they often do not have access to sales and customer behaviour information controlled by the party selling to the final consumer (e.g., retailer). Knowing the demand patterns at the final consumer level can give marketers good insight into how the reseller may order.

Developing strong relationships with the holder of consumer information can result in the reseller sharing this information with the marketer. In fact, some retailers allow marketers direct access to real-time, store-level inventory information so the marketer can monitor how products are selling in stores and be in a position to respond quickly if inventory needs change.

Physical Product Handling

An often overlooked area of inventory management involves the actions and skills needed to prepare a product to move from one point to another. Some products require special attention be given to ensure the product is not damaged during shipment. Such efforts must be carefully balanced against increased costs that arise (e.g., stronger packaging) in order to provide greater protection to products. Because of this, many marketers will accept the fact that some small level of damage to occur during the distribution process.

PRODUCT STORAGE

The second important element in physical distribution concerns storing products for future delivery. Marketers of tangible products, and even digital products, may have storage concerns. Storage facilities, such as warehouses, play an important role in the distribution process for a number of reasons including:

- *Hold Wide Assortment:* Many resellers allow their customers to purchase small quantities of many different products. Yet to obtain the best prices from suppliers, resellers must purchase in large quantities. The need, thus, exists for storage facilities that not only hold a large volume of product, but also can hold a wide-variety of resellers' inventory. Additionally, these facilities must be organized in a way that permits resellers to easily fill orders for their customers.
- *Meet Unanticipated Demand:* Holding products in storage offers a safeguard in cases of unexpected increases in demand for products.
- *Needed for Large Shipping Quantities:* As we noted in our discussion of transportation, manufacturers generally prefer to ship in large product quantities in order to more effectively spread transportation costs. This often means manufacturers must create storage areas in which the manufactured goods can build up in the quantities needed for such shipments to occur.
- *Offer Faster Response:* Additional storage facilities, strategically located in different geographical areas, allows a marketing organization to respond quickly to customers' needs. The ability to respond with quick delivery can be a major value-added feature since it reduces the buyer's need to maintain large inventory at their own locations.
- *Security and Backup:* For digital products, additional storage facilities are not only needed to offer customers faster access to products (e.g., online content and software) but are also needed to protect against technical glitches and security threats.

Types of Warehouses

The warehouse is the most common type of storage though other forms do exist (e.g., storage tanks, computer server farms). Some warehouses are massive structures that simultaneously support the unloading of numerous in-bound trucks and railroad cars containing suppliers' products while at the same time loading multiple trucks for shipment to customers.

Below we discuss five types of warehouses:

- *Private Warehouse:* This type of warehouse is owned and operated by channel suppliers and resellers and used in their own distribution activity. For instance, a major retail chain may have several regional warehouses supplying their stores or a wholesaler will operate a warehouse at which it receives and distributes products.
- *Public Warehouse:* The public warehouse is essentially space that can be leased to solve short-term distribution needs. Retailers that operate their own private warehouses may occasionally seek additional storage space if their facilities have reached capacity or if they are making a special, large purchase of products. For example, retailers may order extra merchandise to prepare for in-store sales or order a large volume of a product that is offered at a low promotional price by a supplier.
- *Automated Warehouse:* With advances in computer and robotics technology many warehouses now have automated capabilities. The level of automation ranges from a small conveyor belt transporting products in a small area all the way up to a fully automated facility where only a few people are needed to handle storage activity for thousands of pounds/kilograms of product. In fact, many warehouses use machines to handle nearly all physical distribution activities such as moving product-filled pallets (i.e., platforms that hold large amounts of product) around buildings that may be several stories tall and the length of two or more football fields.
- *Climate-Controlled Warehouse:* Warehouses handle storage of many types of products including those that need special handling conditions such as freezers for storing frozen products, humidity-controlled environments for delicate products, such as produce or flowers, and dirt-free facilities for handling highly sensitive computer products.
- *Distribution Centre:* There are some warehouses where product storage is considered a very temporary activity. These warehouses serve as points in the distribution system at which products are received from many suppliers and quickly shipped out to many customers. In some cases, such as with distribution centers handling perishable food (e.g., produce), most of the product enters in the early morning and is distributed by the end of the day.

MODERN MARKETING MANAGEMENT

From earliest history, man has been dependent upon agriculture and upon some forms, however crude, of handicraft or manufacturing activity. Only in very recent times have people, especially in the United States, lived in an economy dominated by marketing-oriented organizations. The rather youthful character of our marketing system as it exists today may be better understood by giving very brief attention to historical changes from primitive times, through the emergence of a middleman system, down to current marketing conceptions.

EARLY DEVELOPMENTS

The origin of marketing is lost in antiquity. Certainly there is ample evidence of the existence of trade among the ancient Egyptians. Numerous references to trade are to be found in the Old Testament, and the Phoenicians in their heyday were regarded as a nation of wholesalers. Both wholesale and retail trade were well developed during the era of Greek supremacy and in the period of Roman domination.

To be sure, articles traded in the early days of civilization were few. They were restricted largely to luxuries purchased by the rich, due to the costliness and dangers of transportation and the low standards of living. Differentiation of production in the various parts of a country and deficiencies in essentials such as common salt and spices in certain countries also stimulated trade, but in relatively few items. Even as late as the year 1000, villages were characterized by their agrarian, independent nature and by economic self-sufficiency. In every village attempts were made, by methods now considered crude and wasteful, to raise the necessary food supply and to produce other necessaries of existence. With the fall of the Roman Empire, trade seems to have suffered an eclipse for some centuries.

Beginning with the latter part of the Middle Ages the advance from the manorial or village system to the town was rapid. The town became a place of craftsmen and traders. In this handicraft stage, skilled workers set themselves up in their homes as craftsmen, making goods to order. Enterprising craftsmen began to use apprentices and often produced a surplus which was sold at local markets or fairs. This resulted in the organization of markets and in the holding of fairs at periodic intervals. Craftsmen soon organized into guilds, which controlled both manufacturing and marketing by minute regulations, much to the detriment of progress in both. The domestic system, whereby the products of the craftsmen were sold by businessmen, superseded the handicraft stage. With increased protection by stronger and more stable governments, towns grew rapidly and markets gradually expanded. Toward the close of the fifteenth century a period of discoveries began.

It resulted in marked improvements in maritime transportation, thereby supplying an added impetus to commerce. With the development of national governments, guilds finally outlived their usefulness, and during the early part of the sixteenth century mercantilism became the guiding principle of state policy. In brief, mercantilists argued that a country could become opulent if it sold more merchandise and services to foreigners than it bought from them. Only in this way could it increase its stock of precious metals that was received in payment required by a "favorable balance of trade" and which, at that time, was considered the ultimate desideratum. Naturally, this movement stimulated commerce to no small degree.

The Industrial Revolution

In the latter part of the eighteenth century the Industrial Revolution began to usher in marked improvements in form utility production. These were continued throughout the early part of the nineteenth century, but were greatly accelerated in the United States in the period following the Civil War. The domestic stage of manufacture was supplanted almost entirely by factories in which large numbers of specialized workers were employed. Elaborate steam- or motor-driven machinery replaced handicraft methods. Industry became localized, largescale output became the goal of manufacturers, and a minute division of labour began to be considered an essential prerequisite to efficient operation.

Specialization reached such a point that whole communi-ties or areas sometimes devoted a major part of their energy to the making of a single commodity.

Thus, Pittsburgh and Gary became known for iron and steel products; Detroit for automobiles; Wisconsin for cheese and other dairy products; California, Florida, and the Rio Grande valley for citrus fruits; and so on. xhe geographical chasm separating farm or factory and consumer widened considerably.

The agricultural producer, the processor, or the manufacturer cannot ordinarily seek out the final consumer or user of his wares. He finds it more economical to devote his major effort to physical production, where he is presumably of maximum service, and for the most part allows a marketing system to dispose of his finished goods and even to assemble his raw materials for him. Similarly, the consumer or business user finds that any attempt on his part to purchase the numerous commodities necessary to satisfy his increasing and varied wants, directly from their makers, is the height of absurdity. He is, therefore, only too glad in the vast majority of cases to be relieved of the necessity of buying direct and to let the marketing system do it for him.

Effect of Industrial Revolution

It thus becomes obvious that the present middleman system is the outgrowth of changed conditions, the outcome of a growing civilization and industrial progress. As long as towns were economically self-sufficient, producer-consumer contact was feasible except for trade between countries. As localized, large-scale physical production developed, and cities grew in importance, maladjustments made their appearance, marketing risks increased, and an elaborate middleman system was called into existence to bridge over the ever-widening gap that separated the consumer or business user from the manufacturer. To these factors may be added the constant pressure to increase both the scale of industrial output and production for sale instead of own use, both of which are direct results of our factory system.

Need for Middlemen

From this brief historical sketch it is apparent that few, if any, middlemen existed in primitive society—a condition that still obtains in underdeveloped parts of the globe. There is hardly any surplus to exchange in primitive or highly underdeveloped communities. Each family is making practically all that is used in the home. Whenever any surplus of products of the soil, chase, or craftsman's art becomes available, the members of the tribe or village effect exchanges directly among themselves. Even during the early part of the handicraft stage in Europe, consumers either visited the shops of craftsmen or the latter abandoned their loom or bench at frequent intervals in order to find buyers for their wares.

On the other hand, whenever a country advanced in civilization, trade flourished as it did in ancient Sumeria, Babylonia, Phoenicia, and Egypt. In later years the Persians, Greeks, and Romans engaged in trade to a considerable extent, which decreased in importance as these nations declined in power. In modern times the ascendancy of trade resulted

largely from the Industrial Revolution. This presented in its early days what appeared to be insuperable marketing problems. Marketing functions were therefore shifted more and more to middlemen who specialized in their performance, so that in the latter part of the nineteenth century the basis for the present system of marketing was fairly well established.

Even today in the transfer of title to goods, direct contact may be established. Manufacturers sometimes buy raw materials directly from original producers, and they often purchase semimanufactured goods, parts, equipment, and supplies direct.

Similarly, the consuming public buys a limited amount of merchandise direct from farmer or manufacturer. The bulk of farm products and manufactured goods, however, is bought and sold indirectly through one or more middlemen. *Middlemen are, then, individuals, firms, or corporations that stand between prime producers and ultimate consumers, assume title or assist directly in its transfer, and receive a profit for the risks they assume in addition to being paid for the cost of their services or take whatever losses are incident to the assumption of an entrepreneur's functions.* Salesmen are excluded from this group, for they are not in business for themselves and, consequently, assume none of the risks of entrepreneurs and receive no profit, nor do they sustain losses from their sales efforts as such.

Classification of Middlemen

Undoubtedly the most useful classification of middlemen is that based on ownership of the goods. From both legal and practical aspects the relationship to the transfer of title is a most significant factor in defining the position of any group of middlemen. On this basis, *all middlemen can be divided into merchant and functional middlemen. Merchant middlemen buy the goods outright and necessarily take title to them.* Wholesalers and retailers are common examples. *Functional,* or nonmerchant, middlemen ordinarily assist directly in effecting a change in ownership, but they *do not themselves take title to the goods in which they deal. They specialized in the performance of a single marketing function or of a limited number of such functions,* one of which is usually related to the transfer of title. Functional middlemen are best represented by auction companies, brokers, commission houses, manufacturers' agents, and selling agents. Growing out of the major distinction between merchant and functional middlemen is a difference in degree of risk. All middlemen bear entrepreneurial risks, since they are in business for themselves and they may or may not be successful in securing the necessary volume for profitable operation. Merchant middlemen must, however, bear the additional risk resulting from the uncertain ability to dispose of the goods they own at remunerative prices. Functional middlemen, on the other hand, act for others in the purchase or sale of goods; hence the risks of a changing price level and of uncertain demand or supply conditions are borne by the principals in whom title to the goods vests. There are, of course, other organizations, institutions, or agencies which facilitate the performance of marketing functions by acting in some specialized capacity.

They are not, however, generally regarded as middlemen or as strictly marketing institutions, chiefly because they render no direct assistance in the transfer of title to goods—a characteristic peculiar to all bona fide middlemen and marketing organizations. Among these are railroads, commercial banks, insurance companies, ordinary warehouses, cold storage plants, marketing research agencies, inspectors, and graders. To the extent that they perform distributive and selling functions in certain lines of merchandise, warehouses may be classed among the functional middlemen, and to that extent they constitute an integral part of the marketing system.

Evolution of the Marketing Concept in Industry

Even though marketing functions have long been performed and a middleman system of marketing was well established in the last century, great changes have taken place in the significance attached to marketing by all kinds of companies. In general, this has been a transition from emphasis on selling what a company had to the producing of goods and services that are wanted by the customers that made up the demand side of the market. In the marketing literature of the late 1950's and early 1960's, the newer emphasis has been described as *the marketing concept, marketing orientation, or marketing management philosophy.*

Example of Transition

The evolution may be illustrated by the experience of a well-known manufacturer, The Pillsbury Company, which, like many other organizations, moved through four eras of emphasis. First, there was the era of *manufacturing dominance.* The company was founded in 1869 by Charles A. Pillsbury on the basis of availability of high-quality wheat and proximity of water power.

Major concern was with manufacturing—not marketing. According to a company executive, company philosophy in the era of manufacturing dominance might be stated as follows: "We are professional flour millers. Blessed with a supply of the finest North American wheat, plenty of water power, and excellent milling machinery, we produce flour of the highest quality. Our *basic function is to mill high-quality flour,* and of course (and almost incidentally). The second era was one of *sales orientation.* By the 1930's, competition had become more significant and the problems of reaching the market had grown much more complex. Company officials became somewhat aware of consumer wants and needs, and formed a commercial research department to develop facts about markets. More attention was given to strengthening the distributing organization, consisting of wholesale and retail grocers. Company philosophy in this era is described as follows: "We are a flour milling company, manufacturing a number of products for the consumer market. We must have a first-rate sales organization which *can dispose of all the products we can make* at a favorable price. We must back up this sales force with consumer advertising and market intelligence. We want our salesmen and our dealers to have all the tools they need for *moving the output of our plants to the consumer.*"

A third era of *marketing orientation* did not begin until the early 1950's. The company had experienced substantial post-World War II sales growth in new products, principally cake mixes. It realized that it could produce hundreds of new products, and faced the necessity of selecting the best ones. It was considered essential to build into the company organization *a new function* which would coordinate the heretofore separate company responsibilities of selling, advertising, marketing research, and product planning, and provide guidance for other areas. This function was called "marketing," and marketing developed the criteria for determining which products to market. Emphasis shifted from manufacturing and mere sales considerations to a determination of which products would best fit the needs of the company's customers. Company policy for the 1950's was stated as follows: "We make and sell products *for consumers.*"

At the beginning of the 1960's the company was moving into a fourth era of *marketing control,* described by a company official as follows: "Marketing today sets company operating policy short-term. It will come to influence long-range policy more and more.... At Pillsbury, as our fourth era progresses, marketing will become the basic motivating force for the entire corporation. Soon it will be true that every activity of the corporation—from finance to sales to production—is aimed at satisfying the needs and desires of the consumer."

3

Marketing Environment

ELEMENTS OF THE MARKETING ENVIRONMENT

Elements of the environment. The marketing *environment* involves factors that, for the most part, are beyond the control of the company. Thus, the company must *adapt* to these factors. It is important to observe how the environment changes so that a firm can adapt its strategies appropriately.

Consider these environmental forces:

- *Competition*: Competitors often "creep" in and threaten to take away markets from firms. For example, Japanese auto manufacturers became a serious threat to American car makers in the late 1970s and early 1980s. Similarly, the Lotus Corporation, maker of one of the first commercially successful spreadsheets, soon faced competition from other software firms. Note that while competition may be frustrating for the firm, it is good for consumers. Note that competition today is increasingly global in scope. It is important to recognize that competition can happen at different "levels." At the brand level, two firms compete in providing a very similar product or service. Coca Cola and Pepsi, for example, compete for the cola drink market, and United and American Airlines compete for the passenger air transportation market. Firms also face less direct—but frequently very serious—competition at the product level. For example, cola drinks compete against bottled water. Products or services can serve as substitutes for each other even though they are very different in form. Teleconferencing facilities, for example, are very different from airline passenger transportation, but both can "bring together" people for a "meeting." At the budget level, different products or services provide very different benefits, but buyers have to make choices as to what they will buy when they cannot afford—or are unwilling to spend on—both. For example, a family may decide between buying a new car or a high definition television set. The family may also have to choose between going on a foreign vacation or remodeling its kitchen. Firms, too, may have to make choices. The firm has the cash flow either to remodel its offices or install a more energy efficient climate control system; or the firm can choose either to invest in new product development or in a promotional campaign to increase awareness of its brand among consumers.

- *Economics*: Two economic forces strongly affect firms and their customers:
  - *Economic Cycles*: Some firms in particular are extremely vulnerable to changes in the economy. Consumers tend to put off buying a new car, going out to eat, or building new homes in bad times. In contrast, in good times, firms serving those needs may have difficulty keeping up with demand. One important point to realise is that different industries are affected to different degrees by changes in the economy. Although families can cut down on the quality of the food they buy—going with lower priced brands, for example—there are limits to the savings that can be made without greatly affecting the living standard of the family. On the other hand, it is often much easier to put off the purchase of a new car for a year or hold off on remodeling the family home. If need be, firms can keep the current computers—even though they are getting a bit slow—when sales are down. The economy goes through cycles. In the late 1990s, the U.S. economy was quite strong, and many luxury goods were sold. Currently, the economy fluctuates between increasing strength, stagnation, or slight decline. Many firms face consequences of economic downturns. Car makers, for example, have seen declining profit margins as they have had to cut prices and offer low interest rates on financing. Generally, in good economic times, there is a great deal of demand, but this introduces a fear of possible inflation. In the U.S., the Federal Reserve will then try to prevent the economy from "overheating." This is usually done by raising interest rates. This makes businesses less willing to invest, and as a result, people tend to make less money. During a recession, unemployment tends to rise, causing consumers to spend less. This may result in a "bad circle," with more people losing their jobs due to lowered demands. Some businesses, however, may take this opportunity to invest in growth now that things can be bought more cheaply.
  - *Inflation*: Over time, most economies experience some level of inflation. Therefore, it is useful to explicitly state whether a reference to money over time involves the actual dollar amount exchanged at any point or an "inflation adjusted" figure that

"anchors" a given amount of money to the value of that money at some point in time. Suppose, for example, that cumulative inflation between 1960 and 2007 has been 1,000%—that is, on the average, it costs ten times as much to buy the same thing in 2007 as it did 47 years earlier. If the cumulative inflation between 1960 and 1984 had been 500%, we could talk about one 1984 dollar being worth fifty 1960 cents or two 2007 dollars. It is important to note that inflation is uneven. Some goods and services—such as health care and college tuition—are currently increasing in cost much higher than the average rate of inflation. Prices of computers, actually decline both in absolute numbers and in terms of the value for money paid once an adjustment has been made for the improvement in quality. That is, two years later, the computer has not only declined in price by 20%, but it may also be 30% better. In that case, then, there has actually been, over the period, a net deflation of 38.5% for the category.

- *Political*: Businesses are very vulnerable to changes in the political situation. For example, because consumer groups lobbied Congress, more stringent rules were made on the terms of car leases. The tobacco industry is currently the target of much negative attention from government and public interest groups. Currently, the desire to avoid aiding the enemy may result in laws that make it more difficult for American firms to export goods to other countries. Many industries have a strong economic interest in policies that benefit the industry may have a negative impact on the nation as a whole but enhance profits for the industry. For example, regulations that limit the amount of sugar that can be imported into the United States is estimated to cost each American approximately $10.00 a year. The total increase in profits to the sugar industry is difficult to estimate because many of the large producers of refined sugar are privately held corporations, but it is likely that the net gain to the industry is as much as the roughly $3 billion lost by Americans a whole. However, the interests of the industry are much more concentrated. The industry can rally its stockholders, unions and employees, and suppliers together to lobby for their special interests. In turn, the industry can join forces with other agricultural interests which each support each other's prigrammes.
- *Legal:* Firms are very vulnerable to changing laws and changing interpretations by the courts. Firms in the U.S. are very vulnerable to lawsuits. McDonald's, for example, is currently being sued by people who claim that eating the chain's hamburgers caused them to get fat. Firms are significantly limited in what they can do by

various laws—some laws, for example, require that disclosures be made to consumers on the effective interest rates they pay on products bought on installment. A particularly interesting group of laws relate to antitrust. These laws basically exist to promote fair competition among firms. As suggested, consider such laws when we cover pricing later in the term.

- *Technological:* Changes in technology may significantly influence the demand for a product. For example, the advent of the fax machine was bad news for Federal Express. The Internet is a major threat to travel agents. Many record stores have been wiped out of business by the trend toward downloading songs. Although technological change eliminates or at least greatly diminishes some markets, it creates opportunities for others. For example, although Federal Express has lost a considerable amount of business from documents that can now be faxed or sent by the Internet rather than having to be physically shipped, there has been a large increase in demand for packages to be delivered overnight or "second day air." Just-in-time manufacturing techniques, in addition to online sales, have dramatically increased the market for such shipments. Online sites such as eBay now makes it possible to sell specialty products that, in the old days, would have been difficult to distribute. Although it has been possible for more than a hundred years to sell merchandise by catalog, buyers of these specialty products often had no easy access to the catalogs.
- *Social*: Changes in customs or demographics greatly influence firms. Fewer babies today are being born, resulting in a decreased demand for baby foods. More women work outside the home today, so there is a greater demand for prepared foods. There are more unmarried singles today. This provides opportunities for some firms but creates problems for others. Today, there are more "blended" families that result as parents remarry after divorce. These families are often strapped for money but may require "duplicate" items for children at each parent's residence.

MARKETING TERM OF MARKETING ENVIRONMENT

The market environment is a marketing term and refers to all of the forces outside of marketing that affect marketing management's ability to build and maintain successful relationships with target customers. The market environment consists of both the macroenvironment and the microenvironment.

The microenvironment refers to the forces that are close to the company and affect its ability to serve its customers. It includes the company itself, its suppliers, marketing intermediaries, customer markets, competitors, and publics.

The company aspect of microenvironment refers to the internal environment of the company. This includes all departments, such as management, finance, research and development, purchasing, operations and accounting. Each of these departments has an impact on marketing decisions. For example, research and development have input as to the features a product can perform and accounting approves the financial side of marketing plans and budgets.

The suppliers of a company are also an important aspect of the microenvironment because even the slightest delay in receiving supplies can result in customer dissatisfaction. Marketing managers must watch supply availability and other trends dealing with suppliers to ensure that product will be delivered to customers in the time frame required in order to maintain a strong customer relationship. Marketing intermediaries refers to resellers, physical distribution firms, marketing services agencies, and financial intermediaries. These are the people that help the company promote, sell, and distribute its products to final buyers. Resellers are those that hold and sell the company's product. They match the distribution to the customers and include places such as Wal-Mart, Target, and Best Buy. Physical distribution firms are places such as warehouses that store and transport the company's product from its origin to its destination. Marketing services agencies are companies that offer services such as conducting marketing research, advertising, and consulting. Financial intermediaries are institutions such as banks, credit companies and insurance companies.

Another aspect of microenvironment is the customers. There are different types of customer markets including consumer markets, business markets, government markets, international markets, and reseller markets. The consumer market is made up of individuals who buy goods and services for their own personal use or use in their household. Business markets include those that buy goods and services for use in producing their own products to sell. This is different from the reseller market which includes businesses that purchase goods to resell as is for a profit. These are the same companies mentioned as market intermediaries. The government market consists of government agencies that buy goods to produce public services or transfer goods to others who need them. International markets include buyers in other countries and includes customers from the previous categories.

Competitors are also a factor in the microenvironment and include companies with similar offerings for goods and services. To remain competitive a company must consider who their biggest competitors are while considering its own size and position in the industry. The company should develop a strategic advantage over their competitors.

The final aspect of the microenvironment is publics, which is any group that has an interest in or impact on the organization's ability to meet its goals. For example, financial publics can hinder a company's ability to obtain funds affecting the level of credit a company has. Media publics include newspapers and magazines that can publish substances of interest regarding the company and editorials that may influence customers' opinions.

Government publics can affect the company by passing legislation and laws that put restrictions on the company's actions. Citizen-action publics include environmental groups and minority groups and can question the actions of a company and put them in the public spotlight. Local publics are neighbourhood and community organizations and will also question a company's impact on the local area and the level of responsibility of their actions.

The general public can greatly affect the company as any change in their attitude, whether positive or negative, can cause sales to go up or down because the general public is often the company's customer base. And finally, the internal publics include all those who are employed within the company and deal with the organization and construction of the company's product.

The macroenvironment refers to all forces that are part of the larger society and affect the microenvironment. It includes concepts such as demography, economy, natural forces, technology, politics, and culture.

Studying human populations in terms of size, density, location, age, gender, race, and occupation. This is a very important factor to study for marketers and helps to divide the population into market segments and target markets. An example of demography is classifying groups of people just as to the year they were born. These classifications can be referred to as baby boomers, who are born between 1946 and 1964, generation X, who are born between 1965 and 1976, and generation Y, who are born between 1977 and 1994. Each classification has different characteristics and causes they find important. This can be beneficial to a marketer as they can decide who their product would benefit most and tailor their marketing plan to attract that segment. Demography covers many aspects that are important to marketers including family dynamics, geographic shifts, work force changes, and levels of diversity in any given area.

Another aspect of the macroenvironment is the economic environment. This refers to the purchasing power of potential customers and the ways in which people spend their money. Within this area are two different economies, subsistence and industrialized. Subsistence economies are based more in agriculture and consume their own industrial output. Industrial economies have markets that are diverse and carry many different types of goods. Each is important to the marketer because each has a highly different spending pattern as well as different distribution of wealth.

The natural environment is another important factor of the macroenvironment. This includes the natural resources that a company uses as inputs and affects their marketing activities. The concern in this area is the increased pollution, shortages of raw materials and increased governmental intervention. As raw materials become increasingly scarcer, the ability to create a company's product gets much harder. Also, pollution can go as far as negatively affecting a company's reputation if they are known for damaging the environment. The last concern, government intervention can make it increasingly harder for a company to fulfill their goals as requirements get more stringent.

The technological environment is perhaps one of the fastest changing factors in the macroenvironment. This includes all developments from antibiotics and surgery to nuclear missiles and chemical weapons to automobiles and credit cards. As these markets develop it can create new markets and new uses for products. It also requires a company to stay ahead of others and update their own technology as it becomes outdated. They must stay informed of trends so they can be part of the next big thing, rather than becoming outdated and suffering the consequences financially.

The political environment includes all laws, government agencies, and groups that influence or limit other organizations and individuals within a society. It is important for marketers to be aware of these restrictions as they can be complex. Some products are regulated by both state and federal laws. There are even restrictions for some products as to who the target market may be, for example, cigarettes should not be marketed to younger children. There are also many restrictions on subliminal messages and monopolies. As laws and regulations change often, this is a very important aspect for a marketer to monitor.

The final aspect of the macroenvironment is the cultural environment, which consists of institutions and basic values and beliefs of a group of people. The values can also be further categorized into core beliefs, which passed on from generation to generation and very difficult to change, and secondary beliefs, which tend to be easier to influence. As a marketer, it is important to know the difference between the two and to focus your marketing campaign to reflect the values of a target audience.

When dealing with the marketing environment it is important for a company to become proactive. By doing so, they can create the kind of environment that they will prosper in and can become more efficient by marketing in areas with the greatest customer potential. It is important to place equal emphasis on both the macro and microenvironment and to react accordingly to changes within them.

INDIAN MARKETING ENVIRONMENT

India is the second most populated country in the world, with nearly one billion people. It has a reasonably favourable pro-business environment that aims to attract multinational companies. Because of this enormous market size and positive business climate, scores of American firms—including General Electric, General Motors, McDonald's, Kellogg's, and Microsoft—have recently entered the Indian market. As a result, the country has forged strong commercial interests with the United States, with trade and business relations across many industrial sectors. In fact, the U.S. is India's leading source of technology and her most valuable investor.

However, any company that desires to enter the Indian market must realise the serious challenges of doing business there: segmenting the marketplace properly, understanding the country's economic and political situations, getting through the government bureaucracy, and understanding deep-seated cultural biases and attitudes. It is hoped that a discussion of the Indian marketplace in terms of market potential, culture, consumer behaviour, and selling aspects can add to other substances published recently in Business Horizons* and aid MNC executives in facing those challenges successfully. Sprinkled with numerous success tales and war stories, the discussion offers insights gleaned from a survey of Indian businesspeople—insights that can help provide a reality check on the Indian market potential.

TRUE MARKET POTENTIAL

A fairly large country, India is nearly 2,000 miles from north to south and some 1,800 miles from east to west. The current population of nearly one billion is growing at about 1.7 per cent per annum. Only about a quarter of the population live in an urban environment; the rest reside in rural settings.

When American executives reflect on the size and situation of India's potential customers, they erroneously conclude that the Indian middle class is analogous to the middle class in the United States or Europe. The reality, however, is that the income levels characterizing the Western middle class represent only a tiny upper class in India.

The Indian market can be divided into four levels in terms of purchasing power. The reality for American businesses is that only Level 1 customers are willing to purchase foreign-based firms' goods and services, with only a marginal hope of selling to Level 2 consumers. Hence, the Indian market potential for American firms is only 73 million consumers, not the almost one billion population of the country. Nevertheless, though only 7.5 per cent of the country's population, 73 million is still quite a large market when compared to many other developing nations.

Two particularly attractive segments are urban youth and the rural population. Krishna Rao Gowd, General Marketing Manager for India's Sunku Auto Ltd., stated in the survey that "the new generation is showing an inclination toward impulsive buying." However, he cautions,

Lots of purchase decisions of youngsters are still to be blessed by the elders. For example, buying a TV or a refrigerator is a collective decision, even though it is to be used by a newly married couple living 400 kilometres away from parents. Another survey respondent added, "Increasingly, India's rural market will become important."

MARKET DIVERSITY

A second reality of the Indian market structure is the fact that India has 17 official languages and an ethnic diversity as wide as that from Britain to the Middle East—not to mention 26 states, dozens of castes, and six major religions. The 5.7 million people in Chennai have vastly different tastes than the 8.5 million people from New Delhi, the 11.2 million in Calcutta, and the 12.8 million in Mumbai. Such a diverse marketplace has a tremendous impact on product labelling, product variety, and where products can be sold successfully. McDonald's provides a good example of adapting to the diverse Indian marketplace. Though famous for its beef patty entrees, it has introduced vegetable burgers to the large Hindu population and mutton patties to Indian Muslims.

Tailoring goods and services to the local preferences is not a trivial undertaking. American firms must realise that much market research is needed to understand the regional consumer demands. And they must be willing to modify offerings at the local level.

ECONOMIC AND POLITICAL ENVIRONMENTS FOR DOING BUSINESS IN INDIA

To better understand the Indian marketplace, it is important to gain some perspectives on the country's economic and political environments. So our discussion will shift to India's political system, recent policies for opening the economy to foreign businesses, agreements with the United States, and strategies for getting through bureaucratic hurdles.

The Political System

India is a federal republic of 26 states and seven union territories. The country has a two-house parliamentary legislative system: the indirectly elected Upper House, the Rajya Sabha; and the directly elected Lower House, the Lok Sabha. The judicial system is an independent branch of government; the legal system is based on English common law. National and state legislatures are elected for five-year terms, although terms may be extended in a state of emergency and elections may be held early if the government loses Parliament's confidence. The Prime Minister is elected from the majority ruling party in Parliament.

ECONOMIC IMPACTS ON SPECIFIC STAKEHOLDER GROUPS

As women are often involved in very small-scale fisheries, the economic contribution these make can be easily underestimated. In some areas, women have special skills which have developed into important money-earning fisheries. In coastal areas of Bangladesh, for example, women are among the most important producers in the very extensive fishery for shrimp fry which is vital for the expanding shrimp culture industry.

The economic contributions to the fishery made by women may not always be obvious or may be difficult to analyse in the same way as more formal "commercial" enterprises operated by men. Some apparently very unproductive fisheries with little "economic" importance in comparison to other fisheries may be relatively far more important for those actually involved in them. For very poor or vulnerable households, which are often female-headed households, the small amounts of fish they obtain from pushnetting in nearby swamps may play a far more important role in providing them with a livelihood than a much more commercially oriented fishery carried out by other households as one among a range of enterprises and not necessarily the most important.

Sociologists need to assist in first identifying the range of activities carried out by women which contribute to the fisheries economy and in measuring their importance.

Gender-specific Impacts of Fisheries Interventions

Some fisheries interventions can have direct impacts on women's access to the fisheries in which they are active. The effects of interventions or changes can also be more subtle. Involvement of formal fisheries agencies in attempting to develop or regulate the fisheries in which women are engaged may improve the status and productivity of those fisheries and lead to their being taken over by men, at the expense of women's ability to contribute to the household economy.

Where women are displaced from a fishery, for whatever reason, their social status, cultural norms regarding their behaviour and their reproductive roles within the household are likely to affect their mobility and their ability to take up alternative forms of income-generating or income-substituting activities.

Age Issues

Potentially significant economic contributions by young and old people involved in fisheries also need to be considered.

Like women, older people in fishing communities may depend on open access fishing for a relatively important part of their diet even though the amount of fish they catch may be small.

Also, old people sometimes play significant roles in activities servicing the fisheries sector such as the repair of fishing gear and in fish processing. This may be one of the only ways in which older people in fishing communities can contribute to the family's livelihood and be important in maintaining their status within the household. Clearly such contributions can be affected by changes in the types of gear promoted by fisheries development programmes or by the introduction of new fish-processing technology.

INTERACTIONS IN THE LOCAL AND REGIONAL ECONOMY

Sociological analysis of fishing activity at the community level needs to consider a variety of economic factors which are likely to influence the structure of the fishing community, patterns of dependency and patronage and the flows of benefits within the community.

Interdependence of Fisheries and other Economic Activities

In some areas, particularly remote coastal communities, fisheries may be the "motor" of the community which effectively drives all other activities by providing income and employment. In such circumstances, changes which might affect the contribution of the sector to the local economy, or threaten the sustainability of the sector, need to be carefully studied with a full awareness of possible "ripple effects".

The degree to which other activities in the community and surrounding area depend on particular types of fishing activity has to be clearly understood before interventions are recommended which might change the productivity or locations of fishing activity. Apparently minor shifts in the types of fisheries being targeted may result in changes in patterns of handling of catches which can radically change local economies.

For example, a change in the fishery from targeting fish primarily for processing to targeting fish for fresh sale may lead to a change in landing-place or change in handling procedures which could negatively affect a whole range of sideline activities which may have depended on fish landings - servicing of fishing operations, informal sales of food, cigarettes and other goods, provision of fuelwood for smoking, scavenging of fish discards, and any number of local services could suddenly be deprived of their customers by an "improvement" in fisheries production.

Support Networks for Fisheries

Small-scale fisheries operations are often dependent on flows of resources, notably credit, which are linked to fish marketing channels. The relationships between fishers and credit providers are extremely complex. On the one hand, bonds of obligation and dependence may bind fishers to particular buyers/moneylenders in a way which effectively prevents them from obtaining economic independence. Interest rates, measured by normal financial tools, are often usurious and exploitative.

But frequently these links between primary producers and various middlemen responsible for channelling fish back to the consumer are essential for the support of risky, small-scale operations.

Middlemen/moneylenders are often the only source of easily available credit in remote rural and coastal communities and they often provide flexible terms and a range of other services and assistance which it is difficult for formal credit institutions to imitate. Perhaps most importantly, they may be related to fishers themselves or at least come from the same community, speak the same language and be familiar with the needs and problems of local fishers.

Economic Diversification

The degree of diversification of the economy in areas where fisheries interventions are planned will affect both people's motivations to enter fisheries, in the case of fisheries development programmes, and their ability to find alternative sources of livelihood, in the case of fisheries management programmes.

Sociologists have to take into account the extent to which the economies of fishing communities or particular areas may be linked and integrated with other communities and centres of trade and consumption through such channels. This will enable managers to understand how impacts at different points of the production chain may affect groups and individuals at other points.

Fisheries, particularly coastal marine fisheries, tends to be an activity which "catches" people falling out of other sectors. Therefore fishing pressure is often sensitive to shifts in other sectors which result in people looking for alternative employment. The perception is often that fishing is open to anyone who can afford a net.

Therefore developments in other adjacent sectors need to be carefully looked at in order to understand what is happening in fisheries. Box describes a case from Melanesia where the links between fisheries and other sectors were of considerable importance in determining intensity of exploitation of the fisheries resource and therefore very significant for fisheries managers.

INDEBTEDNESS

Particularly in small-scale fisheries, levels of indebtedness among fishing households can be an important economic factor which managers need to be aware of before considering recommendations which might require further investment of resources among fishers or fish-processors.

Problems can arise where debts are"informal", as is often the case where loans from fish traders or middlemen are concerned. These debts may be difficult to quantify as they are"paid back" through regular sale at preferential prices rather than by any fixed repayment at a set interest rate. However, such debts may still constitute a set of obligations which will be extremely important for fishers as they are also linked with more complex sets of social exchange mechanisms and obligations.

CRITERIA FOR MEASURING BENEFITS AND NEGATIVE IMPACTS

Most introduced changes will generate benefits and negative impacts which need to be measured in order to assess the effects of those interventions. Measurement of these positive and negative impacts in economic terms is clearly important but sociologists also have to assist in identifying benefits and disbenefits as they are perceived by local people. In some cases there may be important benefits which cannot be readily measured in economic terms but which can be very important for local communities.

In some cultures, assumptions that wealth maximisation is a key criteria for engagement in a particular occupation are invalid. In many rural communities greater importance is attached to networks of reciprocal obligations and efforts to raise social status than to accumulating personal wealth and"developing" fishing enterprises through reinvestment. Understanding how people express value and and measure benefits or success is critical if interventions are to be designed which effectively respond to real needs and priorities among local people.

Perceptions of Advantages and Disadvantages of Management

Understanding people's perceptions of what is important is likely to be particularly crucial in fisheries management programmes where fishers and those dependent on fisheries may be asked to renounce immediate benefits with a view to ensuring that the exploitation of the resource as a whole performs better in economic terms and is sustainable into the future.

While the argument in favour of management may seem extremely clear to fisheries scientists and fisheries economists, other forms of argument may be given far higher priority by resource users.

Communities living at a minimum level of subsistence and generating little or no surplus may simply not be able to afford any kind of renunciation of the exploitation of whatever resources are at their disposal, including fish. In such circumstances, fisheries managers' arguments for ensuring the sustainability of resources for the future are unlikely to carry much weight unless supported by tangible alternatives and concrete forms of compensation.

Arguments regarding future economic benefits resulting from current management will also be strongly affected by the extent to which specific groups or communities can control access to the resource being managed.

Compensation—Evaluating the Impacts of Management

Efforts to mitigate the impacts of management measures often rely on monetary compensation as a means of softening the impact on people's livelihoods. In most "developed" economies, such an approach is more likely to be acceptable as the notion of putting a monetary value on people's means of livelihood is more familiar and fairly precise data on earnings can be obtained to help in the evaluation of people's livelihoods. Debate tends to centre around the relative levels of compensation.

However, even in a relatively developed economic context, problems can arise where management measures force people to abandon fisheries altogether. Besides forcing people to change their livelihood, this may also require changes in life-style and place of residence. In these conditions, compensation packages may need to include measures to facilitate the movement of people affected into other occupations and all assistance to overcome the problems which may arise from such a move.

This in turn may require specific programmes of retraining and access to credit facilities. Generally, in more developed economies, there should be more opportunity for fish workers who lose their livelihood as a result of management to invest their compensation package in other sectors and occupations. But support services and access to good advice regarding alternative activities and investment opportunities is likely to be very important.

Compensation—Non-quantifiable Impacts

While the social and cultural boundaries between fishing communities and non-fishing communities in "developed" countries may be less marked than in some "traditional" societies, fishing communities the world over tend to have a distinct identity linked to the nature of the profession. Changes in profession will lead to a loss of social identity which can be very disorienting for the individuals and families involved. In addition, such communities often have cultural practices and sets of beliefs and customs which may risk being lost when shifts are made out of fishing.

The extent to which the customs peculiar to fishing communities represent a part of the nation's cultural heritage, and the value which is attached to such a heritage will depend very much on national priorities. But, in any case, the extent to which such a heritage might be threatened by changes in fisheries, whether through management or development, needs to be assessed as part of the sociological analysis.

In artisanal fisheries, compensation may represent a more complex proposition. Compensation for loss of livelihood is generally viewed as a means for assisting people to establish themselves in alternative occupations. In poor rural areas where alternative economic opportunities are extremely limited, compensation packages may end up being used up by their recipients for short-term survival without any opportunity arising for reinvestment in new, sustainable activities. Movement into alternative occupations may have very little to do with having access to the required capital and more to do with having ties of kinship or traditional associations with people within that occupation.

In some parts of South Asia, in particular, it can be socially and culturally impossible for a fisher to simply change professions, no matter what economic support they are given. It may take generations of gradual change for a shift in occupation to be accepted.

In many high-density rural areas there is often such intense pressure on any form of employment niche that movement at any point within the system is liable to cause considerable disruption all around - for example if fishers want to become agricultural labourers what happens to the people already working as agricultural labourers who they are likely to displace?

The social and cultural impacts and general viability of compensatory packages in "less developed" countries therefore need to be carefully considered. Interventions to limit or eliminate certain types of fishery or significantly change the structure of the sector may have to be inserted into quite complex, integrated programmes which train resource users in alternative occupations and, at the same time, look at the entire local economy to ensure that local livelihood strategies are not seriously compromised by changes in fisheries. Credit availability, small enterprise development and the acquisition of new marketing skills are liable to be key components in any such programme.

GOVERNMENTAL ENVIRONMENT IN MARKETING

Marketing decisions must be made with an understanding of how they are impacted by international, national, regional and local laws and regulations. For marketers, laws (i.e., acts past by governmental ruling bodies) and regulations (i.e., requirements put in place by governmental agencies) identify rules and procedures that guide certain marketing activities.

Failure to conform to requirements established by the governments and their agencies may result in fines, sanctions or other legal action.

The governmental environment is a difficult external force to monitor for two key reasons. First, the number and variety of laws and regulations can be overwhelming even for the most seasoned marketer.

For instance, in the U.S. alone there are potentially hundreds of laws and regulations that are either directly or indirectly targeted to marketing decisions. The table below provides a sampling of the issues covered by U.S. laws and regulations and the primary marketing decision areas these affect:

Affected Decision Area	Coverage
General	Unfair competition, restraint of trade, environmental
Target Market	Discrimination, online registration, privacy
Product	Product safety, labeling, intellectual property, warranties
Promotion	Deceptive and misleading claims, advertising to children, telemarketing, email spam
Distribution	Tying contracts, exclusive dealerships, transportation safety
Pricing	Price discrimination, predatory pricing, consumer credit purchasing

The second reason the governmental environment proves difficult is due to the complexity inherent in understanding laws and regulations which often makes it impossible for marketers to handle these issues on their own. Seeking legal assistance is necessary (and often costly) for most marketers no matter their size.

Dealing with the Government

In addition to seeking legal assistance, marketing organizations may find value by engaging in either direct discussion between company employees and governmental personnel or indirect discussion through firms hired to serve as a representative for the marketing company (e.g., consultants, lobbyist).

Representatives are particularly important when selling internationally where existing relationships between government personnel and a hired representative can effectively reduce bureaucratic red tape.

In situations where proposed legislation is likely to impact an entire industry, communication with the government may occur through a marketer's participation in an industry trade group. These groups perform many tasks on behalf of their members including maintaining relations with governmental groups to ensure the industry's voice is heard with regard to pending legislation that affects the industry.

Finally, marketers should not view the governmental environment as always erecting obstacles. In many cases laws and regulations present marketing opportunities. For example, the U.S. Federal government recently instituted airline travel regulations limiting the size of liquid, gel and aerosol products that may be carried on a plane. Several companies that produce personal care products (e.g., shaving cream, hair care, toothpaste, etc.) have viewed the new regulations as an opportunity to market their products in new packaging that they promote as being approved for airline travel.

INFLUENTIAL STAKEHOLDERS

Besides dealing with various governmental groups, marketers must also pay close attention to other groups that can affect marketing activity. The most important of these groups are those that have an interest or stake in the company. While such groups are not backed directly by the power of a government they can still command a great deal of power especially in terms of swaying public opinion, which sometimes leads to governmental action.

Influential stakeholders can be divided into two categories:

- *Connected Stakeholders:* These stakeholders consist of groups that regularly interact with the marketing organization and often hold important roles in helping the marketer succeed. Examples include: supply and distribution partners (e.g., distributors, material suppliers), industry standards groups, and support companies (e.g., advertising agencies). To address concerns raised by these groups often requires direct communication by management with the stakeholders.

- *Peripheral Stakeholders:* These stakeholders consist of groups that may not routinely impact the marketer unless a specific issue arises that draws their attention. Examples include: religious organizations, community activists, and cause supporters. To address concerns raised by these groups marketers often use public relations professionals as their first line of communication.

CULTURAL AND SOCIETAL CHANGE

Society is made up of many different cultural groups. Members of a cultural group share similar values and beliefs which are learned and reinforced by others within the same cultural group. These shared values and beliefs, lead members of a cultural group to behave in similar ways (e.g., customs, traditions, likes/dislikes, attitudes, perceptions, etc.).

Cultural groups can be viewed on several levels. At a broad level, a cultural group consists of a very large number who share basic values (e.g., ethnicity, religious affiliation). While looking at the broad level can offer some insight into how a general cultural group behaves, marketers are much more concerned with examining cultural groups at narrower levels where individuals share more specific interests.

Narrow level analysis of cultural groups leads to the study of sub-cultures, which consists of individuals sharing values and beliefs that revolve around special interests. For instance, a large cultural group may exist in a certain region of a country. While they share basic cultural values with others in their country (e.g., sense of patriotism), they may also share values (e.g., work ethic, taste in food, etc.) with those in their region that are not shared consistently throughout the country.

Examining these sub-cultures even more closely will reveal thousands of smaller sub-cultures (e.g., sports interests, type of shopper, music preference, online gaming enthusiast, etc.). It should be evident that a single consumer may belong to many different sub-cultures. It should also be evident that members of a sub-culture sharing similar values are also likely to have similar needs and, this suggests that sub-cultures are natural for market segmentation.

Evolution of Cultural Change

Cultural values and beliefs are not stagnant; these do evolve and change. However the pace of change will differ depending on the level examined. At the broad cultural level changes often evolves slowly. For instance, consider how people in the United States and Japan view the importance of saving money. People in the United States are more inclined to spend their earned income than they are to save resulting in a low personal savings rate for Americans. Those living in Japan are more concerned with saving and thus show a high personal savings rate. The difference in values toward savings has been consistent for many years and no one expects consumers from either country to alter their values in the near future.

While broad cultures tend to shift values and beliefs slowly, changes within sub-cultures can occur relatively quickly. For instance, the music industry often experiences rapid shifts as a sub-culture of music enthusiasts discovers new artists. The key for marketers targeting sub-cultures is to maintain close contact with these groups through regular marketing research. In this way marketers can see how different sub-cultures behave and also spot trends, which the marketer can capitalize on through new marketing tactics (e.g., new products, new sales channels, added value, etc.).

INNOVATION

Arguably the external force possessing the greatest potential for changing how marketers and industries compete are those associated with innovation. When most people think of innovation they immediately assume it has to do with computers and other high-tech equipment. While the majority of innovative new products rely in some way on computer technology, it is not a requirement for something to be considered innovative.

Instead, an innovation is viewed as anything new that solves needs by offering a significant advantage (e.g., more features, more convenient, easier to use, lower cost, etc.) over existing ways (e.g., products, services). For example, a designer of automobiles may develop a new layout for a car's dashboard using existing products (no new technologies). This new design reduces the amount of time a driver must take his eyes off the road in order to select a new music station. If this new layout is viewed positively by customers, governmental groups and the media it may gain widespread acceptance by other vehicle manufacturers who will make similar designs available in their products.

As noted in the above example, for an innovation to be truly important it must be widely adopted within a targeted group (e.g., within an industry, by a target market). Once adopted an innovation becomes important if it leads to behavioral changes including changing how consumers and business satisfy their needs. These changes present both opportunities and threats to marketers.

For instance, over the last few years several small companies have created productivity software products (e.g., word processing, spreadsheet) that operate over the Internet. These products do not require the software be downloaded to a user's computer. While these innovative products are not new in terms of the features they offer, they are new in terms of convenience in accessing documents from anywhere and the ability to share with others. It remains to be seen whether these products will alter behaviour, though it appears that one leading maker of traditional productivity software, Microsoft, has recognized this as a threat and is expected to respond with its own version of web-based software.

Because of the potential innovation has in affecting products and industries it is no surprise that many marketing organizations direct a significant amount of funds to researching this external force. In fact, in many industries, such as pharmaceuticals and computers, spending on technological research and development represents a significant portion of a company's overall budget.

Innovation in Marketing

Marketers in many industries know that innovation through new product development is vital to remain competitive. But product decisions are not the only areas affected by new developments. Innovation can affect almost all marketing areas. Below is a sampling of how innovation has affected different marketing areas:

Marketing Area	Effect of Innovation
Marketing Research	Creates new ways to conduct research including more sophisticated methods for monitoring and tracking customer behavior and analyzing data.
Targeting Markets	Allows for extreme target marketing where marketing-to-person is replacing mass marketing. For customer service, technology makes it easier to manage relationships and allows for rapid response to customer's needs.
Product	Creates new digital products/services. Incorporation of innovation into existing product/service enhances value by offering improved quality, features & reliability at a lower price.
Promotion	New techniques allow better matching of promotion to customer activity and individualized promotion. Makes it easier for sellers to offer product suggestions and promotional tie-ins.
Distribution	Creates new channels for distribution and transaction (e.g., electronic commerce) that include making it easier for buyers to place orders. Allows more control over inventory management and closer monitoring of product shipment
Pricing	Enables the use of dynamic pricing methods.

Many of the benefits shown above are driven by the evolution of the Internet. The Internet is transforming how all functional areas of an organization perform work. However, it can be argued that no functional area has been more affected than marketing. Throughout the Principles of

Marketing Tutorials we have seen evidence of how the Internet has impacted marketing. Over the next decade it is expected that the Internet's effect on marketing will continue to grow and marketers are well served to embrace this.

COMPETITORS

For many marketers the final external force is the one most relevant to immediate day-to-day decision making. While the other external forces we've discussed tend to be examined periodically (or in some cases rarely), monitoring competitor activity is often a daily undertaking.

Monitoring competitors can serve several goals:

- *Competitors as Threats:* The most obvious reason to monitor the competition is to see how they are responding in the same markets in which the marketer operates.

  Many larger companies recognize the importance of keeping tabs on their competition and create specific positions or even departments that focus on gathering and analyzing competitor data. These competitive intelligence programs mainly employ high-tech methods, and principally the Internet, to locate information about competitors such as news reports, government filings (e.g., patents, stock reports) and changes to competitors' websites. Even small sized marketers can more easily track competitor actions. For instance, there are several news and information services that will alert a marketer (usually via email) when a competitor is mentioned in the news.
- *Competitors as Partners:* While many may consider competitors as representing the enemy, there are situations where competitors can present opportunities. This happens often to large companies that offer a broad product line serving many target markets. In some markets a company may compete aggressively with another firm but in other markets both firms may be lagging and it may make more sense for both to work together. This can be seen in the computer industry where Apple Inc., which for many years viewed computers built with Intel processors as competitors since these run Microsoft operating systems, has now accepted Intel processors and is building computers powered by this chip.
- *Competitors of Tomorrow*: In many industries and, in particular, those in technology-focused industries where there is heavy emphasis on research and development, the most dangerous competitors are the ones that have yet to emerge. Because technology-dependent industries, such as computers, consumer electronic and pharmaceuticals, rely heavily on innovative new products, serious competitors can emerge quickly from what seems to be out of nowhere. For instance, the evolution of online video and its impact

on the news and entertainment industry grew very rapidly with the introduction of online video services (e.g., YouTube) which was previously an unknown project developed in a garage. However, in less than 18 months it came to dominate the online video industry.

PERFORMANCE MANAGEMENT AND APPRAISAL

The hardest task in respect to HRM of small businesses is to convince owners and managers that there is much to be gained in the long term if financial and time investments are made in the short term. Of all the functional aspects of HRM, it is most difficult to convince small business managers of the need for taking a strategic approach to developing formal performance appraisal systems. Partly, the choice is cost related but it also results from the over-confidence of small business managers that employees are prepared to trade-off extrinsic benefits that are seen to exist in large businesses for the intrinsic benefits they perceive as characteristic of small businesses.

Performance management involves a series of processes focused on managing employee performance. It includes work and job design, reward structures, the selection of people for work, the training of these employees, assessment of work performance and policies associated with rewarding and improving performance. Thus, like other HR functions, performance management is in no small way related to all other HR functions. It is but one part of a performance management system.

Performance Appraisal

Performance appraisal is the HRM activity by which organisations assess the extent to which employees are performing their jobs effectively. The purposes of performance appraisals are to improve performance; identify potential candidates for promotion; provide feedback to employees; communicate between supervisor and subordinate; assist HR planning; and develop management.

A formal performance appraisal system encompasses a method for gathering appraisal data, identification of standards of criteria for analysing data, knowledge of the validity and reliability of the method being utilised for appraisal, understanding of the characteristic of the rater and ratee, a defined process for utilising the information acquired, and an evaluation of the appraisal and its stated objectives. While small businesses may recognise the value of performance appraisals, very few utilise formal appraisal systems. Most small businesses communicate with employees in a personalistic style that places little emphasis on formal and standardised methods and techniques. Assessments of performance are usually made on the basis of employee conversations with the owner, family and co-workers, although the process may be more explicit in the larger 'small' companies that have a hired manager with prior HRM experience.

There are six usual methods used in performance appraisals including comparative standards; absolute standards; objectives based; direct or objective indices; accomplishment records; and means based. The form that is used is determined by what is being measured; what people are, what people do, or what people achieve. Whichever method is used, it is important that it has been tested for validity and reliability and standards are measurable. Interviews are the most commonly used form of undertaking a performance appraisal and may utilise four styles: tell and sell (directive); tell and listen; problem-solving; or mixed. Appraisal interviews should include a review of job responsibilities; a review of performance standards; a review of the employee's performance; a discussion of strengths and weaknesses; setting of goals and targets; a discussion of career plans; and development of an action plan. The major advantage of such formalised approaches is that they allow employees to actively engage in their own setting of goals and objectives and to work with a supervisor to improve their performance.

Performance Appraisal in Small Businesses

As most small businesses do not engage in formal appraisal systems, they open themselves up to accusations of being subjective in their assessment of employees' performance and bias in their appraisal. It should be noted, however, that in small businesses in the professional service areas and high technology sector, there might be greater job autonomy and more formal appraisal. This does not reflect management strategy per se but rather the nature of the work in this particular market environment. Further, informal conversations with employees and cursory summaries of their performance do not provide much scope for development of career plans and management potential from within an existing workforce. Divergence in management abilities across small businesses also means divergence in potential to develop employees as the role of the supervisor is key to small business performance.

This is supported by Jennings and Beaver's (1997) finding that emphasises that small business success or failure hinges on managerial skills and decision-making. As they argue, the role of small business managers being, in general, more multifaceted than their large company counterparts, makes them a key factor at both the strategic and operational level.

The other difficulty that small businesses face in not implementing formal performance appraisal systems is that employees' understanding of the psychological contract and the conditions they have been offered (rewards and promotion prospects) are a matter of perception and what is offered may be changed by management at any time. This has consequences for employee satisfaction and performance as well as turnover.

Though there are certainly costs to a small business of implementing a formal performance appraisal system, the short-term costs may be counteracted by long-term reductions in turnover, absenteeism, poor job performance, job dissatisfaction and hostile attitudes towards management by employees.

So, in developing formal performance appraisal systems, small businesses not only are able to ensure that performance management may become strategically aligned with organisational goals, but also increase accountability, decrease underutilisation of human resources, address concerns of productivity, and decrease employees' concerns about fairness and accuracy.

Reward Management

It has been consistently argued that the rewards offered in small businesses differ markedly from those in larger businesses. Ram (1998) argued that pay determination is usually an individualistic affair in small businesses and rarely pursued in a systematic manner. Further, pay is not usually regularly reviewed, pay increases are normally a product of individual bargains and most small businesses have no recognised pay structure. In sum, issues associated with pay are opaque at best.

Yet while small businesses may not have taken a strategic approach to developing monetary rewards, it is also often argued that many individuals join small businesses for non-monetary rewards such as the sense of organisational loyalty and commitment they find and that the work itself may be viewed as a means of self-expression and self-development. While it is recognised that small businesses may not viably compete with large organisations in terms of extrinsic compensatory rewards, Golhar and Deshpande (1997) maintain that the ability to adequately provide competitive compensation (at least internal pay equity) and employee participation initiatives are crucial factors associated with the effective and efficient operations of small businesses.

Defining Rewards

An organisation's reward system may be defined as the need to attract, retain and motivate employees. A total reward package includes base pay (possibly award-set or minimum standards) + performance-based pay (if applicable) + compulsory employer-provided benefits (such as superannuation) + discretionary employer-provided benefits (such as bonuses). While the ability to attract, retain and motivate individuals is partly explained by the value that money has for individuals, people are often willing to perform work for non-monetary gains such as status and prestige, job security, responsibility and variety, power, affiliation, or softer rewards such as travel or camaraderie. These non-monetary rewards often explain an individual's choice to take one job over another, or to choose one organisation over another when the monetary gains may be higher elsewhere. Rewards may be defined as extrinsic and intrinsic. Extrinsic rewards are those that receive external recognition, such as pay, bonuses and promotion. Intrinsic rewards are those that may not be recognised by others but hold considerable worth to the individual, such as job variety, and autonomy.

Some forms of rewards are useful in attracting employees, yet it is acknowledged that other forms of rewards are required to retain and motivate employees. Ting (1997) suggests that factors of non-monetary motivation decrease in effectiveness when implemented without consideration to pay satisfaction. Yet, it is also argued that pay satisfaction is not sufficient in itself and that pay equity within an organisation is often more important a linkage between compensation and employee loyalty/ retention and compensation. It is suggested that rewards such as hiring bonuses, paid holidays, and benefits will induce applicant attraction while promotion possibilities and new employee training were significantly related to retention rates. While motivational factors such as organisational culture, customer focus, teamwork and problem-solving are cited as having a positive relationship in the context of implementing quality improvements, job enrichment is viewed as the best way of increasing employee motivation and productivity.

Though small businesses in the professional service and high technology sectors offer high rates of pay, reflecting the market power of such individuals (Ram 1998:22), most small businesses offer more to their employees in terms of intrinsic rewards, though these may not include the job enrichment cited as the key factor in motivation (Grensing 1996). Small businesses often use non-traditional benefits to give employees a feeling of greater control over the destiny of their work lives. Benefits may include more responsibility and autonomy, latitude in direction of product marketing, flexibility in handling personal matters, leave and leisure-time activities. Other rewards offered can include liberal dress codes, personnel counseling, assistance with tax preparation, subsidised childcare and welfare programmes.

In many industrialised nations, a key determiner of pay rates and benefits is the award systems that set minimum rates of pay for particular jobs, occupational, industries and sectors. Moreover, legislation also establishes minimum conditions that organisations need to provide. These conditions usually include workers' compensation, superannuation schemes, sick leave, holidays and holiday pay, and long service leave. In some nations, organisations are also required by law to provide paid maternity leave and carers' leave. However, it should be noted that a small number of organisations fail to provide the minimum standards legislated by government to their employees. While small businesses are noted for offering non-traditional benefits, unfortunately they are also overly represented among those businesses that do not provide minimum legal standards.

While small businesses should be providing their employees with minimum conditions, they are not as open to litigation as large corporations. Essentially, the onus falls to employees (where unionisation does not exist in the workplace) to make themselves aware of their entitlements under the law and to seek redress where these standards are not being met. However, where those employees are very young, uneducated, illegal immigrants or immigrants with poor language skills, employers can usually count on the employees remaining uninformed of their rights.

Performance and Pay

Reward planning and management requires organisations to consider four key issues: determing the value of jobs; establishing a pay structure; building a link with performance; and communication and administration. One of the most neglected aspects of this process in small businesses is determining the value of jobs and relates to the lack of initial HR planning and job analysis characteristics of small businesses. Determining the value of jobs entails evaluating a job from job analysis, considering compensable factors, designing a system for evaluation and determining who will do the evaluation e.g. management or peers. From this initial analysis it is then possible to rank and classify jobs, and tie this to the development of selection criteria and other HRM functions.

Employees need some acknowledgement of their accomplishments and validation of task accomplishment is a strong predictor of employee satisfaction. Hence, performance appraisal also has an important link to rewards, particularly where performance-related pay and promotion are offered within an organisation. Without a valid and accepted performance appraisal system, diminished motivation and lowered performance may result. Again it should be noted that the performance appraisal system should also take account of the value of non-monetary or intrinsic rewards such as prestige, job recognition and job enrichment and variety. Building a link between pay and performance needs to involve the development of outcomes to be sought and may entail performance-based pay systems, merit pay plans, individual incentive plans, and managerial incentive plans (that focus on the workgroup rather than specific individuals).

Communicating Rewards

The management and administration of a reward system also has the potential to be a significant form of employee communication. The rewards are clear indications of human resource values, goals and priorities of the organisation. There are three primary reasons why it is important: it ensures the organisation is aware of business trends; it ensures links with overall business objectives of the organisation; and it ensures that employees are aware of how their pay and benefits are determined and how the organisation fits relative to its competitors. There are four important aspects raised by this. First, whether employees should be involved in their own pay determination, e.g. a flexible approach. Second, whether there should be pay secrecy or whether pay rates for particular grades of work as they are in the public sector (market loadings not negated). Third, whether pay equity has an impact on absenteeism and turnover. Fourth, whether all employees should receive annual salaries or whether organisations should have a mix of salaried and performance-based pay employees.

There are non-monetary approaches that may be used to gain firm attractiveness in obtaining and keeping valuable human assets. Appelbaum and Kamal argue that job enrichment, employee recognition, pay equity and managerial skill affect job satisfaction in small business. It is acknowledged that small businesses do not have the financial resources available to offer monetary rewards competitive with larger organisations. However, we suggest that there are practices that small businesses can employ that will ensure that they meet some non-monetary rewards for their employees and are responsive communicators and are of minimal financial cost to the business.

Small businesses can improve their practices in respect to how they communicate benefits and rewards to their employees. They have been known to rely on informal techniques to assist employees to understand the psychological contract. Uncertainty and ambiguity about remuneration need to be removed. While in small businesses the promises made to employees may not be made explicit through formal HRM procedures as they are in large organisations, promises can be made explicit by being actioned.

For instance, promises made may satisfy an employee's extrinsic needs by pay and bonuses and benefits being tied to performance, and promises made may satisfy an employee's intrinsic needs in the form of increased responsibilities and opportunities for personal growth that may lead to promotion. Doing so would ensure that small businesses can minimise negative feelings and attitudes of employees towards the business, increase levels of commitment and minimise absenteeism and turnover. Employees who feel that their organisation gives them challenges and opportunities or more responsibility, freedom to develop new skills, and autonomy and control, are likely to demonstrate more loyalty toward their employer and hence contribute to the growth of the business. Thus, for small businesses to communicate better with their employees and action opportunities for their employees are critical factors in building a committed and quality workforce and organisation.

In addition to removing ambiguity about rewards, small businesses can also ensure that they provide feedback to their employees, both constructive criticism at the time of errors being made and praise when a job is well done. If a manager has no time to give praise, then it should be delegated to someone else. Given the value stowed on independence and autonomy of owner-managers and the concern for loss of control through delegation this may take some time to infiltrate the organisational culture. Moreover, Appelbaum and Kamal suggest that small businesses should hire managers that have the skill to implement incentive programmes and ensure that existing managers understand the value of incentives so that they show commitment to accomplishing tasks. Despite the investment involved, the savings realised through lower employee turnover and anticipated benefit to revenues through more efficient functioning should more than compensate.

Further, instituting communication mechanisms that inform employees about how decisions are made and implementing procedures that allow employees to challenge or appeal decisions made by the business also contributes to employees' intrinsic self-worth. Kickul suggests that small businesses can openly communicate to employees what they can reasonably expect in terms of organisational inducements and practices through open-book management. By sharing an array of organisational information (promises and obligations as well as financial and marketing practices), Kickul argues that small businesses help their employees recognise their contribution and significance to the success of the business. Effective communication between employees and management also must entail information from employees being acted upon by management and efforts made to bring employees on board to implement required changes.

Managing Diversity and Thinking Globally

From the late 1970s most industrialised nations began to implement employment policies targeted at removing discrimination in workplaces on grounds of gender, marital and pregnancy status, race, age, disability, religious belief or political persuasion. These policies were designed to ensure that all individuals had equal employment opportunity in respect to recruitment and selection, training and development, pay and other rewards, and promotion opportunities.

Legislation was also enacted to ensure that individuals would not be subjected to sexual or other harassment in the workplace and could take legal action against perpetrators of such harassment. By the mid-1980s most industrialised nations had also brought in affirmative action policies that suggested or mandated organisations to employ techniques and methods to create equal employment opportunity. While it may be argued by some that small businesses are not as concerned with implementing such policies due to their nepotistic hiring practices, close proximity to their employees, their size, and lesser unionisation, legislatively they are just as obligated to comply as are large corporations. Beyond just the legislative compliance to which organisations must adhere, there is a moral and economic imperative to manage diversity and think globally.

Managing Diversity

The effects of internationalisation and the changing nature of the labour market (partially because of increased international migration) mean that business owners can no longer be assured of the culturally and ethnically homogenous workforces that characterised businesses in the past. This means that there is now an onus on employers and supervisors to manage increasingly diverse workforces that much of the popular press has argued is intrinsically good for organisations. Managing diversity refers to valuing differences between stakeholders and developing and implementing policies to manage those differences. Managing diversity can be argued to be a moral issue, but it is also an economic imperative for organisations in the sense that managing the needs of a diverse workforce can contribute to an organisation's ongoing survival.

Diversity issues confronting organisations include the obvious legislative requirements of equal employment opportunity and anti-discrimination as well as concerns for tolerance of individual difference, communicating with and motivating ethnically diverse populations, managing workers with family responsibilities, conflict resolution among diverse workforces, managing older workers, managing career paths diversely, managing diverse teams, and meeting the needs of those with disabilities. Further, being effective at managing diversity can contribute to an organisation's competitive advantage through the arguments of costs, resource acquisition, marketing, creativity, problem-solving and system flexibility.

Though small businesses may not be confronted with the same demands to manage diversity as larger organisations that have much greater numbers of employees and consequently the likelihood of more diversity, it is also in the interests of small businesses to develop an appreciation of diversity and to engender an organisational culture that supports diversity. Benefits to organisations of thinking diversely include breadth of perspectives in decision making; larger talent pools in acquisition; and greater marketing to ethnically diverse communities domestically and internationally. Potential disadvantages include: difficulties in recruiting, training and managing a diverse workforce; and increased potential for organisational conflict.

Despite the disadvantages, the ever-increasing diversity of modern industrialised nations suggests that there are on-going strategic advantages in employing a diverse workforce. While many small employers may argue that it is cost prohibitive to provide special conditions or facilities for employees with 'divergent' needs, there is no increased financial cost in simply showing respect for difference within their workplaces. Moreover, it may make those organisations more competitive (as employers and businesses) in the future.

Thinking Globally

Increasing numbers of organisations are recognising that effectively managing their human resources also necessitates recognition and incorporation of the global context. While we would not suggest that the vast majority of small businesses would ever be in a position, or indeed have the desire to, take their businesses offshore, it is almost impossible in an age of internationalisation to conceive of any business as being purely domestic in its focus. Though most small businesses may never sell their products internationally or establish subsidiaries in other nations, they are affected by global fiscal and monetary trends, fluctuations in stock markets and swings in economic conditions. Small businesses will also increasingly find that some, if not most of, the products or services they buy and sell, or the components from which they make their products, are produced overseas. Further, the increasing international mobility and cultural diversity of workforces will mean that thinking globally will be essential to business survival, and to this end, there is much that small businesses may learn from the disciplines of international human resource management and cross-cultural management.

The essence of international human resource management (IHRM) is knowledge of conditions in a variety of nations and knowledge of how to manage both within and across them. Strategic international human resource management (SIHRM) is thecollective of HRM issues, functions and practices that result from the strategic activities of multinational organisations and that impact the international concerns and goals of those enterprises.

SIHRM includes issues associated with people management through acquisitions and mergers, expatriate selection and preparation, creation of global thinking managers, managing, motivating, leading and negotiating in other nations, and corporate social responsibility. While management of expatriates and the human resource aspects of mergers and acquisitions will never be necessary for most small businesses, the cross-cultural management aspects of SIHRM do have application to domestic small businesses and all managers may benefit from cross-cultural competence.

In essence, cross-cultural differences arise from culturally divergent attitudes and behaviour and differences in understanding, interpretation and application. Culture may impact on the values people have in the workplace, the manner in which decisions are made, negotiations are conducted, jobs are designed and disputes resolved. As such being able to appreciate and work with differences is essential to achieving organisational harmony and is dependent upon undertaking a comprehensive analysis of the culture of an organisation and its HRM practices. In so doing, Cox and Blake (1991) argue that it will be possible to uncover sources of potential bias unfavourable to some, and to identify ways that corporate culture may place some members at a disadvantage.

GLOBAL MARKETING ENVIRONMENT

The changing behaviour of customers and proliferation of new marketing channels setups the new issues in the business world. In international market competition it's becoming harder and harder to maintain the life time relation with customers. Selling quality product and service in affordable price is not enough to gain the customer loyalty there are also many other dimensions of care. These all changes make profit secondary and modify organizations to customer-focused organizations and born the new theories and approaches. Today's marketing has come out with the circle of 4P's (Product, Price, Place and Promotion) and in the broader sense it is taking as an organizational function. The modified form of marketing is to provide greater value to customer and develop and maintain a healthy relationship.

According to the American Marketing Association today's Marketing is: "Marketing is an organizational function and a set of processes for creating, communicating and delivering value to customers and for managing customer relationships in way that benefit the organization and its stakeholders."

MACRO ENVIRONMENT

The global marketing environment comprises the intermediate and the macro environment. The intermediate environment contains those factors which are semi-controllable through contracts and they will be categorized as suppliers, Distributors, facilitators and shareholders.

For example in software industries the different vendors, application sellers, temporary specialist staffs and subcontractors etc are part of intermediate environment. The macro environment is made up of those factors and forces which are generally uncontrollable.

For the Global strategic marketing planning to evaluate and investigate the threats, opportunities and for risk assessment usually organizations used the PESTLE analysis here PESTLE stands for Political, Economic, Social, Technological, Legal, and Environmental Factors.

Mostly external auditor is used to audit the impact of these forces. Some countries have more relaxed and easy polices for import and export. Countries history of friendly relation and healthy business deals have also a positive impact in the future trades. Similarly if countries have better infrastructure for trading polices and legislations it also goes in the favour of the international traders. It helps to minimize the time and provide the secure dealings and especially newcomers feel comfortable to trade in such environment. With all these reasons the fresh literature tells us about the twelve factors involvement in the international trading. In 2005 according to the Geri Clarke the HELPS FREDICT is a more complete framework for the international marketing environmental analysis.

H History
E Economic
L Language
P Politics
S Social

F Financial
R Rules-International Trade
E Environment
D Demographic
I Infrastructure
C Culture
T Technology

CHANGES AND CHALLENGES

In 1998 article in the Economist Magazine Sums it up nicely: "Marketing has become a complex art. Technology and trade have increased the potential for global brands. The fragmentation of audiences and rising costs of television and print advertising are making other media attractive. And direct marketing and the internet are rewriting all the marketing rules." 55 years back, the television invention opens the new ways of the mass marketing and with the visual demonstration many local brand and now take the status of the world class brand.

This technology changes the language of the advertising. In old age mostly people preferred to buy things from market search and mainly radio transmitted about the market affairs and new coming products. Then TV gave the new confidence to its viewers and globally advertised the real market position. The visual demonstration also teach the people and guide them correctly and it also answered the question that why they need and want this specific product. Now World Wide Web is taking the position of the TV and Similarly the Digital TV and the Smart mobile are writing the new rules of the marketing. Today mobile and pager is the basic need of people and every one is in range just because of a small piece of technology. Here telecommunication was playing an important role. Now in the end of 20th century, the emergence of internet and telecommunication introduce m-commerce.

First mobile companies simply provide an updates information like weather reports, games online information, latest movies and songs information etc just to provide better services and to satisfy customer. From that time the m-commerce became the part of our life and no one feel this addition of the new business technique, today banks and other financial services are also providing mobile commerce services and this tiny device has become the source of market transactions.

This was the small overview of emergence of the technology. On the other hand the destructive incidents like 9/11 and 7/7 etc. and other country wars (War against terrorism) are destroying the developed markets and the investors are feeling fear to invest money in these risky areas. The customer buying behaviour and its quality perception is also changing and now he is demanding the rich added value products and services.

The multinational companies and chain store also create a strong competition globally and it's becoming more difficult to retain a long term relation with existing customer. However the last decade of the twentieth century bought major changes that redefine the role and concept of marketing. The rapid change of market made customer more sophisticated and value added demanding. Products/service development and management has changed radically, the internet and third party securities made more easy transactions and virtualized payment and distribution channels introduce new way to approach market.

4

Marketing Planning and Strategy

INTRODUCTION

The area of marketing planning involves forging a plan for a firm's marketing activities. A marketing plan can also pertain to a specific product, as well as to an organization's overall marketing strategy. Generally speaking, an organization's marketing planning process is derived from its overall business strategy. Thus, when top management are devising the firm's strategic direction or mission, the intended marketing activities are incorporated into this plan. There are several levels of marketing objectives within an organization. The senior management of a firm would formulate a general business strategy for a firm. However, this general business strategy would be interpreted and implemented in different contexts throughout the firm.

MARKETING STRATEGY

Plans and Planning

Plans are needed to clarify what kinds of strategic objectives an organization would like to achieve and how this is to be done. Such plans must consider the amount of resources available. One critical resource is capital. Microsoft keeps a great deal of cash on hand to be able to "jump" on opportunities that come about. Small startup software firms, on the other hand, may have limited cash on hand. This means that they may have to forego what would have been a good investment because they do not have the cash to invest and cannot find a way to raise the capital.

Other resources that affect what a firm may be able to achieve include factors such as:

- *Trademarks/brand names*: It would be very difficult to compete against Coke and Pepsi in the cola market.
- *Patents*: It would be difficult to compete against Intel and AMD in the microprocessor market since both these firms have a number of patents that it is difficult to get around.
- *People*: Even with all of Microsoft's money available, it could not immediately hire the people needed to manufacture computer chips.

- *Distribution*: Stores have space for only a fraction of the products they are offered, so they must turn many away. A firm that does not have an established relationship with stores will be at a disadvantage in trying to introduce a new product.

Plans are subject to the choices and policies that the organization has made. Some firms have goals of social responsibility, for example. Some firms are willing to take a greater risk, which may result in a very large payoff but also involve the risk of a large loss, than others. Strategic marketing is best seen as an ongoing and never-ending process.

Typically:

- The organization will identify the *objectives* it wishes to achieve. This could involve profitability directly, but often profitability is a long term goal that may require some intermediate steps. The firm may seek to increase market share, achieve distribution in more outlets, have sales grow by a certain percentage, or have consumers evaluate the product more favourably. Some organizations have objectives that are not focused on monetary profit—e.g., promoting literacy or preventing breast cancer.
- An analysis is made, taking into consideration issues such as *organizational resources, competitors, the competitors' strengths, different types of customers, changes in the market*, or *the impact of new technology*.
- Based on this analysis, a plan is made based on *tradeoffs between the advantages and disadvantages* of different options available.
- This strategy is then carried out. The firm may design new products, revamp its advertising strategy, invest in getting more stores to carry the product, or decide to focus on a new customer segment.
- After implementation, the results or outcome are evaluated. If results are not as desired, a change may have to be made to the strategy. Even if results are satisfactory, the firm still needs to monitor the environment for changes.

Levels of Planning and Strategies

Plans for a firm can be made at several different levels. At the *corporate* level, the management considers the objectives of the *firm as a whole*. For example, Microsoft may want seek to grow by providing high quality software, hardware, and services to consumers. To achieve this goal, the firm may be willing to invest aggressively.

Plans can also be made at the *business unit* level. For example, although Microsoft is best known for its operating systems and applications software, the firm also provides Internet access and makes video games. Different managers will have responsibilities for different areas, and goals may best be made by those closest to the business area being considered. It is also more practical to hold managers accountable for performance if the plan is being made at a more specific level. Boeing has both commercial aircraft and defence divisions. Each is run by different managers, although there is some overlap in technology between the two. Therefore, plans are needed both at the corporate and at the business levels.

Occasionally, plans will be made at the *functional* level, to allow managers to specialize and to increase managerial accountability. Marketing, for example, may be charged with increasing awareness of Microsoft game consoles to 55% of the U.S. population or to increase the number of units of Microsoft Office sold. Finance may be charged with raising a given amount of capital at a given cost. Manufacturing may be charged with decreasing production costs by 5%.

The firm needs to identify the business it is in. Here, a *balance* must be made so that the firm's *scope is not defined too narrowly or too broadly*. A firm may define its goal very narrowly and then miss opportunities in the market place. For example, if Dell were to define itself only as a computer company, it might miss an opportunity to branch into PDAs or Internet service. Thus, they might instead define themselves as a provider of "information solutions." A company should not define itself too broadly, however, since this may result in loss of focus. For example, a manufacturer of baking soda should probably not see itself as a manufacturer of all types of chemicals. Sometimes, companies can define themselves in terms of a customer need. For example, 3M sees itself as being in the business of making products whose surfaces are bonded together. This accounts for both Post-It notes and computer disks.

A firm's mission should generally include a discussion of the *customers served*, the kind of technology involved, and the markets served. Several issues are involved in selecting target customers.

As suggested, consider these in more detail within the context of segmentation, but for now, the firm needs to consider issues such as:

- The *size* of various market segments;
- How well these segments are being *served by existing firms*;
- *Changes* in the market—e.g., growth of segments or change in technology;
- How the firm should be *positioned*, or seen by customers. For example, Wal-Mart positions itself as providing value in retailing, while Nordstrom's defines itself more in terms of high levels of customer service.

The Boston Consulting Group matrix provides a firm an opportunity to assess *how well its business units work together*. Each business unit is evaluated in terms of two factors: *market share* and the *growth prospects* in the market. Generally, the larger a firm's share, the stronger its position, and the greater the growth in a market, the better future possibilities.

Four combinations emerge:

1. A *star* represents a business unit that has a high share in a growing market. For example, Motorola has a large share in the rapidly growing market for cellular phones.
2. A *question mark* results when a unit has a small share in a rapidly growing market. The firm's position, then, is not as strong as it would have been had its market share been greater, but there is an opportunity to grow. For example, Hewlett-Packard has a small share of the digital camera market, but this is a very rapidly growing market.
3. A *cash cow* results when a firm has a large share in a market that is not growing, and may even be shrinking. Brother has a large share of the typewriter market.
4. A *dog* results when a business unit has a small share in a market that is not growing. This is generally a somewhat unattractive situation, although dogs can still be profitable in the short run. For example, Smith Corona how has a small share of the typewriter market.

Firms are usually best of with a portfolio that has a *balance* of firms in each category. The cash cows tend to *generate cash but require little future investment*. On the other hand, stars generate some cash, but *even more cash is needed to invest in the future*—for research and development, marketing campaigns, and building new manufacturing facilities. Therefore, a firm may take excess cash from the cash cow and divert it to the star. For example, Brother could "harvest" its profits from typewriters and invest this in the unit making colour laser printers, which will need the cash to grow. If a firm has cash cows that generate a lot of cash, this may be used to try to improve the market share of a question mark. A firm that has a number of promising stars in its portfolio may be in serious trouble if it does not have any cash cows to support it. If it is about to run out of cash—regardless of how profitable it is— is becomes vulnerable as a takeover target from a firm that has the cash to continue running it.

A SWOT analysis is used to help the firm *identify effective strategies*. Successful firms such as Microsoft have certain strengths. Microsoft, for example, has a great deal of technology, a huge staff of very talented engineers, a great deal of experience in designing software, a very large market share, a well respected brand name, and a great deal of cash. Microsoft also has some weaknesses, however: The game console and MSN units are currently running at a loss, and MSN has been unable to achieve desired levels of growth. Firms may face opportunities in the current market.

Microsoft, for example, may have the opportunity to take advantage of its brand name to enter into the hardware market. Microsoft may also become a trusted source of consumer services. Microsoft currently faces several threats, including the weak economy. Because fewer new computers are bough during a recession, fewer operating systems and software packages. Rather than merely listing strengths, weaknesses, opportunities, and threats, a SWOT analysis should suggest how the firm may use its strengths and opportunities to overcome weaknesses and threats. Decisions should also be made as to how resources should be allocated. For example, Microsoft could either decide to put more resources into MSN or to abandon this unit entirely. Microsoft has a great deal of cash ready to spend, so the option to put resources toward MSN is available. Microsoft will also need to see how threats can be addressed. The firm can earn political good will by engaging in charitable acts, which it has money available to fund. For example, Microsoft has donated software and computers to schools. It can forego temporary profits by reducing prices temporarily to increase demand, or can "hold out" by maintaining current prices while not selling as many units.

Criteria for Effective Marketing Plans

Marketing plans should meet several criteria:

- The plan must be *specific* enough so that it can be implemented and communicated to people in the firm. "Improving profitability" is usually too vague, but increasing net profits by 5%, increasing market share by 10%, gaining distribution in 2,000 more stores, and reducing manufacturing costs by 2% are all specific.
- The plan must be *measurable* so that one can see if it has been achieved. The plans involve specific numbers.
- The goal must be *achievable* or realistic. Plans that are unrealistic may result in poor use of resources or lowered morale within the firm.
- The goals must be *consistent*. For example, a firm cannot ordinarily simultaneously plan improve product features, increase profits, and reduce prices.

MARKETING PLAN

The central point in planning for marketing decisions is the Marketing Plan.

As we note in the highly detailed How to Write a Marketing Plan tutorial, the plan serves several functions including:

- Forcing marketing personnel to look internally in order to fully understand the results of past marketing decisions.
- Forcing marketing personnel to look externally in order to fully understand the market in which they operate.
- Setting future goals and providing direction for future marketing efforts that everyone within the organization should understand and support.

- Serving as a key component in obtaining funding to pursue new initiatives.

The scope of the Marketing Plan depends on the company and industry. A small technology startup company may, for instance, have a less elaborate plan that is highly flexible to meet the needs of a rapidly changing market.

A more established marketing organization, such a large consumer products firm, may create a very structured plan that clearly identifies all activities that take place over a 12-month period.

Whether the marketer is creating a short plan intended to cover a narrow timeframe or a full-blown document laying out plans for a year or more, any plan requires undertaking significant market research to better understand the market.

COMPONENTS OF THE MARKETING PLAN

The Marketing Plan is often a complex and diverse document that examines many areas.

For most plans the key components found in the document include:

- *Organizational Mission*: Represents the guiding force of an organization by identifying the long-run vision for what the organization hopes to achieve. The mission comes from the top leaders of the organization and often remains unchanged for many years.
- *Objectives*: Reflects what the organization expects to achieve with its marketing efforts. As with the mission, objectives also flow from the top of the organization down to the marketing department. Objectives can be in the form of financial goals or marketing goals.
- *Marketing Strategy*: Achieving objectives requires the marketer engage in marketing decision-making which indicates where resources will be directed. However, before spending begins on individual marketing decisions the marketer needs to establish a general plan of action that summarizes what will be done to reach the stated objectives.
- *Tactical Prigrammes*: Marketing strategy sets the stage for specific actions that will take place. Marketing tactics are the day-to-day actions that marketers undertake and involve the major marketing decision areas. As would be expected, this is the key area of the Marketing Plan since it explains exactly what will be done to reach the organization's objectives.
- *Marketing Budget*: Carrying out marketing tactics almost always means that money must be spent. The marketing budget lays out the spending requirements needed to carry out marketing tactics. While the marketing department may request a certain level of funding they feel is required, in the end it is upper-management

that will have final say on how much financial support will be offered.

IMPORTANCE OF MARKETING PLANNING

Marketers consider many factors when making decisions. Of course the main factors are those directly associated with how customers (including distribution partners) respond to an organization's marketing efforts, such as how they may react to changes in a product, new advertisements, special pricing promotions, etc.

But when making decisions marketers face other concerns that are not directly customer related. For instance, we have discussed how marketing decisions (e.g., lowering price) may place pressure on other areas of the organization (e.g., production, shipping). Other examples include:

- As we noted in our definition of marketing, decisions must be made with an understanding of the value these provide not only to customers but to the marketing organization. Consequently, marketers must be well aware of how their decisions fit with the overall objectives of the company. For example, a company whose goal is to be the low-price leader may have concerns if the company's marketing department wants to market a very high-end product, since this would go against the reputation and core strengths of the company.
- We showed that marketers' decisions may affect peripheral stakeholders who are not directly connected to the marketing organization but have the potential to impact the organization if issues arise that draw their attention.
- Marketing decisions also directly affect an organization's financial condition. Marketers' efforts generate the funds (i.e., sales) needed for the company to survive, but do so while using company resources, in particular, expenditure of funds. Controls must be put in place to insure the results of what the organization spends through marketing (i.e., return on investment) meet expectations.

Because marketing decisions have both internal and external impact, marketers are wise to make their decisions only after engaging in a careful, disciplined planning process. Marketers who make hasty, off-the-cuff decisions without regard to the implications are taking risks that may lead to problems. Instead, marketing decisions should be made with consideration of how these affect others and the resources (e.g., funds) required to carry out the plan.

TYPES OF MARKETING STRATEGY

One of the most important concepts of the marketing planning process is the need to develop a cohesive marketing strategy that guides tactical programs for the marketing decision areas. In marketing there are two levels to strategy formulation: General Marketing Strategies and Decision Area Strategies.

General Marketing Strategies

These set the direction for all marketing efforts by describing, in general terms, how marketing will achieve its objectives. There are many different General Marketing Strategies, though most can be viewed as falling into one of the following categories:

- *Market Expansion*: This strategy looks to grow overall sales in one of two ways:
  - *Grow Sales with Existing Products*: With this approach the marketer seeks to actively increase the overall sales of products the company currently markets. This can be accomplished by: 1) getting existing customers to buy more; 2) getting potential customers to buy (i.e., those who have yet to buy); or 3) selling current products in new markets.
  - *Grow Sales with New Products:* With this approach the marketer seeks to achieve objectives through the introduction of new products. This can be accomplished by: 1) introducing updated versions or refinements to existing products; 2) introducing products that are extensions of current products; or 3) introducing new products not previously marketed.
- *Market Share Growth:* This strategy looks to increase the marketer's overall percentage or share of market. In many cases this can only be accomplished by taking sales away from competitors. Consequently, this strategy often relies on aggressive marketing tactics.
- *Niche Market*: This strategy looks to obtain a commanding position within a certain segment of the overall market. Usually the niche market is much smaller in terms of total customers and sales volume than the overall market. Ideally this strategy looks to have the product viewed as being different from companies targeting the larger market.
- *Status Quo*: This strategy looks to maintain the marketer's current position in the market, such as maintaining the same level of market share.
- *Market Exit*: This strategy looks to remove the product from the organization's product mix. This can be accomplished by: 1) selling the product to another organization, or 2) eliminating the product.

PLANNING WITH THE PRODUCT LIFE CYCLE

As we have seen, there are many components, both internal and external, that must be considered within the marketing planning process. In fact, for many marketers creating the Marketing Plan represents one of the most challenging and burdensome tasks they face.

Fortunately, over the years marketing academics and professionals have put forth theories, models and other tools that aid planning. Possibly the most widely used planning tool within marketing is the Product Life Cycle (PLC) concept. The basic premise of the PLC is that products go through several stages of "life" with each stage presenting the marketer with different challenges that must be met with different marketing approaches. By understanding a product's position in the PLC, the marketer may be able to develop more effective plans.

There have been several attempts over the years to define the stages that make up the PLC. Unfortunately, the PLC may be different for different products, different markets and different market conditions (e.g., economic forces). Consequently, there is not a one-model-fits-all PLC. Yet there is enough evidence to suggest that most products experience patterns of activity that divide the evolution of the product into five distinct stages. These stages are:

- *Development*: Occurs before the product is released to the market and is principally a time for honing the product offering and preparing the market for product introduction.
- *Introduction*: Product is released to the market and sales begin though often gradually as the market becomes aware of the product.
- *Growth*: If the product is accepted it may reach a stage of rapid growth in sales and in profits.
- *Maturity*: At some point sales of a product may stabilize. For some products the maturity phase can be the longest stage as the product is repeatedly purchased by loyal customers. However, while overall sales may grow year-over-year, percentage sales increases may be small.
- *Decline*: All products eventually see demand decline as customers no longer see value in purchasing the product.

LEVELS OF ANALYSIS OF THE PLC

The Product Life Cycle is commonly referenced in many business publications as a way of describing the current conditions facing a market or product. The fact it is used to describe either markets or individual products points out the need to understand the different levels of analysis for which the PLC can be used. These levels include:

- *Product Category*: This level considers the macro market view for the general category of products that meet a general need. For instance, automobiles would be a general category that meets the need for personal motorized transportation (obviously there are others, such as motorcycles, scooters and trucks but we will focus only on automobiles) and includes hundreds of products. Since the PLC for a product category includes sales for all products, the timeframe for the automotive PLC is quite long with the Introduction stage beginning around 1900.

- *Product Form*: This level looks at product groupings that fall within a product category. The product form contains many different groupings that, taken together, make up the product category. These groupings include products that not only satisfy the general need of the product category, but do so by also offering additional benefits. In our example, hybrid cars would be a product form, since it satisfies the general need for personal motorized transportation and offers additional benefits in the form of fuel efficiency and environmental friendliness. Other product forms in the product category include sports cars, minivans, luxury sedans, etc. Clearly there can be a unique PLC for each form of a product. Marketers are very concerned with analysis at this level since it provides evidence for what is occurring in specific markets and for this reason is considered the most important level of analysis.
- *Individual Brand*: This level concerns the life cycle of a specific brand within a product form. In our example this would include the Toyota Prius. While it may seem marketers would be most concerned with this level, they actually gain more value from analyzing what is happening in the overall market (i.e., product form). For instance, a marketer may make a serious mistake if she assumes the entire market has entered the Decline stage just because her company's brand has seen a sales drop. Doing so may mean a total misread of what is happening in the market and lead to the marketer missing out on additional opportunities if the market for the product form is still growing.

We should note that in most cases the PLC considers what is happening for the total market (i.e., worldwide sales). However, more information could be obtained by applying the concepts of the PLC to individual market segments, such as geographic regions or customer characteristics (e.g., by age, education level, etc.).

ADOPTION OF NEW PRODUCTS

The PLC is tied closely to the concept of Diffusion of Innovation, which explains how information and acceptance of new products spread through a market, innovation is anything new that solves needs by offering a significant advantage over existing methods (e.g., other products) customers use. Innovation can encompass both highly advanced technology products, such as new computer chips, and non-technological products, such as a new soft drink. In fact, the seminal work of the Diffusion of Innovation concept occurred in the 1950s when researchers in the agricultural industry observed how new corn seeds were adopted by farmers in Midwest U.S. states.

For marketers a key concept to emerge from research on new product diffusion is the identification of adopter categories into which members of a market are likely to fall. These categories include:

- *Innovators*: Represent a small percentage of the market that is at the forefront of adopting new products. These people are often viewed as enthusiasts and are eager to try new things, often without regard to price. While a good test ground for new products, marketers find that Innovators often do not remain loyal as they continually seek new products.
- *Early Adopters*: This group contains more members than the Innovator category. They share Innovators' enthusiasm for new products though they tend to be more practical about their decisions. They also are eager to communicate their experiences with the Early Majority (next group) and because of their influence they are important to the future success of the product (i.e., act as opinion leaders).
- *Early Majority*: This represents the beginning of entry into the mass market. The Early Majority account for up to one-third of the overall market. The Early Majority like new things but tend to wait until they have received positive opinions for others (i.e., early adopters) before purchasing. Adoption by the Early Majority is key if a new product is to be profitable. On the other hand, many new products die quickly because they are not accepted beyond early trials by Innovators and Early Adopters and never reach mass market status.
- *Late Majority*: Possibly as large as the Early Majority, this group takes a wait-and-see approach before trying something new. Marketers are likely to see their highest profits once this group starts to purchase.
- *Laggards*: This is the last group to adopt something new and, in fact, may only do so if they have no other choice. Depending on the market this group can be large though because of their reluctance to accept new products marketers are not inclined to direct much attention to them.

Adopter Categories and the PLC

The adopter categories help explain the shape of the life cycle for many products. For instance, consider how a new household cleaning product may become successful. First, Innovators may experience the product during the developmental stage and then become the key targeted customers at the beginning of the Introduction stage. Early Adopters will also be targeted during the Introduction stage and their adoption will determine whether the product makes it to the Growth stage.

If the product survives the Innovator and Early Adopters it moves to the Growth stage where acceptance by the Early Majority means the product is entering the mass market. The product can continue to be successful as it is adopted by the Late Majority and, to a much lesser extent, by Laggards. Eventually product sales decline as Innovators and Early Adopter move to something new and the cycle starts over.

It should be noted that an assumption of a person's placement in a certain adopter category for one product does not imply that person will also occupy the same category for other products.

For example, someone who is an Innovator for one product may be a Laggard for another. However, with research, marketers may find that an individual's adopter classification for one product applies across a similar set of products.

For instance, those classified as Innovators for computer hardware may have a high probability of being categorized the same for computer software. This assumption may be necessary as a software company develops its target marketing strategies in advance of the launch a new product.

Finally, it should be noted that each adopter category may consist of multiple smaller market segments. For example, the Early Majority is made up of smaller markets that can be segmented on variables such as geography, age, income, etc.

THE PLC AND MARKETING PLANNING

With a basic understanding of the PLC, we now turn to how this is used in marketing planning. As we will see, the PLC helps the marketer understand that marketing decisions must change as a product moves from one stage to another. For example, marketers will find that what works when appealing to Innovators in the Introduction stage is different than marketing methods used to attract Early Majority during the Growth stage.

For much of the rest of this tutorial we offer a detailed discussion of how the PLC can aid marketing planning. The discussion is presented using the following assumptions and techniques:

- The chief scope of analysis is at the product form level (i.e., what is happening in a specific industry) where we show how certain characteristics of the market change over time. We break down each stage and discuss the market characteristics in terms of:
  - Level of Competition
  - Nuances of the Target Market
  - Available Product Options
  - Average Price Level
  - Promotional Focus
  - Distribution Strategy
  - Total Industry Profits

- While market characteristics are evaluated for the product form, we offer strategy guidance for individual brands that compete within these specific industries.
- While at the general level the PLC is divided into five main stages, we view most stages as consisting of sub-stages that result from noticeable changes in market characteristics.

DEVELOPMENT STAGE

The Product Life Cycle begins long before a product is brought to market. While technically sales do not start until the next stage, marketers must address many of the same issues they will face once the product is launched. Much of what happens in the Development stage follows our discussion of New Product Development in the Managing Products, where market research is the key element in planning. Most of what occurs in this stage is experienced only by companies who are on the forefront of innovation of a new product form. In our discussion, the Development stage is divided into two distinct sub-stages: early and late.

Early Development Stage

Characteristics

- *Competition*: No real competition exists since the product is in early development much of which is in-house and not readily viewable to competitors. However, from a research perspective competitors are now being identified.
- *Target Market*: The target market exists only in market research terms. Possibly a small number of target customers are used to assist with research.
- *Product*: The product exists only in the form of ideas and prototypes. Inventory is not yet available.
- *Prices*: Non-existent unless the company charges research customers a fee to be part of early product testing.
- *Promotion*: Promotion has yet to occur as companies continue to refine the product form and build their marketing plan.
- *Distribution*: Mostly limited to internal analysis of possible distribution alternatives, though there may be some communication with a limited number of distribution partners in order to gauge interest.
- *Profits*: At this stage there are costs only.

Brand Strategy

For firms developing a new product form this stage is primarily concerned with market research. This stage matches the Concept Development and Testing step for New Product Development.

Customers and distribution partners are only involved to aid in information gathering often through focus group research. Because the product form is still in early development the marketer has yet to determine whether the company will move forward with a full product launch.

Late Development Stage

Characteristics

- *Competition*: While a marketer may not face competition in terms of sales, they may face competitive pressure from companies developing similar products, such as competition to acquire materials or technologies for product development, competition to line up product evaluators, and competition to get early word out about the product to the news media. Additionally, competition may exist in the form of other types of products that potential customers currently use to satisfy needs targeted by the new product form. If these competitors are aware that a new product form is being developed, they may increase efforts to sell their product with the intention of reducing the market's need for the new product.
- *Target Market*: Companies may test market the product among a small group of customers or within a selected geographic market.
- *Product*: Companies researching the product form begin to produce small quantities of the product, primarily for testing or to build initial awareness (e.g., for display at trade shows).
- *Prices*: Initial market price is discussed and if there are active test markets the company may be testing different price levels.
- *Promotion*: Promotion often begins prior to product launch as marketers prime the market. Emphasis may be on public relations in an attempt to encourage the media to discuss the product prior to launch. If a real test market is used the companies may be using several promotional options including advertising and sales promotion.
- *Distribution*: For product sold through distributors, the ground work is being laid to build the distribution network. In some cases distributor education and training will start prior to product launch.
- *Profits*: A small amount of revenue may be generated if real test markets are used, but overall marketers continue to experience substantial costs.

Brand Strategy

Products that have moved to the late stage of development have done so because market research suggests there is strong potential for success. By this point a marketer has a real product (not just ideas) and is in the position to test it in the market.

Consequently, this stage matches the Market Testing step for New Product Development. Firms electing to test their product in real "test markets" will do so using all their marketing tools.

COMPONENTS OF STRATEGIC PLANNING

Strategic planning's three main components are plan development, plan execution, and plan review. Many of the functional areas within these components are similar in that all three require a team concept that is based on: ensuring the member's roles are defined, educating team members about the process, and using quality communication when interacting.

PLAN DEVELOPMENT

Plan development is the first component of strategic planning.

During this stage, the following steps should be completed:

- *Assess the association's history and significant accomplishments*: Develop a history of the association. List important milestones that brought the association to where it is today. In order to help visualize how the association has changed over the years, include items where impact occurred in the association's operations, such as: hiring additional staff, upgrade computer hardware/software, changing processes significantly, raising dues, building additional facilities, rebuilding/renovating existing facilities, etc., by dates and quantities/ dollars, as appropriate.
- *Assess the association's current status*: Determine the association's current status by looking at such things as the state of the facilities, infrastructure of the operations, the financial statements, the demographics of the population, and so forth.
- *Evaluate the association's current governance structure*: Review the operations to determine how responsi-bilities are assigned, defining communi-cations and authorities. Examine policies, procedures, and desk guides available to determine the chain of command within the association's staff, within the board, and for oversight and communications between the staff or property management company and the board of directors. Critical is the point of contact for the staff or management company and the board, to preclude misunderstandings, duplications of effort, things falling through the cracks, etc.
- Determine the board's responsibilities versus that of the staff or management company's responsibilities. An example of a delineation of responsibilities between the staff or management company and the board is covered in Policy Governance, which simply stated,

assigns the board's function as that of policy making, the "what is" of the subject/issue, while the staff's or management company's function is that of carrying out the policies, the "how to" of the subject/issue.

- *Develop mission and vision statements*: The vision statement is the image or state to which the association aspires. It emphasizes the dream of where the association will be at a specific time. The mission statement is the organization's purpose stated in a memorable phrase. In short, an association's mission statement describes the business it's in. It should be geared toward fulfilling the association's purpose and what it is intended to do with some specifics contained in the governing documents. Mission and vision statements should not be a list of goals.
- *Determine operating values*: Also called guiding principles, these values state the association's intentions and expectations. They are used to judge the association's policies and actions, as well as individual conduct. Associations should include values such as: the importance of customers and customer service; commitment to quality and innovation; importance of honesty; integrity and ethical behaviour; corporate citizenship; respect for the employee and duty the association has to its employees; and importance of safety and protecting the environment, etc.
- *Perform a needs assessment*: Determine the needs of the association by analyzing the present state of the community, addressing any critical issues, and identifying the association's strengths, weaknesses, opportunities, and threats.
  - *Determination of key result areas*: Define five to ten areas in which the association must be successful in order to accomplish its mission, based on customer expectations.
    a. *Determine customer expectations*: Determine the customer [members, suppliers, and employees] expectations of the association as stakeholders. Group the expectations into five to ten key results areas.
- *Determine critical issues*: List the critical issues faced by the association that must be addressed for the association to achieve its mission and vision, based on an assessment of its strengths, weaknesses, opportunities, and threats.
  - Assessment of strengths, weaknesses, opport-unities, and threats (SWOT)
    a. *Strengths*: List the organizational attributes that promote the association's ability to meet its mission and vision.
    b. *Weaknesses*: List those organizational attributes that hamper the association's ability to meet its mission and vision. Some

examples include inadequate technology or use of technology, lack core competency training, poor service, and so forth.

c. *Opportunities*: List those factors, internal and external, that would enable the association to meet its mission and vision. Some examples include technological advances in needed areas, consolidating functions, etc.

d. *Threats*: List those factors, internal or external, that would hamper the association from meeting its mission and vision. Some examples include high rate of foreclosures, drawn out worker strike, change in developer focus, etc.

- *Define the roles of key players*: Who will be the key people responsible for each aspect of the strategic plan? Answer questions such as: What level of control will the board have? Is the manager going to be a proactive leader or an administrator? Are the homeowners going to be active as committee members or are they going to be less involved? Role definition is extremely important so that efforts are not duplicated-or neglected overall. One way to establish a team and define specific roles is to adopt a model similar to a city council and city manager form of government. The city council (board of directors) sets policies, votes on contracts and bids, and is the on-site eyes and ears (oversight) of the community. The city manager (management) should be the professionally educated, proactive, paid leader who manages the day-to-day operations and then implements the board's decisions. The citizens (homeowners) should attend meetings, serve on committees, and elect competent individuals to the board of directors. This concept of team roles goes much deeper than this discussion allows, especially in the areas of compliance, budgeting, and homeowner interaction.
- *Educate and communicate the plan*:Without education and communication, team members can neither perform their roles nor effectively interact with each other. Make sure that every player has the necessary documents and basic knowledge to perform effectively. Further ensure that each of the players communicate with each other-provide updates as necessary and always ask for others' input. Better to catch a potential problem earlier rather than later. In the event that there is a change in management, association boards should also be sure to communicate their strategic plans to the new manager, and revise it, if necessary. Also, if the Strategic Plan calls for specific management participation, make sure it is spelled out in the management contract.
- *Listen and take notes*: During the strategic planning process it is important for all parties to actively listen and take notes. Many type-A personalities, who may be involved with the association at any

level, will want to solve the community's issues quickly and efficiently. If they do this without listening to the board of directors, homeowners, and vendors, they may be executing a plan, but not a quality strategic plan.

- *Develop and prioritize long-range goals*: Develop long-range goals to address the critical issues identified through the needs assessment; then prioritize those goals.
- *Develop short-term goals and action plans*: Establish short-term goals and specific action plans along with scheduled completion dates.
- *Monitor the progress*: Establish a monitoring process to assess the progress made on both short-term and long-range goals.

MODELS OF STRATEGIC PLANNING

Strategic planning is a relatively new genre of planning, adapted from primarily two sources. Business schools have equipped leaders with institutional planning processes, which were developed from decision making and production control. Community planning schools have prepared planning staffs with models of social planning and physical land-use planning. The business model is more often tailored for a hierarchical organization with top-down control, although this has softened in the dot-com era. The community-planning model is more grass roots, bottom-up, consensus building and is better suited for non-profit organizations and local governments. The former is market share and profit oriented, and the latter is empowerment and constituent needs oriented. In between, there is a range of blended approaches.

MODEL 1: NON-PROFIT ORGANIZATIONS (NPOS)

Brian W. Barry details strategic planning for NPOs in the pamphlet and workbook *Strategic Planning Workbook for Nonprofit Organizations*. The workbook is oriented to organizations such as soup kitchens, nascent neighbourhood groups, and other human services groups. It outlines the strategic planning process, but is tailored to a small organiza tion with a narrow focus. It also assumes that all of the stakeholders are represented, that they speak with authority, and that the constituencies they represent are fairly homogeneous. In order to be applied to community associations, this model must be modified to accommodate multiple missions in more complex organizations, which offer many services to very heterogeneous constituencies. However, it lacks attention on soliciting feedback and developing consensus.

NPO Strategic Planning includes:

- Recruiting stakeholders, power brokers, and leadership.
- Reviewing the organization's history and current situation.
- Reviewing and revising (or developing) the organization's mission statement.

- Identifying the organization's opportunities and threats.
- Identifying organizational strengths and weaknesses.
- Identifying the most critical issues arising from any of the organization's opportunities, threats, strengths, and weaknesses.
- Setting goals to remove weaknesses, blunt threats, and seizing opportunities.
- Brainstorming, evaluating, and selecting strategies to empower leaders.
- Critiquing and reviewing the plan.
- Revising goals, and re-implementing goals, as appropriate.

MODEL 2: APPLIED STRATEGIC PLANNING

The Applied Strategic Planning approach is described in the pamphlet *Applied Strategic Planning, An Introduction* by Leonard D. Goodstein, Timothy M. Nolan, and William J. Pfeiffer. Business and military executives tend to favour this model. It assumes a top-down hierarchy with a plans and operations department, that is responsible for running the models and recruiting and involving appropriate and key personnel. It also presumes the existence of a fair degree of quantifiable data and business modeling decision making where one finds targets and executes prigrammes. This method might be well suited for solving problems where constituents have an identifiable problem and are unified in the opinion that better service is needed. The process also incorporates scanning the environment, brainstorming solutions, establishing a future orientation, and looking at the behaviour of competitors and new products on the horizon.

Applied Strategic Planning includes:

- Identifying consultants and key internal players.
- Garnering CEO support, identifying stakeholders, and setting planning goals.
- Scanning organizational values, philosophy, and culture.
- (Re)defining the organization's mission statement.
- Identifying new futures and new venture opportunities.
- Auditing threats, opportunities, strengths, and weaknesses.
- Identifying critical gaps between where the organization is and its future.
- Selecting strategies to expand or retrench as a means to close performance gaps.
- Implementing the strategies to acquire or divest.
- Monitoring actions, updating conditions, and restarting the cycle.

MODEL 3: ICMA STRATEGIC DEVELOPMENT

This model is the least relevant to community planning as it focuses very narrowly on the special issue of economic development. It makes a strong case for inventorying existing capacities and capabilities. It also contains several good elements that would stimulate association planning groups' thinking on consensus building. ICMA Strategic Development is described in *Economic Development: A Strategic Approach for Local Governments*, a 68-page leaders guide and student workbook for an International City/County Management Association (ICMA) course on local economic development.

ICMA Strategic Development includes:

- Augmenting existing planning structure with stakeholders.
- Conducting an environmental scan of community conditions.
- Identifying and evaluating the community resources.
- Identifying and rating different community business activities.
- Identifying and rating different community development agencies and prigrammes.
- Conducting an inventory of congruent and divergent values and visions in the community.
- Imagining and describing multiple visions of different community economic sectors.
- Developing visions into goals and establishing objectives to reach the goals.
- Describing who, what, when, how, and where resources are needed.
- Monitoring, reporting, updating, and reallocating efforts as targets are hit.
- Restarting the process again by recruiting a new group and conducting scans.

THE FIVE-FACTOR MODEL

MODEL

One of the long held goals of psychology has been to establish a model that can conveniently describe human personality, and disorders therein, with the intent to use this model in the remedying of personality disorders and improving general understanding of personality. Currently, a handful of models have risen to prominence, and have thus far stood the test of time. Some models are more generally accepted than others. Support for some models seems to come and go in cycles.

One of the more prominent models in contemporary psychology is what is known as the five-factor model of personality. This theory incorporates five different variables into a conceptual model for describing personality.

These five different factors are often referred to as the "Big 5". The five-factor theory is among the newest models developed for the description of personality, and this model shows promise to be among the most practical and applicable models available in the field of personality psychology. Thorough critical attention is given to the proposal that the five-factor model is in fact a great theory.

Five Factors

As it became evident to many psychologists that, mathematically, combinations of five factors were useful in describing personality, there was a need to clearly define what these factors were. Indeed, this process led to some dissent in the ranks. One dissenter from the five-factor theorists was renowned psychologist H. J. Eysenck. Eysenck felt that, due to overlaps in the five factors and their correlates, in fact a three-factor model was more appropriate and accurate. His theory is called the PEN model or sometimes is even shortened to the two factor E-IN model. "Factor analysis has improved the situation...but the problem of naming factors is of course still with us".

Many psychologists support Eysenck's PEN model. However, of the major "factor-analytic models...the Big Five dominates the landscape of current psychological research". Through extensive debating and experimenting, there is currently a general consensus in the realms of scholarly psychology as to the identity of the five factors, and their basic interpretations and values to analysis of personality. The five factors are extroversion-introversion, neuroticism, agreeableness, conscientiousness, and openness.

Extroversion has long been one of the traits that has appeared in factor-analytic models, and is one of the two traits to appear in both the five-factor model and Eysenck's PEN and E-IN models. Extroversion also is sometimes referred to as social adaptability, though the popularity of this term seems to be waning. Extroversion is defined as "a trait characterized by a keen interest in other people and external events, and venturing forth with confidence into the unknown".

Neuroticism is the other trait to play a role in most of the contemporary factor models for personality. In some studies, adjustment is examined as a factor, instead of neuroticism. In this case, higher scores will indicate a positive result, consistent with the other four factors. This is because the term neuroticism has an inherent negative denotation. The bases of neuroticism are levels of anxiety and volatility. Within these bounds, neuroticism is "a dimension of personality defined by stability and low anxiety at one end as opposed to instability and high anxiety at the other end".

Openness, agreeableness, and conscientiousness are all terms with which most people outside the realm of psychology are familiar. In general, openness refers to how willing people are to make adjustments in notions and activities in accordance with new ideas or situations. Agreeableness measures how compatible people are with other people, or basically how able they are to get along with others. Conscientiousness refers to how much a person considers others when making decisions.

As with the two factors in the big five from Eysenck's E-IN, these three are also placed on sliding scales. These three scales, like neuroticism and extroversion, slide between their limits to give a clear picture of personality. The limits of these scales give a clear idea of their applications and are defined as "trusting and helpful versus suspicious and uncooperative, hard working and reliable versus lazy and careless, and nonconformist and creative versus conventional and down-to-earth.

Clinical Use of the Five Factors

With the five factors themselves more or less firmly established, the model is of little importance to psychology if it can not somehow be applied. Clinically, the five-factor model works much like Freud's psychoanalysis. People who have a certain characteristic that falls at an extreme on the chart of one or more of the five variables are likely to have some sort of psychological abnormality associated with that trait. People are likely to select their environment in such a way that this trait is perpetuated. To keep this cycle from iterating, psychologists make their patients come to terms with the flawed trait, allowing the patient to break the cycle. The five-factor model is perhaps even more useful in research and learning than it currently is for psychological patients. To this end, supporters of the five-factor model point to the fact that factor analysis"serves as a useful bridge between the more clinical theories...and the learning, behavioural theories".

Determining the Greatness of the Theory

To determine the greatness of a psychological theory, it is necessary to examine several key factors. First, to truly be labeled a great theory, it should be established that the theory does not contradict currently held or accepted theories. Also, once this is established, a great theory would include some kind of taxonomy. In addition, a truly great theory would be applicable. In other words, the theory would have some sort of clinical uses and would be able to predict experimental results without contradiction and with a relatively high level of consistency. Also, a great theory requires a ring of originality. It is not a great deed by anyone's standards to simply restate a long existing belief, or to remold it slightly and call it new. Finally, a great personality theory also needs to be universal. Cultural or situationally dependent models, although certainly of some relevance, are not worthy of being called great.

Compatibility

To establish the five-factor model's compatibility with other models, it is necessary to examine other popular or long held psychological theories. First and foremost, it is easy to see that the five-factor model is consistent with other factor-analytical models. Eysenck developed his PEN model from Cattell's sixteen-factor model. In this same vein of factor-analytic models, it is now proposed that"the structure of personality is best conceptualized as consisting of five major traits, rather than Eysenck's three types". Still, it seems natural that any factor analytic model should not directly contradict other factor analytic models.

It has been established in recent years that the five-factor model is quite compatible with other popular psychological theories as well, not just those concerned with factor analysis. It has been a recent endeavor of some psychologists to build bridges between the five-factor model and Freud's theories of psychoanalysis. For example, recent experiments have shown correlates between Freud's concept of the ego and the five variables in the five-factor model. As stated in the report of one such experiment conducted by Huey and Weisz, focusing on ego resiliency and ego control in adolescent boys,"Ego resiliency seems to reflect, in part, the well adjusted pole of each FFM dimension, whereas Ego undercontrol...reflects high extroversion, low agreeableness, and low conscientiousness". The correlation between elements of Freud's theory of psychoanalysis and elements of the five-factor model helps demonstrate the compatibility of the five-factor model.

Taxonomy

With the five factors placed on sliding scales, it becomes only an exercise in persistence to associate various human characteristics with one or more of the five factors. Strong correlates quickly become evident, and as trends develop it becomes possible to assign very accurate descriptions about people via their placement on the sliding scales associated with the five factors. Certainly, it seems plausible that these results can be used to extrapolate many behavioural characteristics, including such dependent traits as financial success and depth of religious faith.

Psychologists are currently working towards this end, attempting to empirically establish what Langston and Sykes called"a taxonomy of personality". Naturally, this taxonomy has long been the goal of personality psychologists, though it seems that, of late, somewhat of a snag has developed in trying to extrapolate past the very broadest of personality traits. This problem with the five-factor model is that, although often very categorical and taxonomic, it does not delve deeply into the causation of certain correlates. In fact, some relationships are even somewhat counterintuitive, making extrapolation by common sense difficult. For example, one recent study found that type A behaviour, which is characterized by general optimism and ambitiousness, had a low correlation to conscientiousness

Application

In accordance with the aforesaid flaw in the second criterion for greatness, the five-factor model runs into the most trouble when approached through the standards set forth by the third criterion. This criterion calls for a great theory to be applicable. McAdams states,"Personality theories do more than specify traits". In essence, what he is getting at is that the five-factor model falls short of attaining or ever having a chance to attain the title of the unified psychological theory.

As stated, the five-factor model is used effectively in application. Because of this, it can be said that it is applicable, even though this does not address McAdams' claim that the five-factor theory should not really be considered a theory, but more appropriately just a list of five variables that are useful when attempting to identify and classify personality traits. In general, though, most of the applications of the five-factor model as it now exists seem to come in the academic and experimental forum. In reference to the model's usefulness in academics, Digman, "At a minimum, research on the five-factor model has given us a useful set of very broad dimensions that characterize individual differences. These dimensions can be measured with high reliability and impressive validity". In summary, Digman states that the five variables that compose the five-factor model "provide a good answer to the question of personality structure".

Originality

It would be possible to argue that the five-factor model does not meet the criterion of originality. Indeed, when Fiske first derived a model for predicting behaviour that consisted of five factors, Cattell's sixteen-factor system was already nearly five years old. Despite this, the five-factor model could arguably be considered distant enough from Cattell's model to warrant the label of originality. Perhaps instead, though, it is more useful to think of the factor models together, as a single set of theories that, although very different individually, all fit into one family. This family of models, starting with Cattell's sixteen-factor system, and including Eysenck's model and the five-factor model, grew from a study of language initiated by German psychologists Allport and Odbert, who were inspired for their studies by two other German psychologists, Baumgarten and Klages. Through this family history of the factor models, it is easy to see that they came to exist more or less independently of any other major psychological theories.

Universality

The fulfillment of the fourth criterion listed for a great theory in personality is that the theory should be nearly universally true. In a non-physical science, like psychology, it is naturally too much to ask that a theory always hold true. The basic premise, though, is that the theory should transcend culture and situation. As the premise is in two parts, so too shall be the response.

It appears that the five-factor model holds very well across cultural and linguistic lines. Digman gives three examples of other cultures in which the five-factor theory has held up nicely. His three studies took place in Japan, the Philippines, and Germany, and in all three cases, a five-factor solution was clearly evident at the end of testing. On the subject of the ability of the five-factor model to cross cultural and linguistic barriers, Digman writes, "something quite fundamental is involved here. Is this the way people everywhere construe personality, regardless of language or culture?".

A current fault of the five-factor model seems to be that it fails to anticipate behaviour in many situations. The same virtue that allows the five-factor model to hold true across cultural boundaries is its fault in specific situations: The five variables are too broad. McAdams accurately sums up this problem by saying, "Because the Big Five operate at such a general level of analysis, trait scores...may not be especially useful in the prediction of specific behaviour in particular situations".

ISSUES DESCRIPTIVE AND EVALUATIVE

In"The Five-Factor Model: Emergence of a Taxonomic Model for Personality Psychology," Popkins summarizes and evaluates a factor analytic description of personality that has risen to prominence in the last decade. However, there are problems with both Popkins' summary and his evaluation that this commentary will bring to light.

Perhaps Popkins is well within the scope of mainstream psychology when he discusses the five-factor model as a single, unitary development. However, proponents of the five-factor model prefer to make more fine-grained distinctions. Two related, yet distinct, five-factor models can be distinguished: the OCEAN model of Costa and McCrae, and the big five of Goldberg and colleagues. Costa and McCrae's OCEAN model is known by its acronym for the five factors: openness, conscientiousness, extraversion, agreeableness, and neuroticism. This naming of factors has the advantage of making them memorable to newcomers, but the disadvantage that the order is not meaningful, and the further disadvantage that the factors are not all named just as to the positive pole of each axis. In the big five variant, Goldberg prefers to name the factors just as to their positive poles, and in the order derived from the amount of variance each explains, as follows: surgency, agreeablenss, conscientiousness, emotional stability, and intellect. Currently, debates rage over whether the fifth factor is a'60's style openness to experience construct, or whether it represents a general intellect factor--and if the latter, then how intellect differs from general intelligence.

A further difference between the OCEAN and big five models is that the former is hierarchical whereas the latter is circular. The big five are circular because many variables have large loadings on two factors as opposed to only one, or three or more. Because the big five are circular, they have swallowed up both the interpersonal circumplex and the affective circumplex, incorporating these into a broader taxonomy

Another important difference between the OCEAN model and the big five is the theoretical basis that exists for the latter, but not for the former--

namely, the lexical hypothesis. This hypothesis contends that those individual differences that are most salient and socially relevant will come to be encoded as terms in the natural language. This conjecture makes into a meaningful activity the culling of all personality-relevant terms from an unabridged dictionary, and the subjecting of self- and peer-ratings on these terms to factor analysis.

Having now discussed the descriptive errors of omission in Popkins' paper, One will go on to point out some evaluative errors of commission. Popkins concludes that the five-factor model is not a great theory because it is not a theory, but only a taxonomy. In corroboration of Popkins' thesis, two leading big five researchers go so far as to state,"we would ban the use of the term'theoretical'...in favour of more exact terms such as'premises,''assumptions,' and'hypotheses,' as well as more meaningful distinctions such as'broad versus narrow' and'phenotypic versus genotypic' attributes".

Popkins to specify what is the difference between a theory and a taxonomy. The difference is not so obvious as it might appear at first blush. Prefer the more neutral term"research prigramme", because research can be done to challenge and improve both theories and taxonomies. Popkins' metatheory dictates that theories should be compatible. This idea, however, is incompatible with the history of science. Instead, scientific progress tends to come about when rival theories clash, and when there are many critics on every side.

Take the example of the Copernican revolution. Galileo insisted that Copernicus' heliocentric theory of the solar system be taken as literally true, rather than as merely a possible alternative to Ptolemy's geocentric theory. His insistence won him the retribution of the Church of that time, but the veneration of generations of scientists ever since. Moreover, this change from one contradictory theory to another is generally thought of as a paradigmatic case of scientific progress. Back when Copernicus was insisting that his theory and Ptolemy's were mutually consistent, progress languished. Similarly, one believe that the science of personality will progress most when various theories are found to be mutually contradictory, and the results of scientific tests are used to determine which is superior.

This idea of progress through contradiction can be applied to models of personality. Perhaps the OCEAN and big five models are not all that compatible after all. Certainly one substantive area on which they disagree is the interpretation of the fifth factor--is it intellect or openness? If these models contradict each other, then they almost surely contradict such alternative models as Eysenck and company's psychoticism-extraversion-neuroticism model and Ainsworth and company's attachment styles. Theoretical elaboration on the reasons for these divergences would likely engender progress in the science of personality, just as in other sciences.

BASICS OF STRATEGIC PLANNING

Strategic planning is more than ensuring your association will remain financially sound and be able to maintain its reserves—it's projecting where your association expects to be in five, ten, or fifteen years—and how your association will get there. It is a systematic planning process involving a number of steps that identify the current status of the association, including its mission, vision for the future, operating values, needs (strengths, weaknesses, opportunities, and threats), goals, prioritized actions and strategies, action plans, and monitoring plans.

Strategic planning is the cornerstone of every common-interest community. Without strategic planning, the community will never know where it is going—much less know if it ever got there. An important concept of strategic planning is an understanding that in order for the community to flourish, everyone needs to work to ensure the team's goals are met.

Team members include all association homeowners, the board of directors, professional management—whether onsite or through a management company— and various service professionals such as accountants and reserve professionals. This team needs to work as a collective body to be successful. Part of the team concept is the establishment of roles for the team players. Teams usually perform poorly if everyone or no one is trying to be the quarterback.

GOALS, OBJECTIVES AND TARGETS

Strategic planning is a very important business activity. It is also important in the public sector areas such as education. It is practiced widely informally and formally. Strategic planning and decision processes should end with objectives and a roadmap of ways to achieve those objectives.

One of the core goals when drafting a strategic plan is to develop it in a way that is easily translatable into action plans. Most strategic plans address high level initiatives and over-arching goals, but don't get articulated (translated) into day-to-day projects and tasks that will be required to achieve the plan. Terminology or word choice, as well as the level a plan is written, are both examples of easy ways to fail at translating your strategic plan in a way that makes sense and is executable to others. Often, plans are filled with conceptual terms which don't tie into day-to-day realities for the staff expected to carry out the plan.

The following terms have been used in strategic planning: desired end states, plans, policies, goals, objectives, strategies, tactics and actions. Definitions vary, overlap and fail to achieve clarity. The most common of these concepts are specific, time bound statements of intended future results and general and continuing statements of intended future results, which most models refer to as either goals or objectives (sometimes interchangeably). One model of organizing objectives uses hierarchies. The items may be organized in a hierarchy of means and ends and numbered as follows: Top Rank Objective (TRO), Second Rank Objective, Third Rank Objective, etc. From any rank, the objective in a lower rank answers to the question "How?" and the objective in a higher rank answers to the question "Why?" The exception is the Top Rank Objective (TRO): there is no answer to the "Why?" question. That is how the TRO is defined.

People typically have several goals at the same time. "Goal congruency" refers to how well the goals combine with each other. Does goal A appear compatible with goal B? Do they fit together to form a unified strategy? "Goal hierarchy" consists of the nesting of one or more goals within other goal(s).

One approach recommends having short-term goals, medium-term goals, and long-term goals. In this model, one can expect to attain short-term goals fairly easily: they stand just slightly above one's reach. At the other extreme, long-term goals appear very difficult, almost impossible to attain. Strategic management jargon sometimes refers to "Big Hairy Audacious Goals" (BHAGs) in this context. Using one goal as a stepping-stone to the next involves goal sequencing. A person or group starts by attaining the easy short-term goals, then steps up to the medium-term, then to the long-term goals. Goal sequencing can create a "goal stairway". In an organizational setting, the organization may co-ordinate goals so that they do not conflict with each other. The goals of one part of the organization should mesh compatibly with those of other parts of the organization.

DEVELOPMENT OF STRATEGIC MANAGEMENT

Strategic management as a discipline originated in the 1950s and 60s. Although there were numerous early contributors to the literature, the most influential pioneers were Alfred D. Chandler, Jr., Philip Selznick, Igor Ansoff, and Peter Drucker.

Alfred Chandler recognized the importance of coordinating the various aspects of management under one all-encompassing strategy. Prior to this time the various functions of management were separate with little overall coordination or strategy. Interactions between functions or between departments were typically handled by a boundary position, that is, there were one or two managers that relayed information back and forth between two departments. Chandler also stressed the importance of taking a long term perspective when looking to the future. In his 1962 groundbreaking work Strategy and Structure, Chandler showed that a long-term coordinated strategy was necessary to give a company structure, direction, and focus. He says it concisely, "structure follows strategy."

In 1957, Philip Selznick introduced the idea of matching the organization's internal factors with external environmental circumstances. This core idea was developed into what we now call SWOT analysis by Learned, Andrews, and others at the Harvard Business School General

Management Group. Strengths and weaknesses of the firm are assessed in light of the opportunities and threats from the business environment.

Igor Ansoff built on Chandler's work by adding a range of strategic concepts and inventing a whole new vocabulary. He developed a strategy grid that compared market penetration strategies, product development strategies, market development strategies and horizontal and vertical integration and diversification strategies. He felt that management could use these strategies to systematically prepare for future opportunities and challenges. In his 1965 classic Corporate Strategy, he developed the gap analysis still used today in which we must understand the gap between where we are currently and where we would like to be, then develop what he called "gap reducing actions".

Peter F Drucker was a prolific strategy theorist, author of dozens of management books, with a career spanning five decades. His contributions to strategic management were many but two are most important. Firstly, he stressed the importance of objectives. An organization without clear objectives is like a ship without a rudder. As early as 1954 he was developing a theory of management based on objectives. This evolved into his theory of management by objectives (MBO). According to Drucker, the procedure of setting objectives and monitoring your progress towards them should permeate the entire organization, top to bottom. His other seminal contribution was in predicting the importance of what today we would call intellectual capital. He predicted the rise of what he called the "knowledge worker" and explained the consequences of this for management. He said that knowledge work is non-hierarchical. Work would be carried out in teams with the person most knowledgeable in the task at hand being the temporary leader.

In 1985, Ellen-Earle Chaffee summarized what she thought were the main elements of strategic management theory by the 1970s:

- Strategic management involves adapting the organization to its business environment.
- Strategic management is fluid and complex. Change creates novel combinations of circumstances requiring unstructured non-repetitive responses.
- Strategic management affects the entire organization by providing direction.
- Strategic management involves both strategy formation (she called it content) and also strategy implementation (she called it process).
- Strategic management is partially planned and partially unplanned.
- Strategic management is done at several levels: overall corporate strategy, and individual business strategies.
- Strategic management involves both conceptual and analytical thought processes.

MISSION

Mission is the description of an organization's reasons for existence, its fundamental purpose. It is the guiding principle that drives the processes of goal and action plan formulation, "a pervasive, although general, expression of the philosophical objectives of the enterprise."

Mission should focus on "long-range economic potentials, attitudes toward customers, product and service quality, employee relations, and attitudes toward owners."

It provides identity, continuity of purpose, and overall definition, and should convey the following categories of information.

- Precisely why the organization exists, its purpose, in terms of
  - Its basic product or service,
  - Its primary markets,
  - Its major production technology.
- The moral and ethical principles that will shape the philosophy and character of the organization.
- The ethical climate within the organization.

Thus mission outlines the firm's identity and provides a guide for shaping strategies at all organizational levels. The role played by mission in guiding the organization is an important one.

Specifically it:

- Serves as a basis for consolidation around the organization's purpose.
- Provides impetus to and guidelines for resource allocation.
- Defines the internal atmosphere of the organization, its climate.
- Serves as a set of guidelines for the assignment of job responsibilities.
- Facilitates the design of key variables for a control system.

Deal and Kennedy claim that a strong culture is the key to long-term corporate success and that culture has five elements: business environment, values, heroes (people who personify values), rites and rituals (routines of day-to-day corporate life), and the cultural network (communication systems).

The mission statement describes primarily the second of these cultural factors, corporate values. The strong cultural companies studied by Deal and Kennedy all had "a rich and complex system of values that were shared by the employees." The mission statement must be believable in that the company's behaviour should correspond to it over both the short and long term. In this way it can serve as the foundation for the development of respect for and pride in the firm by management, employees, owners, customers, suppliers, and others who interact with it. Broad-based acceptance of the values represented by mission can lead to three characteristics of firms that accomplish this acceptance:

- They stand for something—the way in which business is to be conducted is widely understood.
- From the topmost levels of management down through the firm's organization structure to the lowest level of production jobs, the values are accepted by all employees.
- "Employees feel special because of a sense of identity which distinguishes the firm from other firms."

Many examples of firms that have these characteristics as a result of a finely honed sense of cooperation and value acceptance are presented by Deal and Kennedy. A few of these are listed here, along with the slogans that have come to represent their value systems.

- *Dupont*: "Better things for better living through chemistry—a belief that product innovation, arising out of chemical engineering...
- *Sears, Roebuck*: "Quality at a good price—the mass merchandiser from Middle America.
- *Dana Corporation*: "Productivity Though people— enlisting the ideas and commitment of employees at every level in support of Dana's strategy of competing largely on cost and dependability rather than product differentiation...
- *Chubb Insurance Company*: "Underwriting excellence—an overriding commitment to excellence in a critical function.
- *Price Waterhouse and Company*: "Strive for technical perfection" (in accounting).

Mission typically is not considered a part of a firm's strategy set. It reflects the essential preferences of owners and managers for what the firm will do. Strategy will accomplish the task of reducing mission to operational terms.

As such mission is somewhat a personal choice of a firm's dominant group of actors and is an *input* to the strategy formulation process.

TYPES OF MARKETING STRATEGY

One of the most important concepts of the marketing planning process is the need to develop a cohesive marketing strategy that guides tactical prigrammes for the marketing decision areas.

In marketing there are two levels to strategy formulation:

- General Marketing Strategies
- Decision Area Strategies

GENERAL STRATEGIES

Status Quo

This strategy looks to maintain the marketer's current position in the market, such as maintaining the same level of market share.

Market Exit

This strategy looks to remove the product from the organization's product mix.

This can be accomplished by:

- Selling the product to another organization
- Eliminating the product the company's product offerings

DECISION AREA STRATEGIES

These are used to achieve the General Marketing Strategies by guiding the decisions within important marketing areas.

For example, a General Marketing Strategy that centres on entering a new market with new products may be supported by Decision Area Strategies that include:

- *Target Market Strategy*: Employ segmenting techniques
- *Product Strategy*: Develop new product line
- *Pricing Strategy*: Create price prigrammes that offer lower pricing versus competitors
- *Distribution Strategy*: Use methods to gain access to important distribution partners that service the target market
- *Promotion Strategy*: Create a plan that can quickly build awareness of the product

Achieving the Decision Area Strategies is accomplished through the development of detailed Tactical Prigrammes for each area. For instance, to meet the Pricing Strategy that lowers cost versus competitors' products, the marketer may employ such tactics as: quantity discounts, trade-in allowances or sales volume incentives to distributors.

STRATEGIC MANAGEMENT MODEL

We can look at strategic management as a process that generates certain outputs and requires certain informational inputs. Understanding strategic management is a matter of understanding the contents of and the relationship among these three components.

To develop that understanding in this book, we take the strategic management process as our focus and discuss each stage by explaining its management activities, its input requirements, and the nature of the results or outputs of each stage. Thus the chapters correspond to stages in the strategic management process, and each chapter discusses the various inputs and outputs of each stage.

Of course, in practice one does not necessarily follow the sequence of strategic management stages in this fashion. Managers might formulate goals and the means for achieving them (action plans) simultaneously, rather than attempt to accomplish one completely and then the other.

Or some might view organization structure as a prerequisite for strategy; that is, structure might be established before strategy rather than strategy before structure. Still others might prefer to establish the portions of a control system first, before turning attention to the details of strategy formulation.

This could be the case, for example, where strict federal reporting requirements, such as for defence contracting, necessitate structuring the organization and its strategy around particular control features.

This sequence is also similar to structures prepared by other authors. Whereas it serves to identify the milestones for students being introduced to it for the first time, it also could be used as the outline for analyzing an ongoing strategic management system or one portrayed in a case study.

The strategy formulation block contains a section representing the process of goal formulation and another section for the process of action-plan formulation. When we discuss strategy formulation, we mean the development of both goals and action plans, or, as others have said, ends *and* means. An early concern in strategic management is constructing a set of data (facts and supporting information) that defines present and expected influences on, and characteristics of, the organization.

The major categories of information sources for this process are the organization's present strategic management elements (mission and goals and action plans for each of the various levels of strategy), relevant characteristics of present and forecast environment, and pertinent features of internal operations.

Information generated by these analyses can be organized in a strategic data set according to whether it constitutes threats and weaknesses, or strengths and opportunities.

These, in turn, can be further categorized as internal or external factors that are either positive or negative in nature. Mintzberg distinguishes between goal formation and goal formulation by noting that formulation involves a conscious individual decision process. Goal formation is accomplished by implication; individuals form goals implicitly by the decisions they make.

In the first part of Chapter, we are concerned with the process of goal formulation. It results in goals for an organization's performance that apply to the corporate, business, and functional levels of its operation.

Refinement of goals requires understanding of the political processes at work in the organization as well as of the system of individual values and preferences that characterize its managers. Whatever facts and predictions make up a firm's strategic data set, they are filtered through these two influences.

The activity of deriving action-plan choices for the overall process of strategy formulation is described in the second part of Chapter. Just as political processes and personal values and preferences influence goal formulation, they also shape the ways in which strategy choices are made.

Also, relevant portions of the firm's strategic data set constitutes vital information inputs to this process.

Chapter discusses several approaches that have appeared in the literature to explain the processes by which strategies are evaluated and selected.

Both existing and new strategies have to be evaluated to:

- Determine their acceptability in the present time frame,
- Estimate how well they can be expected to meet future goals in light of the firm's pro forma data set,
- Ultimately select the particular strategy set to be implemented.

Thus either an existing or a new strategy can be rejected as a whole, retained as is, or retained with alterations. Of course, evaluation of existing strategy ideally would take place during the first stage of the strategic management process as part of the internal analysis; proposed new strategies could be evaluated only after formulation.

The formulation and content of six areas of functional strategy—marketing, finance, personnel, research and development, production, and external relations—are addressed in chapter.

Since functional strategy is formulated to put into motion strategies developed at higher levels, it logically could be called either a formulation or an implementation process. We have chosen the former for two reasons.

First, there is a necessary interplay between the formulation of functional strategy and the formulation of the other levels of strategy. Second, even for those who consider functional strategy an implementation problem, it still must be formulated before it can be used to implement business and corporate strategy.

The next stage in strategic management is to implement the entire set of strategies. This process is explained in the first part of Chapter. Strategy implementation is essentially an administrative process; the other processes of strategic management are primarily analytical in nature.

Strategy implementation involves the structural and behavioral aspects of assigning responsibility for carrying out strategic components. It results in an organization structure, complete with appropriate vertical and lateral linkages specifically related to the strategy elements selected.

The final strategic management process, control, is discussed in the second part of Chapter. In practice, strategic control might be the first concern of the manager. Certainly the issues of how to establish performance standards, how to measure results, what corrective actions to take at what time, and other control problems should be considered throughout the strategic management process and not ignored until everything else is decided.

Indeed, control issues may significantly influence the content of strategy. It is discussed last simply to be consistent with tradition. In addition to all the other strategic management process outputs, strategic control takes as an input the technology of control available to the organization. For example, the advent of sophisticated microprocessor-based decision support systems (DSS), customized to the needs of a particular set of strategies, has resulted in many new control method possibilities. The absence of this technology in a particular firm, however, may severely limit the strategic control options available to its managers.

Output of the strategic control process consists of a feedback system that can modify strategic implementation and organization operations so as to alter either strategies or performance as might be reasonably necessary.

Thus one category of input information at each stage of strategic management consists of control system output. In this way evaluation of current performance vis-a-vis the organization's current strategy is always included in the analysis of each stage.

PROCESS STRATEGIES OF MARKETING

The world keeps changing. It always has and always will. This is the fundamental importance of strategic management, for the use of strategic planning is to make decisions now to guide an organization's future directions. In terms of future directions, the basic problem of any company is survival. And to survive over the long term, as Lowell Steele of General Electric succinctly summarized, a company must have two strategic capabilities: the ability to prosper and the ability to change.

Prosperity

The failure to prosper imperils survival because when expenses exceed income over a long enough period a company fails in bankruptcy. Moveover, prosperity now requires not only profitability but long-term growth. Modern stock markets often value long-term asset growth over short-term dividends. In these days of corporate takeovers, continual corporate growth in earnings and sales is necessary for management to retain control. Together, this combination of continuing profitability and continual growth presents a tough strategic problem because all markets eventually mature and growth in a company's business is limited by the growth of its markets.

In the second half of the twentieth century, this need for continual corporate growth not only created both the driving force for corporate diversification but was also a major cause of the dissolution of large companies. Successful management of a portfolio of different businesses in the same company became a major top corporate leadership challenge. An illustration of this was the successful growth of General Electric in the last two decades of the twentieth century. The CEO who provided strategic management for GE during that time, Jack Welch, became well known in the business world growing GE in two decades from a market value of $12 billion to $500 billion—then a rare corporate feat. In his intended last year at GE,Welch bought more growth for GE by acquiring Honeywell:

- "It was vintage Jack Welch. At the Oct. 23 press conference announcing General Eletric Co.'s $45 billion acquisition of the aeospace and industrial conglomerate Honeywell International Inc, the GE chairman and CEO strutted around the stage, boasting of the promise of the deal... Welch spoke bullishly of the acquisition—'It's exciting.... ' "

In the fall of the year before Welch's intended retirement, Welch had learned that the Honeywell was agreeing to be acquired by United Technologies, and Welsh rushed in with a higher offer to buy Honeywell. Honeywell would add 7% growth to GE's earnings. GE had revenues of $131 billion with operating profits of $19 billion. Honeywell had $25 billion revenue and $4 billion profits. Growth was important to GE to maintain a high stock value— through continuing growth.

Then Welch's business fame was so extensive that he had earlier received a $ 7.1 million advance for his projected memoirs. It was one of the highest book advances in publishing history; and the publisher, Time Warner's Doubleday, would have to sell at least 1.6 million copies in North America to make a profit:

- Executives of Doubleday had prepared a complete book jacket and marketing plan to pitch to Mr. Welch. Sitting in his shirt sleeves at a conference table, Mr. Welch preferred discussing his ideas about management over marketing details... At one point, the conversation turned to Lee Iacocca, the legendary chairman of Chrysler Motors whose autobiography sold 2.6 million copies in hardcover and 3.5 million in document back in North America. Mr. Welch told them that he would consider a book like Mr. Iacocca's a failure, because it was about a personality rather than ideas. Mr.Welch said he preferred the 1964 book by Alfred P. Sloan, MyYears with General Motors...

Strategic management is about ideas. Worth magazine asked several successful CEOs about what they thought was important in the job of the CEO.

Two of them, Koichi Nishimura of Solectron and Eric Schmidt of Novell, responded:

1. *Nishimuara*: Four things, I think, are important. First, communicate a vision of where the company is and what you are doing. The second is that when you communicate, you want to be able to motivate people. Third, you want feedback. And fourth, you want to take action.
2. *Schmidt*: I think the job breaks down into three parts. First, setting a strategic vision that is implementable. That's number one. Second

is recruiting and leading great human beings. The third is worrying about shareholder value. If you follow those three rules, then everything else sort of works.... I think the question from an investor should be, Does the CEO have a strategy that you believe can win?

Strategic vision, communicating vision, recruiting and motivating good people, obtaining feedback, and taking action that creates shareholder prosperity—these are essential elements in corporate leadership. Strategy is ideas about the longterm future.

Change

Attaining the kind of growth and prosperityWelch had achieved atGErequired him to make great changes within the company. On taking office back in 1981,Welch first sold off a hundred of GE's businesses and then consolidated the rest into 14 business groups.

This massive restructuring gaveWelch a tough reputation:

- Neutron Jack, as he is sometimes called, is widely regarded as one of the world's most ruthless managers. The truth is more complex. Some of his actions are indeed harsh, and he antagonized people inside the company and out by fixing something they didn't think was broke. What is becoming clear only now is how those moves fit into a larger plan to strengthen the enterprise and to make its remaining employees more secure.

Welch's success at GE was to strategically change GE from primarily manufacturing businesses into primarily financial service businesses. In 1980, manufacturing produced 70% of GE's revenues, with services contributing 30%. By 1999, manufacturing produced only 26% of revenues, with services having grown to 74%. Welch's strategy was to retain only a selective group of manufacturing businesses and grow financial services: "ChairmanWelch unloaded the consumer electronics division and built financial services into a powerhouse, while keeping GE dominant in turbines and jet engines." Periodic change in a large organization is necessary to help the firm adapt to new times, for new times keep on occurring.

One of Jack Welch's most widely quoted strategic precepts was:

- "Control your own destiny, or someone else will."

The failure to make appropriate changes at the right time, imperials survival because the company may become competitively obsolete in its products, services, and value to customers. Change requires an ability to anticipate the external dynamics of the environments in which a company operates—markets, competition, innovation, government regulation, economic conditions, globalization, and so on. Change also requires an ability to alter a company's directions.

Lowell Steele nicely summarized the emphasis of change as the focus of strategic thinking:

- Strategy is concerned overwhelmingly with questions of change. How much must the enterprise change in order to survive and to continue to prosper? How much change can it finance and manage? How fast can it change? These are profoundly difficult questions.

Strategic management is about the difficult questions of future business—whether it should go and how should it change—a particularly risky set of questions for a large business that is already successful. In many of the older books on strategy, it was presumed that the logic of strategy should begin with a "mission and vision" statement. A mission statement is a statement of what kind of business is the organization; and a vision statement is what kind of business the organization would like to become. However, this older kind of "strategic logic" is not really useful for an ongoing organization, unless the mission changes.

What is useful in vision for an organization is foresight on change to the mission. The "vision thing" is: how should the mission change to take advantage of future market opportunities and meet future competitive threats? Strategic thinking is not about the mission of the business but changes to the mission.

Strategic Thinking

CEOs like Jack Welch become successful and famous because of their ability to think and act strategically. And because of the fundamental importance of strategy to long-term corporate survival, this ability to think strategically became recognized as an important leadership skill for executives.

For example, one can often see specifications for the ability to strategize in common recruitment advertisements for executive positions, such as the following ad, which appeared in The New York Times in May 2000:

- ... Corporation, a publicly traded manufacturer of products... has an excellent opportunity in its Engineered Products headquarters office.... The successful candidate will have hands-on experience in sourcing components. The position will report to Group VP and be responsible for purchasing in (5) divisions.... The individual must thrive on multitasking, have outstanding negotiating skills, be a good manager of people and projects, and be a strategic thinker. Highly competitive compensation package. For confidential consideration, forward resume and salary requirements to..

This is the fundamental management skill which we address in this book. What is a strategic thinker? How can hands-on experience improve a manager's ability to think strategically? Which practical techniques facilitate effective strategic planning in a large organization? What important strategic concepts used by successful leaders such as Sloan and Welch? Change in a company environment always forces strategic redirection. Changes in automobile technology provided the strategic ground for Sloan's successful management of General Motors, and changes in services and medical technologies provided some of the impetus for Welch's successful strategic management of General Electric.

Information Technology

By the end of the twentieth century, progress in information technology had become the strongest and most pervasive force for strategic change in businesses throughout the world.

One example of IT's impact was Thomas Middelhoff's strategic exhortation to his company in 2000:

- We have to reach every brain to explain that we have nothing less than an industrial revolution. That makes it necessary to change how we see and run our business. That means speed is king. That means we have to be decentralized on the one hand and also more corporate. We have without any question a generational change at Bertelsmann.

The growth of the Internet was a rapid phenomena. For example, in the United States, 14% of the population used the Internet in 1996, jumping to 22% in 1997, 31% in 1998, 38% in 1999, and 44% in 2000. In 2000, the average monthly hours a user spent on line was 19 hours. U.S. consumer spending online had grown from a few million in 1996 to $3 billion dollars in 1997, $7 billion in 1998, $19 billion in 1999, and $36 billion in 2000. Of the $36 billion spent in 2000, $11.0 billion was for travel, $7.7 billion for PCs, $2.4 billion for clothes, $13.4 billion for books, and $13.4 billion for other merchandise. In October 2000, advertising revenues of the Internet in the U.S. totaled $600 million. In business history, the decade of the 1990s will likely be called the decade of the Internet. Its innovation and rapid impact on business made it an interesting and challenging time—that brought to everyone's immediate attention the great importance of progress in information technology upon all business strategy.

The dramatic experience of that decade was nicely summarized by Joseph Nocera and Time Carvell:

- The Internet decade has seen the unscrupulous rewarded, the dimwitted suckered, the ill-qualified enriched at a pace greater than at any other time in history. The Internet has been a gift to charlatans, hypemeisters, and merchants of vapour... and despite all that, it still changes everything.

The Internet was an example of a larger class of phenomena in business history called pervasive innovations. William Abernathy and Kim Clark even introduced a new term to strategic management—transilience of innovation—to emphasize the importance of a pervasiveness of an innovation upon the operations of a firm. Transilience means the ability to pass through a system, and it emphasizes the range of business impacts that a transilient innovation may have upon the value-adding capabilities of a firm, passing through its activities to make changes in:

- The kinds of products and way the firm produces products
- The kinds of customers and markets the business serves

Abernathy and Clark classified the types of transilient innovation impacts upon a firm by the innovation's potential to alter either product/production or market/customer competencies:

- In product/production competency, innovations may alter
  - Product design
  - Production systems
  - Technical skills and knowledge base
  - Materials and capital equipment
- Under market/customer competency, innovations may alter
  - Customer bases
  - Customer applications
  - Channels of distribution and service
  - Customer knowledge and modes of communication

  For any of these factors the impact of innovation may range from strengthening existing competencies to making existing competencies obsolete. Accordingly, Abernathy and Clark also classified innovations:

  a. A technological innovation that conserved both existing production and market competencies was called a regular innovation.
  b. A technological innovation that conserved existing production competency but altered market competency was called a niche-creation innovation.
  c. A technological innovation that made an existing production competency obsolete but preserved existing market competency was called a revolutionary innovation.
  d. A technological innovation that obsoleted both existing production and market competencies was called an architectural innovation.

The innovation of the Internet was an architectural innovation. Historically, many firms have usually successfully exploited regular or niche creation innovations, for they sustain current operations. But many large firms have perished during revolutionary or architectural innovations. For example, Clayton Christensen examined reasons why large U.S. firms historically have often failed to profit from revolutionary or architectural innovations:

- Resource dependence in large firms, influenced by investors and current customers.

- The emergent markets of radical innovations are early-on perceived as too small for big firm growth needs.
- The ultimate use of radical innovations are often not known early.
- The performance and features of radical new innovations are often not attractive to current markets.

The architectural impact information technology made on business strategy was summarized by Bill Miller who spent a long career and argued that IT was:

- Altering the competitive dynamics of both products and services, leading to the new importance of dominant designs and platforms in product/service strategy
- Flattening organizational hierarchy or even dissolving boundaries into networked forms, such as "virtual enterprises"
- Impacting management styles through introducing both a "transparency" of the business model to all levels of employees and making their jobs more complex, through the increased need for teaming and direct attention to the bottom-lines of business goals.

Information technologies could strategically impact businesses in different ways:

- A business can be in the information technology business, providing information technology goods and services
- A business can use information technology as a core technology in its production of goods and delivery of services
- A business can use information technology as a supporting technology in its design of products/services;
- A business can use information technology as a marketing tool to attract customers to its product/services.

As suggested, address this new challenge of IT to strategic management, using a strategy process in which information technology integrates with business strategy.

Strategic Management

Strategy, planning, budgeting, and knowledge are the four forward-looking activities of management, and it is important that they be clearly distinguished. Budgeting is the allocation of resources for the future operations of an organization. Budgeting is neither planning nor strategy. All organizations budget, but they do not necessarily plan nor strategize. Organizations annually budget in order to allocate the resources for continuing operations. Thus the managers of all organizations do formulate budgets; but not all managers plan or formulate strategy. Planning is thinking out of tactics for the continuing operations of an organization. Planning is not strategy but the implementation of strategy. Managers plan when the tactics of operations change from year to year. Organizations that need to annually plan are those with significant changes in tactics and operations from one year to the next.

Strategy is neither planning nor budgeting. Strategy is the perspective for long term change. Many organizations do not even begin to formulate strategy until an immediate emergency requires change; but by then, it may be too late to formulate effective strategy. Effective strategy requires looking out ahead, anticipating the need for change and preparing for it. A strategy is a change in the direction of the objectives of the operations over a course of years.

Few organizations do strategy when external conditions, markets, and competition all are stable. Strategy is needed when external conditions change—change in technology, change in markets, change in competitors. Knowledge is the basis for improving and controlling the future value-adding operations of a business enterprise. Progress in information technology provides new tools for managing the development of the knowledge assets of the business. Knowledge has been and continues to be the major force in strategic changes in business.

EVOLUTION OF STRATEGIC MANAGEMENT

Gluck, Kaufman, and Walleck propose a model of the evolution of strategic management within organizations whose managers have a propensity to plan. The model is based on a study undertaken by McKinsey and Company. Part of the reason for including a summary of their model here is to help students recognize the strategic management stage in which a particular organization might be.

Such information may provide additional insight into the operation of the firm and help understand the degree of strategic management progress made by managers. More importantly, however, it may be useful in helping students understand strategic management as the highest level of a hierarchy of management activities.

The McKinsey analysis discovered four quite distinct phases of strategic management evolution. In Phase 1, financial planning, management focuses on the preparation of budgets with an emphasis on functional operations. Most organizations have a budgeting process, in at least rudimentary form, as a way of allocating resources among functional units, subsidiaries, or projects. The second, forecast-based planning, follows naturally from the first as managers project budget requirements beyond the one-year cycle. This phase represents an effort to extend managers' attention beyond the immediate future as scenarios are developed which describe their expectations about future time periods.

Budgets are often constructed for several years at a time and are rolled over annually so that the appropriateness of a budgeted amount can be reviewed several times before it is operationalized. Phase 2 planning is very "now" oriented.

Current operations and characteristics are stressed in analyses of the firm and there is little attention to or patience for considering operational options or development of strategic changes. The business portfolio of a Phase 2 firm is often viewed as the final expression of strategy rather than as an input to the strategy formulation process. Current structure and business activities may be considered fixed, not as strategic variables.

Planners are required to adopt an external orientation and tools and procedures for environmental and internal assessment.

Concern centers on understanding the organization's environment and competitive position and generating ideas about how the company might better fit its environment. Several choices, contingency plans, are often devised for how the company might fit its environment. Lower level planners and managers are often involved in the process of generating choices, an activity that soon puts top management in the position of choosing a plan in which it had little involvement in developing.

Strategic management, evolves as top management senses the need to more heavily invest in the planning process because of its lack of understanding of or involvement in the details of earlier plan development. Strategic management is the meshing of Phase 3 planning and operational management into one process.

It is analysis and conclusion that takes place year-round and ties performance evaluation and motivational programmes to strategy.

Deliberateness of Strategy

Sometimes outsiders impute strategy to the behaviour of firms. Obviously, students analyzing case studies are placed in this position when they impute strategy from the data they are able to generate on the firm's operations. Similarly, journalists and the managers of competing firms may impute strategy to a firm's behaviour; and it may or may not accurately reflect the real strategy in place.

Outsiders may also imply intent to an imputed strategy. That is, they assume not only that the strategy they imputed from the firm's behaviour is the real strategy its employees are implementing, but they imply that this strategy is the one intended for the firm by its management. Seldom is this the case.

Mintzberg developed a taxonomy which is useful for discussing the realism and deliberateness of strategy. First, he distinguished between strategy that is the result of a plan, and of a pattern of behaviour.

He referred to them as "strategy as plan" and "strategy as pattern," respectively. Strategy as plan is a chosen course of action; it could be a real strategy (one intended for implementation) or a ploy (a tactical move whereby a competitor may be influenced into making a mistake). Some people think that Coca-Cola's rumored change in Coke's formula in the mid-1980s was such a ploy.

The implication is that Coca-Cola had not intended to really change the formula. Instead, it is thought, they publicized their plan to change formula, intoduced a new product with a different formula that tasted a lot like a competitor's product, and finally graciously conceded to continue producing the old formula product when the public demonstrated a preference for it over the new—"similar to a competitor's—" formula.

Incidentally, if this was in fact a ploy, it has to rank among the top marketing moves ever attempted by any business. Coca-Cola reaped an immediate increase in market share of about 15 per cent that thrust them once again into unquestioned dominance in the huge U.S. softdrink market.

Strategy as plan, when implemented, may or may not be what the firm ends up with. That is, the planned strategy could ultimately be either realized or unrealized.

If it is realized, then the entire process would be a textbook case of strategy formulation and implementation in the sense that the firm successfully implemented what was intended.

But what happens if the planned strategy is implemented and, for some reason, the strategy that is realized is not the intended one? We might say that the planned strategy was unrealized, and the realized strategy (the one that seems to describe what the company is actually doing) arises out of some consistency in the behaviour of the company.

Mintzberg and Waters call this unintended realized strategy, "strategy as pattern," or a pattern in a series of actions by the organization. Strategy as pattern is what you will end up with when you impute strategy to the behaviour of a company you are analyzing in a case study, or what journalists produce when they attribute a strategy to a company based only on its actions.

Thus, a realized strategy could be either a deliberate strategy as plan, or an "undeliberate" strategy as pattern. If the realized strategy was planned and also accurately described the firm's actions, then strategy as pattern and strategy as plan would be synonymous. However, when realized strategy is not intended strategy (that is, it was either not what was intended by management when they drafted a planned strategy, or they drafted no strategy at all), then it simply "grew" out of the activities of the company. In Mintzberg's terms, it "emerged" as a pattern of behaviour in the absence of intension, or despite unrealized intentions.

A realized strategy is what a company is actually doing. If it is the one intended by management, then it is deliberate If not, then the intended strategy wasunrealized, and the realized strategy is emergent. An emergent strategy is, by definition, not deliberate.

However, a manager may choose not to consciously formulate strategy and, instead, "go with" the emergent one. But even here, the resultant emergent strategy would not have been deliberate in the same way an intended strategy would have been.

Often it is convenient to distinguish between intended and emergent strategies. When management performs no strategic management at all, they still will have a realized strategy that is emergent.

This emergent strategy could be recognized by outsiders (and insiders for that matter) even though it may not have been intended my management.

Contingency Strategies

Managers may develop several versions of strategy, each of which is intended to fit a different environmental scenario. An environmental scenario consists of a set of environmental characteristics that describe a firm's external circumstances. By structuring external variables into sets of related variables, different scenarios result.

Thus several scenarios (usually three) can be arrayed on a probability distribution for which the horizonal axis is a measure of the extent to which they are viewed as "good" or "bad"—supportive or not supportive—to the firm.

In the scenarios that fall on the left side of the distribution are considered pessimistic (undesirable but only a small probability that they might have to be dealt with); those on the right as optimistic (desirable but probably will not materialize either); and those in the middle as most likely to occur and having some good and bad features.

Next a strategy set is established for each scenario. These could be entirely different strategies or variations of one. Evaluative criteria then are formulated for each scenario. These are variables to be monitored in order to figure out which of the scenarios is going to apply in the future.

Actually this is a matter of deciding whether the present scenario will continue to be the best description of the firm's environment or, instead, if one of the others seems to be emerging as most correct. By identifying critical values for evaluative criteria, the strategist knows beforehand under what set of conditions to switch from the present strategy set to the pessimistic or optimistic set.

KEY PART OF THE GENERAL CORPORATE STRATEGY

Marketing strategy is a method of focusing an organization's energies and resources on a course of action which can lead to increased sales and dominance of a targeted market niche. A marketing strategy combines product development, promotion, distribution, pricing, relationship management and other elements; identifies the firm's marketing goals, and explains how they will be achieved, ideally within a stated timeframe. Marketing strategy determines the choice of target market segments, positioning, marketing mix, and allocation of resources. It is most effective when it is an integral component of overall firm strategy, defining how the organization will successfully engage customers, prospects, and competitors in the market arena. Corporate strategies, corporate missions, and corporate goals. As the customer constitutes the source of a company's revenue, marketing strategy is closely linked with sales. A key component of marketing strategy is often to keep marketing in line with a company's overarching mission statement.

Basic theory:

- Target Audience
- Proposition/Key Element
- Implementation

TACTICS AND ACTIONS

A marketing strategy can serve as the foundation of a marketing plan. A marketing plan contains a set of specific actions required to successfully implement a marketing strategy. For example: "Use a low cost product to attract consumers. Once our organization, via our low cost product, has established a relationship with consumers, our organization will sell additional, higher-margin products and services that enhance the consumer's interaction with the low-cost product or service." A strategy consists of a well thought out series of tactics to make a marketing plan more effective.

Marketing strategies serve as the fundamental underpinning of marketing plans designed to fill market needs and reach marketing objectives. Plans and objectives are generally tested for measurable results. A marketing strategy often integrates an organization's marketing goals, policies, and action sequences into a cohesive whole. Similarly, the various strands of the strategy, which might include advertising, channel marketing, internet marketing, promotion and public relations can be orchestrated.

Many companies cascade a strategy throughout an organization, by creating strategy tactics that then become strategy goals for the next level or group. Each one group is expected to take that strategy goal and develop a set of tactics to achieve that goal. This is why it is important to make each strategy goal measurable. Marketing strategies are dynamic and interactive. They are partially planned and partially unplanned.

TYPES OF STRATEGIES

Marketing strategies may differ depending on the unique situation of the individual business. However there are a number of ways of categorizing some generic strategies.

A brief description of the most common categorizing schemes is presented below:

- *Strategies based on market dominance*: In this scheme, firms are classified based on their market share or dominance of an industry.

  Typically there are four types of market dominance strategies:

  1. Leader
  2. Challenger
  3. Follower
  4. Nicher

- *Porter generic strategies*: Strategy on the dimensions of strategic scope and strategic strength. Strategic scope refers to the market penetration while strategic strength refers to the firm's sustainable competitive advantage. The generic strategy framework comprises two alternatives each with two alternative scopes. These are Differentiation and low-cost leadership each with a dimension of Focus-broad or narrow.

- Product differentiation
- Cost leadership
- Market segmentation

- *Innovation strategies*: This deals with the firm's rate of the new product development and business model innovation. It asks whether the company is on the cutting edge of technology and business innovation.

  There are three types:

  1. Pioneers
  2. Close followers
  3. Late followers

- *Growth strategies*: In this scheme we ask the question, "How should the firm grow?".

  There are a number of different ways of answering that question, but the most common gives four answers:

  1. Horizontal integration
  2. Vertical integration
  3. Diversification
  4. Intensification

A more detailed scheme uses the categories:

- Prospector
- Analyser
- Defender
- Reactor
- Marketing warfare strategies - This scheme draws parallels between marketing strategies and military strategies.

STRATEGIC MODELS

Marketing participants often employ strategic models and tools to analyse marketing decisions. When beginning a strategic analysis, the 3Cs can be employed to get a broad understanding of the strategic environment. An Ansoff Matrix is also often used to convey an organization's strategic positioning of their marketing mix. The 4Ps can then be utilized to form a marketing plan to pursue a defined strategy.

There are many companies especially those in the Consumer Package Goods market that adopt the theory of running their business centred around Consumer, Shopper & Retailer needs. Their Marketing departments spend quality time looking for "Growth Opportunities" in their categories by identifying relevant insights on their target Consumers, Shoppers and retail partners. These Growth Opportunities emerge from changes in market trends, segment dynamics changing and also internal brand or operational business challenges.The Marketing team can then prioritize these Growth Opportunities and begin to develop strategies to exploit the opportunities that could include new or adapted products, services as well as changes to the 7Ps.

REAL-LIFE MARKETING

Real-life marketing primarily revolves around the application of a great deal of common-sense; dealing with a limited number of factors, in an environment of imperfect information and limited resources complicated by uncertainty and tight timescales. Use of classical marketing techniques, in these circumstances, is inevitably partial and uneven. Thus, for example, many new products will emerge from irrational processes and the rational development process may be used to screen out the worst non-runners.

The design of the advertising, and the packaging, will be the output of the creative minds employed; which management will then screen, often by'gut-reaction', to ensure that it is reasonable. For most of their time, marketing managers use intuition and experience to analyse and handle the complex, and unique, situations being faced; without easy reference to theory. This will often be'flying by the seat of the pants', or'gut-reaction'; where the overall strategy, coupled with the knowledge of the customer which has been absorbed almost by a process of osmosis, will determine the quality of the marketing employed. This, almost instinctive management, is what is sometimes called'coarse marketing'; to distinguish it from the refined, aesthetically pleasing, form favoured by the theorists.

PRODUCT MARKETING

Product marketing deals with the first of the"7P"'s of marketing, which are Product, Pricing, Place, and Promotion, Packaging, Positioning & People. Product marketing, as opposed to product management, deals with more outbound marketing tasks. For example, product management deals with the nuts and bolts of product development within a firm, whereas product marketing deals with marketing the product to prospects, customers, and others. Product marketing, as a job function within a firm, also differs from other marketing jobs such as marketing communications, online marketing, advertising, marketing strategy, etc.

A Product market is something that is referred to when pitching a new product to the general public. The people you are trying to make your product appeal to is your consumer market. For example: If you were pitching a new video game console game to the public, your consumer market would probably be the adult male Video Game market. Thus you would carry out market research to find out how best to release the game. Likewise, a massage chair would probably not appeal to younger children, so you would market your product to an older generation.

ROLE OF PRODUCT MARKETING

Product marketing in a business addresses five important strategic questions:

1. What products will be offered?
2. Who will be the target customers?
3. How will the products reach those?
4. At what price should the products be offered?
5. How will customers be introduced to the products?

PRODUCT MARKETING VS. PRODUCT MANAGEMENT

Product marketing frequently differs from product management in high-tech companies. Whereas the product manager is required to take a product's requirements from the sales and marketing personnel and create a product requirements document, which will be used by the engineering team to build the product, the product marketing manager can be engaged in the task of creating a Marketing Requirements Document which is used as source for the product management to develop the PRD.

In other companies the product manager creates both the MRDs and the PRDs, while the product marketing manager does outbound tasks like giving product demonstrations in trade shows, creating marketing collateral like hot-sheets, beat-sheets, cheat sheets, data sheets, and white documents. This requires the product marketing manager to be skilled not only in competitor analysis, market research, and technical writing, but also in more business oriented activities like conducting ROI and NPV analyses on technology investments, strategizing how the decision criteria of the prospects or customers can be changed so that they buy the company's product vis-a-vis the competitor's product, etc.

One issue that faces Product Marketers is that they are chartered with developing much of the content for the various constituents. Creating content tends to be given more value than the actual research and thinking that is behind all the content.

In smaller high-tech firms or start-ups, product marketing and product management functions can be blurred, and both tasks may be borne by one individual. However, as the company grows someone needs to focus on creating good requirements documents for the engineering team, whereas someone else needs to focus on how to analyse the market, influence the "analysts", and understand longer term market direction. When such clear demarcation becomes visible, the former falls under the domain of product management, and the latter, under product marketing. In Silicon Valley, in particular, product marketing professionals have considerable domain experience in a particular market or technology or both. Some Silicon Valley firms have titles such as Product Marketing Engineer, who tend to be promoted to managers in due course.

The trend that is emerging in Silicon Valley is for companies to hire a team of a product marketing manager with a technical marketing manager. The Technical marketing role is becoming more valuable as companies become more competitive and seek to reduce costs and time to market. Another trend is to have one Product Marketing Manager per group of Product Managers. This is the model that leads to the issue of PMMs being pressured to write content instead of connecting with the market.

QUALIFICATIONS

The typical education qualification for this area of business is a high level Marketing or Business related degree, e.g. an BBA, MBA, not forgetting sufficient work experience in related areas. As a key skill is to be able to interact with technical staff, a background in engineering or computing is also an asset.

DETERMINING OF PRICE

Pricing is the process of determining what a company will receive in exchange for its products. Pricing factors are manufacturing cost, market place, competition, market condition, and quality of product. Pricing is also a key variable in microeconomic price allocation theory. Pricing is a fundamental aspect of financial modeling and is one of the four Ps of the marketing mix. The other three aspects are product, promotion, and place. Price is the only revenue generating element amongst the four Ps, the rest being cost centres. Pricing is thc manual or automatic process of applying prices to purchase and sales orders, based on factors such as: a fixed amount, quantity break, promotion or sales campaign, specific vendor quote, price prevailing on entry, shipment or invoice date, combination of multiple orders or lines, and many others. Automated systems require more setup and maintenance but may prevent pricing errors. The needs of the consumer can be converted into demand only if the consumer has the willingness and capacity to buy the product. Thus pricing is very important in marketing.

QUESTIONS INVOLVED IN PRICING

Pricing involves asking questions like:

- How much to charge for a product or service? This question is that a typical starting point for discussions about pricing, however, a better question for a vendor to ask is - How much do customers value the products, services, and other intangibles that the vendor provides.
- What are the pricing objectives?
- Do we use profit maximization pricing?

- How to set the price?:
- Should there be a single price or multiple pricing?
- Should prices change in various geographical areas, referred to as zone pricing?
- Should there be quantity discounts?
- What prices are competitors charging?
- Do you use a price skimming strategy or a penetration pricing strategy?
- What image do you want the price to convey?
- Do you use psychological pricing?
- How important are customer price sensitivity and elasticity issues?
- Can real-time pricing be used?
- Is price discrimination or yield management appropriate?
- Are there legal restrictions on retail price maintenance, price collusion, or price discrimination?
- Do price points already exist for the product category?
- How flexible can we be in pricing?: The more competitive the industry, the less flexibility we have.
  - The price floor is determined by production factors like costs, economies of scale, marginal cost, and degree of operating leverage
  - The price ceiling is determined by demand factors like price elasticity and price points
- Are there transfer pricing considerations?
- What is the chance of getting involved in a price war?
- How visible should the price be? - Should the price be neutral? should it be highly visible? or should it be hidden?.
- Are there joint product pricing considerations?
- What are the non-price costs of purchasing the product?
- What sort of payments should be accepted?

WHAT A PRICE SHOULD DO

A well chosen price should do three things:

1. Achieve the financial goals of the company
2. Fit the realities of the marketplace
3. Support a product's positioning and be consistent with the other variables in the marketing mix
   - Price is influenced by the type of distribution channel used, the type of promotions used, and the quality of the product
     a. Price will usually need to be relatively high if manufacturing is expensive, distribution is exclusive, and

the product is supported by extensive advertising and promotional campaigns

b. A low price can be a viable substitute for product quality, effective promotions, or an energetic selling effort by distributors

From the marketer's point of view, an efficient price is a price that is very close to the maximum that customers are prepared to pay. In economic terms, it is a price that shifts most of the consumer surplus to the producer. A good pricing strategy would be the one which could balance between the price floor and the price ceiling.

TERMINOLOGY

There are numerous terms and strategies specific to pricing:

Effective Price

The effective price is the price the company receives after accounting for discounts, promotions, and other incentives.

Line Pricing

Line Pricing is the use of a limited number of prices for all product offerings of a vendor. This is a tradition started in the old five and dime stores in which everything cost either 5 or 10 cents. Its underlying rationale is that these amounts are seen as suitable price points for a whole range of products by prospective customers. It has the advantage of ease of administering, but the disadvantage of inflexibility, particularly in times of inflation or unstable prices.

Loss Leader

A loss leader is a product that has a price set below the operating margin. This results in a loss to the enterprise on that particular item in the hope that it will draw customers into the store and that some of those customers will buy other, higher margin items.

Promotional Pricing

Promotional pricing refers to an instance where pricing is the key element of the marketing mix.

Price/quality Relationship

The price/quality relationship refers to the perception by most consumers that a relatively high price is a sign of good quality. The belief in this relationship is most important with complex products that are hard to test, and experiential products that cannot be tested until used. The greater the uncertainty surrounding a product, the more consumers depend on the price/quality hypothesis and the greater premium they are prepared to pay.

The classic example is the pricing of Twinkies, a snack cake which was viewed as low quality after the price was lowered. Excessive reliance on the price/quantity relationship by consumers may lead to an increase in prices on all products and services, even those of low quality, which causes the price/quality relationship to no longer apply.

Premium Pricing

Premium pricing is the strategy of consistently pricing at, or near, the high end of the possible price range to help attract status-conscious consumers. Examples of companies which partake in premium pricing in the marketplace include Rolex and Bentley.

People will buy a premium priced product because:

- They believe the high price is an indication of good quality;
- They believe it to be a sign of self worth - "They are worth it;" it authenticates the buyer's success and status; it is a signal to others that the owner is a member of an exclusive group;
- They require flawless performance in this application - The cost of product malfunction is too high to buy anything but the best - example: heart pacemaker.

Goldilocks Pricing

The term Goldilocks pricing is commonly used to describe the practice of providing a "gold-plated" version of a product at a premium price in order to make the next-lower priced option look more reasonably priced; for example, encouraging customers to see business-class airline seats as good value for money by offering an even higher priced first-class option. Similarly, third-class railway carriages in Victorian England are said to have been built without windows, not so much to punish third-class customers as to motivate those who could afford second-class seats to pay for them instead of taking the cheaper option.

This is also known as a potential result of price discrimination. The name derives from the Goldilocks story in which Goldilocks chose neither the hottest nor the coldest porridge, but instead the one that was "just right". More technically, this form of pricing exploits the general cognitive bias of aversion to extremes. This practice is known academically as "framing". By providing three options you can manipulate the consumer into choosing the middle choice and thus, the middle choice should yield the most profit to the seller, since it is the one chosen most often.

Demand-based Pricing

Demand-based pricing is any pricing method that uses consumer demand - based on perceived value - as the central element. These include: price skimming, price discrimination and yield management, price points, psychological pricing, bundle pricing, penetration pricing, price lining, value-based pricing, geo and premium pricing. Pricing factors are manufacturing cost, market place, competition, market condition, quality of product.

Multidimensional Pricing

Multidimensional pricing is the pricing of a product or service using multiple numbers. In this practice, price no longer consists of a single monetary amount but rather consists of various dimensions. Research has shown that this practice can significantly influence consumers' ability to understand and process price information

NINE LAWS OF PRICE SENSITIVITY

The Strategy and Tactics of Pricing, Thomas Nagle and Reed Holden outlined 9 laws or factors that influence a buyer's price sensitivity with respect to a given purchase:

1. Reference Price Effect Buyer's price sensitivity for a given product increases the higher the product's price relative to perceived alternatives. Perceived alternatives can vary by buyer segment, by occasion, and other factors.
2. Difficult Comparison Effect Buyers are less sensitive to the price of a known/more reputable product when they have difficulty comparing it to potential alternatives.
3. Switching Costs Effect The higher the product-specific investment a buyer must make to switch suppliers, the less price sensitive that buyer is when choosing between alternatives.
4. Price-Quality Effect Buyers are less sensitive to price the more that higher prices signal higher quality. Products for which this effect is particularly relevant include: image products, exclusive products, and products with minimal cues for quality.
5. Expenditure Effect Buyers are more price sensitive when the expense accounts for a large percentage of buyers' available income or budget.
6. End-Benefit Effect The effect refers to the relationship a given purchase has to a larger overall benefit, and is divided into two parts: Derived demand: The more sensitive buyers are to the price of the end benefit, the more sensitive they will be to the prices of those products that contribute to that benefit. Price proportion cost: The price proportion cost refers to the per cent of the total cost of the end benefit accounted for by a given component that helps to produce the end benefit. The smaller the given components share of the total cost of the end benefit, the less sensitive buyers will be to the component's price.
7. Shared-cost Effect The smaller the portion of the purchase price buyers must pay for themselves, the less price sensitive they will be.

8. Fairness Effect Buyers are more sensitive to the price of a product when the price is outside the range they perceive as"fair" or"reasonable" given the purchase context.
9. The Framing Effect Buyers are more price sensitive when they perceive the price as a loss rather than a forgone gain, and they have greater price sensitivity when the price is paid separately rather than as part of a bundle.

APPROACHES

Pricing as the most effective profit lever. Pricing can be approached at three levels.The industry, market, and transaction level. Pricing at the industry level focuses on the overall economics of the industry, including supplier price changes and customer demand changes. Pricing at the market level focuses on the competitive position of the price in comparison to the value differential of the product to that of comparative competing products. Pricing at the transaction level focuses on managing the implementation of discounts away from the reference, or list price, which occur both on and off the invoice or receipt.

PRICING TACTICS

Micromarketing is the practice of tailoring products, brands, and promotions to meet the needs and wants of microsegments within a market. It is a type of market customization that deals with pricing of customer/ product combinations at the store or individual level.

PRICING MISTAKES

Many companies make common pricing mistakes.

Bernstein's object "Supplier Pricing Mistakes" outlines several which include:

- Weak controls on discounting
- Inadequate systems for tracking competitor selling prices and market share
- Cost-Up pricing
- Price increases poorly executed
- Worldwide price inconsistencies
- Paying sales representatives on dollar volume vs. addition of profitability measures

PLACE MARKETING

Marketing experts know that the best product in the world will never make an impact in the business world if no one can locate and obtain it. Keeping this simple, yet vital brick in the house of marketing, McDonald's gives careful consideration to the placement of its restaurants. Within their marketing research, they take into consideration the population of a given area, major roadways in the vicinity of the proposed restaurant site, traffic that passes by the restaurant site, and the demographics of the area, as they know a great deal about their customers.

The construction of a McDonald's restaurant costs millions of dollars, and in order for the operation to be profitable, placement must be in an area that maximizes the customer exposure, therefore increasing the chance of generating business. However, please keep in mind that McDonald's leaves nothing to chance. They do their marketing homework, and it shows. The fact that McDonald's always seems to be "right around the corner" is due to a great deal of extensive marketing research, planning and execution. If you really give this idea a great deal of thought, take into consideration the very low number of McDonald's restaurants that go out of business in a given community. This is not sheer luck, nor is it just something that has happened by chance. It only looks like a coincidence! While other fast food chains come and go, McDonald's is always there for you, right around the corner in most cases.

PROMOTION MARKETING

Promotion is one of the four elements of marketing mix. It is the communication link between sellers and buyers for the purpose of influencing, informing, or persuading a potential buyer's purchasing decision.

The following are two types of Promotion:

1. The line promotion: Promotion in the media in which the advertiser pays an advertising agency to place the ad
2. Below the line promotion: All other promotion. Much of this is intended to be subtle enough for the consumer to be unaware that promotion is taking place. E.g. sponsorship, product placement, endorsements, sales promotion, merchandising, direct mail, personal selling, public relations, trade shows

The specification of five elements creates a promotional mix or promotional plan. These elements are personal selling, advertising, sales promotion, direct marketing, and publicity. A promotional mix specifies how much attention to pay to each of the five subcategories, and how much money to budget for each. A promotional plan can have a wide range of objectives, including: sales increases, new product acceptance, creation of brand equity, positioning, competitive retaliations, or creation of a corporate image. Fundamentally, however there are three basic objectives of promotion.

These are:

1. To present information to consumers as well as others
2. To increase demand
3. To differentiate a product.

There are different ways to promote a product in different areas of media. Promoters use internet advertisement, special events, endorsements, and newspapers to advertise their product. Many times with the purchase of a product there is an incentive like discounts, free items, or a contest. This is to increase the sales of a given product. The term "promotion" is usually an "in" expression used internally by the marketing company, but not normally to the public or the market - phrases like "special offer" are more common. An example of a fully integrated, long-term, large-scale promotion are My Coke Rewards and Pepsi Stuff.

ADVERTISING

Advertising is a form of communication intended to persuade an audience to purchase or take some action upon products, ideals, or services. It includes the name of a product or service and how that product or service could benefit the consumer, to persuade a target market to purchase or to consume that particular brand. These brands are usually paid for or identified through sponsors and viewed via various media. Advertising can also serve to communicate an idea to a large number of people in an attempt to convince them to take a certain action.

Commercial advertisers often seek to generate increased consumption of their products or services through branding, which involves the repetition of an image or product name in an effort to associate related qualities with the brand in the minds of consumers. Non-commercial advertisers that spend money to advertise items other than a consumer product or service include political parties, interest groups, religious organizations and governmental agencies. Nonprofit organizations may rely on free modes of persuasion, such as a public service announcement.

Modern advertising developed with the rise of mass production in the late 19th and early 20th centuries. Mass media can be defined as any media meant to reach a mass amount of people. Different types of media can be used to deliver these messages, including traditional media such as newspapers, magazines, television, radio, outdoor or direct mail; or new media such as websites and text messages. Advertising may be placed by an advertising agency on behalf of a company or other organization.

Industry

In 2007, spending on advertising was estimated at more than $150 billion in the United States and $385 billion worldwide. Internationally, the largest advertising conglomerates are Interpublic, Omnicom, Publicis, and WPP.

Backdrop

Egyptians used papyrus to make sales messages and wall posters. Commercial messages and political campaign displays have been found in the ruins of Pompeii and ancient Arabia. Lost and found advertising on papyrus was common in Ancient Greece and Ancient Rome. Wall or rock painting for commercial advertising is another manifestation of an ancient advertising form, which is present to this day in many parts of Asia, Africa, and South America. The tradition of wall painting can be traced back to Indian rock art paintings that date back to 4000 BC. History tells us that Out-of-home advertising and billboards are the oldest forms of advertising.

As the towns and cities of the Middle Ages began to grow, and the general populace was unable to read, signs that today would say cobbler, miller, tailor or blacksmith would use an image associated with their trade such as a boot, a suit, a hat, a clock, a diamond, a horse shoe, a candle or even a bag of flour. Fruits and vegetables were sold in the city square from the backs of carts and wagons and their proprietors used street callers to announce their whereabouts for the convenience of the customers.

As education became an apparent need and reading, as well as printing, developed advertising expanded to include handbills. In the 17th century advertisements started to appear in weekly newspapers in England. These early print advertisements were used mainly to promote books and newspapers, which became increasingly affordable with advances in the printing press; and medicines, which were increasingly sought after as disease ravaged Europe. However, false advertising and so-called "quack" advertisements became a problem, which ushered in the regulation of advertising content.

As the economy expanded during the 19th century, advertising grew alongside. In the United States, the success of this advertising format eventually led to the growth of mail-order advertising.

In June 1836, French newspaper La Presse was the first to include paid advertising in its pages, allowing it to lower its price, extend its readership and increase its profitability and the formula was soon copied by all titles. Around 1840, Volney B. Palmer established a predecessor to advertising agencies in Boston. Around the same time, in France, Charles-Louis Havas extended the services of his news agency, Havas to include advertisement brokerage, making it the first French group to organize. At first, agencies were brokers for advertisement space in newspapers. N. W. Ayer & Son was the first full-service agency to assume responsibility for advertising content. N.W. Ayer opened in 1869, and was located in Philadelphia.

At the turn of the century, there were few career choices for women in business; however, advertising was one of the few. Since women were responsible for most of the purchasing done in their household, advertisers and agencies recognized the value of women's insight during the creative process. In fact, the first American advertising to use a sexual sell was created by a woman – for a soap product. Although tame by today's standards, the advertisement featured a couple with the message "The skin you love to touch".

In the early 1920s, the first radio stations were established by radio equipment manufacturers and retailers who offered programmes in order to sell more radios to consumers. As time passed, many non-profit organizations followed suit in setting up their own radio stations, and included: schools, clubs and civic groups. When the practice of sponsoring programmes was popularised, each individual radio programme was usually sponsored by a single business in exchange for a brief mention of the business' name at the beginning and end of the sponsored shows. However, radio station owners soon realised they could earn more money by selling sponsorship rights in small time allocations to multiple businesses throughout their radio station's broadcasts, rather than selling the sponsorship rights to single businesses per show.

This practice was carried over to television in the late 1940s and early 1950s. A fierce battle was fought between those seeking to commercialise the radio and people who argued that the radio spectrum should be considered a part of the commons – to be used only non-commercially and for the public good. The United Kingdom pursued a public funding model for the BBC, originally a private company, the British Broadcasting Company, but incorporated as a public body by Royal Charter in 1927.

In Canada, advocates like Graham Spry were likewise able to persuade the federal government to adopt a public funding model, creating the Canadian Broadcasting Corporation. However, in the United States, the capitalist model prevailed with the passage of the Communications Act of 1934 which created the Federal Commu-nications Commission. To placate the socialists, the U.S. Congress did require commercial broadcasters to operate in the "public interest, convenience, and necessity". Public broadcasting now exists in the United States due to the 1967 Public Broadcasting Act which led to the Public Broadcasting Service and National Public Radio.

In the early 1950s, the DuMont Television Network began the modern practice of selling advertisement time to multiple sponsors. Previously, DuMont had trouble finding sponsors for many of their programmes and compensated by selling smaller blocks of advertising time to several businesses. This eventually became the standard for the commercial television industry in the United States. However, it was still a common practice to have single sponsor shows, such as The United States Steel Hour. In some instances the sponsors exercised great control over the content of the show—up to and including having one's advertising agency actually writing the show. The single sponsor model is much less prevalent now, a notable exception being the Hallmark Hall of Fame.

The 1960s saw advertising transform into a modern approach in which creativity was allowed to shine, producing unexpected messages that made advertisements more tempting to consumers' eyes. The Volkswagen ad campaign—featuring such headlines as "Think Small" and "Lemon"—ushered in the era of modern advertising by promoting a "position" or "unique selling proposition" designed to associate each brand with a specific idea in the reader or viewer's mind. This period of American advertising is called the Creative Revolution and its archetype was William Bernbach who helped create the revolutionary Volkswagen ads among others. Some of the most creative and long-standing American advertising dates to this period.

The late 1980s and early 1990s saw the introduction of cable television and particularly MTV. Pioneering the concept of the music video, MTV ushered in a new type of advertising: the consumer tunes in for the advertising message, rather than it being a by-product or afterthought. As cable and satellite television became increasingly prevalent, specialty channels emerged, including channels entirely devoted to advertising, such as QVC, Home Shopping Network, and ShopTV Canada.

Marketing through the Internet opened new frontiers for advertisers and contributed to the "dot-com" boom of the 1990s. Entire corporations operated solely on advertising revenue, offering everything from coupons to free Internet access. At the turn of the 21st century, a number of websites including the search engine Google, started a change in online advertising by emphasizing contextually relevant, unobtrusive ads intended to help, rather than inundate, users. This has led to a plethora of similar efforts and an increasing trend of interactive advertising.

The share of advertising spending relative to GDP has changed little across large changes in media. For example, in the US in 1925, the main advertising media were newspapers, magazines, signs on streetcars, and outdoor posters. Advertising spending as a share of GDP was about 2.9 per cent. By 1998, television and radio had become major advertising media. Nonetheless, advertising spending as a share of GDP was slightly lower—about 2.4 per cent.

A recent advertising innovation is "guerrilla marketing", which involve unusual approaches such as staged encounters in public places, giveaways of products such as cars that are covered with brand messages, and interactive advertising where the viewer can respond to become part of the advertising message.Guerrilla advertising is becoming increasing more popular with a lot of companies. This type of advertising is unpredictable and innovative, which causes consumers to buy the product or idea. This reflects an increasing trend of interactive and "embedded" ads, such as via product placement, having consumers vote through text messages, and various innovations utilizing social network services such as Facebook.

5

Industrial Marketing

INTRODUCTION

Industrial marketing, which some marketing experts have described as a 'sleeping giant', has been the subject of very little research. This text is an attempt to create in the reader an interest in this challenging yet not much talked about subject.

Several developments have transformed industrial marketing in the last few years:

- Technology has become the cornerstone of industrial marketing. New product technologies are emerging and manufacturing processes are evolving. Information technology is being leveraged to develop new products and services, in addition to streamlining operations.
- The Internet has revolutionized industrial marketing. It has helped bring down the communication costs between the industrial marketers and other stakeholders drastically. E-procurement and e-marketplaces have gained popularity among organizational buyers.

The nature of competition has undergone a sea change in the industrial marketplace. "The Business Network is the Business Strategy." Today, competition is between value-chain partnerships rather than between industrial firms. From the 1990s, the Government of India has been supporting liberalization by taking various positive measures, including the permitting of foreign direct investments in capital intensive industries. In addition to setting up joint ventures and subsidiaries, many firms have adopted the outsourcing route. India's progress on both the domestic and export fronts has resulted in a growing demand for professionals to market industrial products, services, and solutions to a wide range of industries.

CHARACTERISTICS OF THE INDUSTRIAL MARKETING

The industrial market differs in a number of important respects from the market for goods sold to ultimate consumers. Because of the diversity of industrial products, generalizations do not, of course, apply equally to all kinds and types of goods entering the industrial market. The present discussion is confined to widely prevalent features that may be deemed generally characteristic, even though some exceptions may be encountered under specific circumstances.

Derived and Widely Fluctuating Demand

There is no demand for industrial products *per se.* Demand is altogether derived from the demand for consumer goods or services or public (governmental) service that flow from the production and marketing of industrial goods. In recession periods the industrial market absorbs a smaller proportion of total production because the lower level of consumer goods output can be maintained without adding to existing productive equipment.

In boom periods the demand for industrial installations and equipment, and for semi manufactured goods and parts that enter into their production, is greatly accelerated. As ultimate consumer demand reaches high levels, additions are made to existing productive equipment which far surpass normal replacement demand. Moreover, there is a tendency for industrial buyers to accumulate inventories in such periods, owing to optimistic sales forecasts and anticipations of price increases, thus greatly accelerating the demand for materials used directly in manufacturing. Under adverse conditions, not only is plant expansion curtailed, but inventories tend to be depleted, thus diminishing the demand for materials.

Discovering the Market

In comparison with industrial goods, the potential market for most consumer goods items is easily defined in terms of persons and families with certain income, type of residence, sex, age, or other characteristics. Furthermore, such markets are relatively easily located geographically by means of Census of Population information or market surveys. By way of contrast, manufacturers of industrial goods are faced with the constant problem of discovering new uses of their products by old customers and additional outlets in other industries in order to maintain or increase sales volume.

The market for some industrial products can be analyzed in a crude manner from data in periodic *Censuses of Manufactures.* Facts are given which indicate the number of manufacturing establishments in each industry classification by geographic area. Also given is the value of each major type of material used within each industrial classification. While such facts are helpful in identifying the types of establishments which are presently the major users of important materials, they are not complete, provide little information about materials or supplies used in relatively small amounts, and are not of much help in determining when one type of material might readily be substituted for another. Industrial marketing research is confronted with unusually complex problems in discovering who uses the product, what it is used for, what conditions surround its use, what are the trends in demand for the products of which it is a part, what new applications are feasible, what are competitors offering, and how well the product in question is meeting the needs of users. This may be illustrated by the market for pressure sensitive tape, which grew rapidly in the 1950's because of new uses discovered by manufacturers of this type of product. Among numerous interesting applications are included the familiar masking tape widely used in automobile painting; holding tapes, used to keep doors of major appliances from coming open in transit or in warehouse handling; strong bond tapes, used in place of wire or steel bands in reinforcing fiberboard cartons; sealing tapes, to keep dust and moisture from packed mechanical items; and printed or colored tapes, used for identification of products or to distinguish parts of complex installations, such as oil from water lines.

Size of Purchase

The industrial market differs markedly from the consumer goods market in size of typical purchase. Ultimate consumers buy one unit of an item or a few units at a time, and their maximum outlay for tangible goods other than real estate is generally for an automobile. Installation sales, on the other hand, often involve dollar amounts in six digits. Many items of industrial equipment involve the expenditure of thousands of dollars. Contracts for parts, semimanufactured goods, and raw materials often involve many thousands and even millions of dollars. Every industrial buyer does, however, have occasional need for some items which are bought only in small lots.

Limited Number of Customers

A further characteristic of industrial marketing is that the possible number of customers for a given type of product is often very limited. When an industrial product is used only by one or a very few industry or trade groups, it is said to have a *vertical market.* The market is narrow, but deep in the sense that most prospective customers in the industry may need the article. Machinery especially designed for shoe manufacturing or for textile weaving is illustrative. In a few cases a vertical market may be limited to less than ten possible customers, but in other instances it may amount to thousands. Manufacturers of dress trimmings have a vertical market, but there are approximately 4,000 dress manufacturing establishments that have use for such items.

A *horizontal market* exists when the product is bought by many kinds of firms in different industries. Most supplies fall in this category, for almost all firms have need for products such as paper towels, small tools, stationery, light bulbs, nails, and screws.

Office machinery, materials handling equipment, and cleaning and maintenance equipment are further examples. While a horizontal industrial market is usually very broad in comparison with a vertical market, numbering perhaps hundreds of thousands or even more than a million possible users, such a market is nevertheless limited in comparison with markets for ordinary consumer goods, where possible consumers are counted in terms of tens of millions.

Concentrated Markets

The industrial market is highly concentrated compared with the market for consumer goods. A group of 100 major industrial market areas includes some 72 per cent of the total number of manufacturing establishments and 83 per cent of the total value added by manufacturing. Vertical markets consisting of customers in specific industries (*e.g.*, apparel manufacturers, coal mining companies, airline transportation companies) are often much more highly concentrated than indicated by total data for the industrial market.

Diffused Buying Responsibility

Marketers of consumer goods accept the housewife as the primary source of responsibility for consumer goods purchasing, recognizing, however, that she is influenced by the wants and needs of other family members. Middlemen in consumer goods channels have little problem in determining who is responsible for purchasing on the wholesale level. Wholesalers soon learn who buys for each store they serve. But industrial purchases may result from any one of a number of factors and any one of several officials.

The purchasing agent in the manufacturing company, public utility company, or large institution has no counterpart in the marketing of consumer goods. In many companies, he is an important executive who passes judgment on all important purchases and in some cases practically every purchase, no matter how routine, is processed through his office. The responsibility and scope of influence of the purchasing agent in the industrial organization has tended to increase under the highly competitive conditions prevailing in the late 1950's and early 1960's. Still, salesmen of industrial products know that he plays only a limited role in determining the kind, quality, and quantity of many items.

Installations are usually purchased only after major decisions by top management relating to plant expansion or modernization and may involve additional careful investigation of the merits of rival lines by the plant engineer, the superintendent, sometimes by foremen, and often by the president and the board of directors. Consulting engineers and architects influence decisions to buy certain products. Equipment is often selected because of the personal wishes of a foreman or plant superintendent. Reciprocity must be considered, and officials often have personal acquaintances who are to be favored, at times even against the best judgment of the purchasing agent.

One problem for the salesman of industrial goods is to ascertain the most influential employees in a company insofar as buying is concerned. Time is wasted talking to the superintendent who has no power but will not admit it. What he learns at one plant may not help greatly in the next call in the same industry, since policies vary with the personalities of the various officials. Likewise it is difficult to avoid waste in direct mail and in periodical advertising when neither advertising nor sales managers can determine who are the most probable prospects.

Buying and Patronage Motives

Industrial purchases are commonly made on a performance basis, with rational motives governing buying decisions to a higher degree than is the case in purchases by ultimate consumers. In terms of product buying motives, the industrial purchaser is likely to be motivated by such considerations as contribution to salability of end product, adherence to specifications or standards, operating costs, ease of repair, economy, portability, freedom from adulterative matter, replacement cost, safety, strength, uniformity, and availability of desired after-sale service. Patronage motives commonly stressed in industrial purchasing include accessibility of seller, rapidity of delivery, terms of sale or credit arrangements, technical services available, speed and reliability of repair services, history of satisfactory business relationships, and other similar rational considerations. This does not mean that industrial buyers are motivated entirely by rational factors. In small firms, industrial purchasing is often haphazard, being carried on by an owner-manager who cannot or does not take time to evaluate alternative proposals. Even among large organizations, purchasing agents and other officials are influenced by emotional factors such as fear of disapproval by superior executives, personal acquaintance with certain salesmen, or prestige of the company making a sale, even though this may contribute little to the value of the product purchased. Nevertheless, it is widely accepted that industrial purchasing is rationally oriented to a much greater extent than is the situation in consumer goods buying.

Value Analysis

Rational approaches to purchasing are carried to an extreme degree in many large industrial companies by means of formal analytical procedures commonly known as value analysis. Such procedures are ordinarily performed as a staff activity in purchasing departments, with a view to providing recommendations to other departments (*e.g.*, engineering, manufacturing, plant maintenance) that may have ultimate responsibility for deciding upon the suitability of alternative parts, equipment, material, or supplies. This may be illustrated by ten highly publicized "Tests for Value," originated at the General Electric Company and widely used, often in modified form, in the purchasing departments of other companies:

- Does the use of the item contribute value?
- Is its cost proportionate to its usefulness?

- Does it need all its features?
- Is there anything better for the intended use?
- Can a usable part be made by a lower cost method?
- Can a standard product be found that will be usable?
- Is the product made on proper tooling, considering the quantities that are used?
- Do material, labour, overhead, and profit total its cost?
- Will another dependable supplier provide it for less?
- Is anyone buying it for less?

The purpose of value analysis is to relate design and function to cost, with a view to reducing cost through modification of design, change in specifications, different method of manufacture, change in source of supply, possible elimination of an item, or incorporation into a related item. The increasing use of value analysis in industrial purchasing has a significant relationship to industrial marketing, since vendors are commonly asked to cooperate with their customers in such a programme.

Reciprocity

Another characteristic of industrial marketing is the importance of reciprocity policies. Many companies give their customers preference when in the market for articles of the class produced by them. Thus the railroad gives preference to the brands of the oil companies which use its services and to the steel companies whose mills and mines are served by the road. Officials of some tire companies have been asked to buy automobiles from manufacturers using their tires for original equipment. While there are occasional instances of purchasing on the basis of reciprocity in the consumer goods field, this is known to be much less significant than in industrial marketing.

SCOPE OF THE INDUSTRIAL MARKET

The magnitude of the industrial market may be judged by the volume of products entering it and by the kind and number of industrial or business buyers. The task of industrial marketing involves about one-half of the output of manufac-turing industries, practically all of the production of the nonfarm extractive industries, about four-fifths of agricultural production, some one-half of the goods imported from other countries, and all industrial and business services.Industrial products are purchased by a large number and variety of concerns operating in many fields, as illustrated by this partial list:

- Manufacturing establishments
- Public utilities (gas, electric, water, communication)
- Transportation agencies (rail, air, motor truck, marine)

- Mining, crude petroleum production, and other extractive industries
- Construction industries (residential, commercial, industrial, public)
- Distributive trades (wholesale, retail, personal and business service establishments—purchases for business use rather than resale)
- Institutional markets (hospitals, schools, etc.)
- Agricultural producers
- Governmental purchasing units (federal, state, local)

TYPES OF INDUSTRIAL GOODS

Special problems incident to the marketing of the various types of industrial goods are treated in detail. The various types of industrial products are, however, briefly outlined and illustrated at this point, in terms of classifications that indicate how purchasers treat such expenditures, to provide an over-all view of the industrial market.

- Products entering directly into manufacture (customarily handled as a direct accounting charge to the cost of goods sold):
    - *Raw materials* from agriculture and other extractive industries: unprocessed primary materials. Examples: wheat, livestock, coffee beans, crude petroleum, iron ore, fruits and vegetables for canning.
    - Semimanufactured goods: products which are the finished output of one manufacturer or processor but which undergo additional changes in form by another. Examples: sheet steel, basic chemicals, textiles sold to garment manufacturers, flour sold to bakeries, lumber sold to furniture manufacturers.
    - *Parts:* manufactured articles which can be installed as a component of another product without further change in form. Examples: electric motors, automobile batteries and tires (original equipment), thermostats for refrigerators, handles for tools.
    - *Contract manufacturing services:* part of the manufacturing process contracted to an outside organization. Examples: dyeing, casting, cutting, or shaping services performed by a company on materials supplied by the customer.
- Supplies of goods and services (ordinarily treated as an expense of business operation):
    - *Maintenance and repair items:* items quickly consumed and regarded as highly expendable for the purpose of insuring the continued satisfactory functioning of plant and equipment. Examples: repair parts, lubricants, cleaning materials, paint.
    - *Operating supplies:* items used directly in and required for

dayto-day operations. Examples: stationery, cash register tape, small tools not purchased on a capital investment basis, staples or fastening items.

  - *Business services:* services provided by others, often involving the use of supplies. Examples: printing and mimeographing service, janitorial or cleaning service, business repair services, equipment maintenance service.

- Capital investment items (major outlays which become a continuing expense burden over part or all of the anticipated period of service through depreciation charges):
  - *Installations:* items usually regarded as part of the fixed plant of the purchaser. Examples: large machine tools, printing presses, electric generators, elevators.
  - *Equipment:* capital investment items not regarded as part of fixed plant. Examples: store fixtures, motor trucks, portable drills, typewriters, farm tractors.

Industrial products have been grouped into broad categories according to the business nature of the purchase and into more homogeneous classes according to use of the products. While this is a useful arrangement for considering special problems of industrial marketing, it is subject to the reservation that many specific products have a *multiple market*. Light bulbs, for one example, are purchased as consumer goods and as industrial goods, and within the industrial goods field they are used as supplies by all firms and as parts by manufacturers of floor lamps and store lighting equipment.

DISTRIBUTION CHANNELS

Four main types of channels of distribution are used to effect transfers in ownership of manufactured industrial goods. These are as follows:

- Direct from factory to user
- From factory, through the manufacturer's own sales branch, to user
- From factory, through agents or brokers who do not take title to the goods, to the industrial user
- Through industrial distributors (wholesalers)

Different combinations are sometimes employed. Some sales are made from sales branches to industrial distributors, and occasionally a functional middleman serves as a connecting link between a factory and the industrial distributor. These are not common situations. It is estimated that about 60 to 65 per cent of the sales of manufactured industrial goods is direct from factory to user without the aid of functional middlemen or a manufacturer's branch wholesaling system; about 17 to 20 per cent is handled through wholesalers or industrial distributors; about 15 to 18 per cent is distributed through manufacturers' sales branches; and from 10 to 15 per cent is made through functional middlemen. The relative importance of each of these channels varies somewhat with different classes of goods.

By way of contrast with consumer products, there is a much greater tendency for the *physical flow* of manufactured industrial goods to move over a route different from that taken in *the channel of transfer of title.* A large proportion of the industrial sales of manufacturers' sales branches, agents and brokers, and even of industrial distributors is not supplied from stocks maintained at the wholesale establishment but rather involves direct physical movement from factory to user, mainly because the large quantities involved make direct shipment feasible and economical. Channels of distribution for business services are almost altogether direct from producer to user. In the marketing of agricultural raw materials, however, long channels are common due to the widely dispersed nature of agricultural production and the relatively small size of output of the typical farmer.

INDUSTRY ANALYSIS

Industry analysis complements analyses of the other dimensions of a firm's environment. It focuses on the industries in which the firm competes.

The breadth and depth of industry analysis and the boundaries for information gathering are defined by these industries.

Thus industry analysis involves the same processes as those identified earlier for environmental analysis, except that it logically must be preceded by identification of the appropriate industries for analysis along with descriptions of the various characteristics of those industries.

Industry analysis is relevant in any of these situations:

- The firm's strategy defines the business in terms of specific industries.
- The firm is facing new forms of extra-industry competition.
- The firm is contemplating entry into a new industry.

An industry perspective is also useful for the student case analyst in that it provides the basis for gaining familiarity with the products, competition, resource requirements, and constraints peculiar to a line of business.

The industry perspective must be used cautiously since an individual firm or business unit can hardly be considered completely protected from direct extra-industry influences.

For example, relaxation in occupational safety and health standards for an industry may come at the same time that an individual firm is singled out for stricter compliance enforcement. The analyst, therefore, is cautioned to assess direct environmental influences as well as the portion of the environment that affects overall industry conditions.

Michael E. Porter developed an assessment model for analyzing industry structure that focuses on the forces imposed on the process of competing by five influences: The intensity of rivalry among competitors, the threat of new entrants, the threat of substitute products, the bargaining power of suppliers, and the bargaining power of buyers or customers. This "Five Forces Model of Competition" is presented in this section.

Some environmental influences affect a firm through the industries in which it competes. These influences, the nature of their present and future effects on the appropriate industries, and characteristics of the relationships between the firm's relevant industries and the firm itself are the subjects of industry analysis. Multiple product/service firms, particularly those that are diversified, will often hold "membership" in more than one industry. This will obviously require multiple analyses and creative cross-cutting of industries in the compilation and analysis of data.

Defining an Industry

In general an industry is nothing more than a cluster of economic units (firms or business units within firms) that are grouped together for analytical or cooperative purposes. Trade associations are the purest manifestation of the latter purpose. Trade associations themselves define criteria for membership and establish networks for information sharing and cooperation.

Thus the American Boat Builders and Repairers Association defines its own industry scope and becomes a private sector information depository (among other functions) within the confines of that scope.

A more universal taxonomy for analytical purposes is that provided by the U.S. Government's Standard Industrial Classification (SIC) scheme. It is designed to furnish a common framework for gathering, tabulating, analyzing, and cross-referencing data in a uniform fashion. The SIC clusters "establishments" (as opposed to legal entities or firms) together on the basis of the primary type of activity in which they are engaged (normally defined by product or service category). These clusters are named and coded to provide the needed uniformity and comparability. The more digits in the code, the more narrowly defined is the cluster.

The coding scheme results in a nesting arrangement of "divisions," "major groups," "groups," and "industries". Industries are assigned a four-digit code. Additional digits are used for subdivisions within industries.

The SIC is useful in a number of respects. First, it provides rather detailed descriptions of the many industries it includes. Perusal of these descriptions can offer the analyst interesting insights into product/market opportunities. Second, the assignment of establishments to specific industries and groups is internally consistent.

This allows comparable data referencing from a variety of public and private sector sources wherever the SIC has been used. Finally, the nesting feature of the SIC places somewhat narrowly defined industries in broader contexts (clusters with fewer digits). This can aid the strategist in overcoming myopic perceptions of a business and can serve as one basis for identifying forms of strategic growth (e.g., concentric versus conglomerate diversification).

As a practical matter, the definition of an industry is left to the analyst and need not be confined to institutional classifications.

Geographic boundaries, customers, suppliers, technologies, or other peculiar dimensions of a business may better serve the purposes of clustering enterprises for competitive analysis. Indeed the creative strategist in search of new product/market opportunities and threats will define and redefine industries at will.

Levels of Analysis

Industry analysis focuses interest on two primary levels:

- The structure and performance of the industry as a whole.
- The strategies and performance of individual competitors.

On the first level, aggregate data are often available from public and private sources that can be used to assess industry trends.

Although U.S. Industry Outlook has not been published since 1994, it has been replaced by several sources of similar information.

Other information of relevance at this level for the industry might be as follows:

- The industry includes about seventy-five companies operating 200 establishments.
- Industry sales are heavily concentrated among four large producers.
- Plastic containers represent a threat to industry volume.
- Use of paper containers in microwave ovens represents significant opportunities.
- Real growth has been limited; rising volume of shipments has resulted largely from price increases.
- Exports are increasing.

These and other data can be used to assess common threats and opportunities across the industry. They may be internally imposed by the industry itself (e.g., sluggishness in adopting new technologies) or may be due to other environmental circumstances (e.g., general economic conditions).

At the second level of analysis, the actions of individual competitors are of interest so that the analyst can identify:

- Competitive differentials
- Key success factors. In essence a search is made to uncover basic prerequisites for success in the industry (e.g., access to well-established distribution channels) and to examine the competitive weaponry wielded by the industry's players (e.g., product modifications).

Here the focus is on the manner in which industry members position themselves vis-a-vis one another in the broader context of overall industry change.

An Industry Study Guide

As with the more broadly based environmental analysis, the output of the industry study should be in the form of prognoses.

That is, assessment of industry conditions should be forward looking, representing opportunities and threats to which the firm might adapt its goals and action plans. This can be expedited in part by focusing on changes in industry structures and practices.

Finally, the analyst is cautioned that there are no single "cookbook" sources of data for a truly comprehensive industry analysis. Gathering and analyzing industry data is a long and arduous process that requires creativity and patience.

Porter's Five Forces Model of Competition

The nature of competition in an industry in large part determines the content of strategy, especially business-level strategy.

Based as it is on the fundamental economics of the industry, the very profit potential of an industry is determined by competitive interactions.

Where these interactions are intense, profits tend to be whittled away by the activities of competing. Where they are mild and competitors appear docile, profit potential tends to be high. Yet a full understanding of the elements of competition within an industry is easy to overlook and often difficult to comprehend.

Porter has identified five basic forces that collectively describe the state of competition in an industry:

- The intensity of rivalry among competitors
- The threat of new entrants to the market
- The amount of bargaining power possessed by the firm's/industry's suppliers
- The amount of bargaining power possessed by the firm's/industry's customers
- The extent that substitute products present a threat to a firm's/industry's products

These forces assist in identifying the presence or absence of potential high returns. The weaker are Porter's five forces, the greater is the opportunity for firms in an industry to experience superior profitability.

More generally, understanding how these forces affect competition within an industry allows the strategist to identify the most advantageous strategic position.

The actors within an industry on whom these forces exert pressure are, respectively, the industry's competing firms themselves, potential new entrants to the industry's markets, suppliers (vendors), customers, and makers of substitute products.

Obviously, the starting point for conducting an analysis of the five forces of competition is to identify all the competitors, potential new entrants, major suppliers, the demographics of customers, and makers of and nature of substitute products.

Competitors would not only have to be identified, but various distinguishing data about the industry would also have to be specified.

For each competitor this data would include market share, product line differences/similarities, market segments served, price/quality relationships represented by products, growth/decline trends, financial strength differences, and any other information that will help describe the industry.

Arranging the five forces and the major actors within an industry produces the "five forces model" as follows:

Porter's Model

Using Porter's model to analyse an industry for a particular firm, involves estimating the strength of each force, identifying its underlying source, and then formulating a strategy that will create an advantage for the firm.

An advantage could be established by defining a position from which to defend itself against strong forces somewhere in the model, drafting an offensive posture to take advantage of weak forces in the industry, or designing a way to favorably alter the forces. The key task of the analyst is to understand the underlying causes of each of the competitive forces at work. With this knowledge, a company's strengths or weaknesses can be clarified, and the most fertile areas for drafting competitive thrusts can be defined. Also, knowing the magnitude of competitive forces allows the strategist to identify the most important trends that are emerging as opportunities and threats.

Next, we'll identify typical characteristics of each competitive force, and the kinds of factors that can create strength for the five sets of competitors.

Intensity of Rivalry among Competitors

Some industries appear "sleepy" because of a low level of rivalry among competitors. An example might be industrial fasteners, the manufacturers of nuts and bolts and other devices used to connect the components of products.

A large number of quite small manufacturers accept low levels of profitability as a cost of staying in business. Competition is low key with little effort and expense devoted to differentiating brands or single products.

Such firms often produce a catalog and send representatives to trade shows to demonstrate products, or use sales forces or independent sales representatives for selling. They usually compete on the basis of price, delivery times, or the convenience of either large or small lot sizes.

There are virtually no screw machine companies advertising on television! On the other hand, some industries are characterized by a high level of competitive activity. For example, the brewing industry has many competitors who battle fiercely with each other over market share.

There is little natural differentiability in beer, so brewing firms develop complex promotional and advertising programs to try to gain the upper hand in consumer awareness.

We have seen ads, appeals, posters, jingles, demonstrations, sales, and many other types of promotional and advertising programme by beer brewers and distributors to differentiate their product on the basis of taste, brewing process, alcohol content, social acceptance, ingredients, price, "naturalness," similarity to foreign beer brands, dissimilarity to foreign beer brands, strength of flavour, weakness of flavour, and so on.

Lately, small retail location-based breweries have been popping up all over the country who make their own beer.

For breweries of a given revenue size, capital investment is large so exit barriers are high. There are few alternative uses of a defunct brewery. So participants fight it out intensely for a share of the huge beer market.

Generally, the factors that tend to precipitate intense rivalry in an industry are the following:

- Relative equilibrium in size and power among a large number of competitors
- Slow or stagnant growth of industry demand such that expansion of one competitor would come at the expense of others
- Undifferentiated products and low switching costs
- High fixed costs or product perishability
- Even small capacity additions generate large volume increases which raise pressure to cut prices
- High exit barriers causing firms to bear low or negative returns on investment
- Wide spectrum of strategies and types of firms which generates confusion and frequent "collisions" in the market. The opposite case might be an oligolopy like the automobile industry where most actions are reactions to another competitor and rivalry is somewhat orderly, albeit intense.

Buyers

For an industry, buyers can usually be broken into three categories: Consumer, industrial, and commercial customers. Consumers, or purchasers of the firm's service or product for their own use, are further divided into "bundles" of demographics which collectively identify all the various market segments that are present.

Firestone, for example, sells tires directly to the people who will be driving on them through its own retail outlets. The various products that make up its line cater to the needs of different sets of demographic descriptions of people.

Industrial buyers are companies that purchase the firm's product or service to be used as a component in its product. Continuing with the Firestone example, automobile manufacturers who put Firestone tires on new cars, would be one group of its set of industrial buyers. By contrast, commercial buyers would be other companies that sell Firestone's products to consumers. An example would be any of the large discount store chains that handle Firestone tires, like Wal-Mart, K-Mart, Sears, etc.

Buyers, whether consumer, industrial, or commercial, can enjoy positions of strength over the firm from which they purchase products by superior bargaining power.

ZFor example, a large retailer ("commercial buyer" to its supplier) with a loyal customer base and high volume of sales of the product in question, may be able to virtually dictate price, shipping arrangements, order quantity, quality level, and other factors to its vendors.

Similarly, an automobile manufacturer could have a powerful bargaining position over a tire maker or the entire tire industry if a large volume of tires was sought for installation on a popular auto line.

Of course, the wise tire maker would prevent itself from becoming too dependent on one buyer by strenuously developing similar relationships with other companies. Toyota uses "multiple sourcing"—buying from several producers of the same components—to prevent dependency on too few suppliers.

Thus it has a strong bargaining position on matters of price, quality, delivery times, etc., as its suppliers compete with one another to gain favour with its buyers.

An industry's buyers tend to be powerful relative to the firms they are buying from when the conditions listed below apply (keep in mind that these factors apply as well to a group of consumers and to industrial and commercial buyers):

- Buyers are concentrated as in cooperatives, or they account for a large volume of purchases.
- Products are undifferentiated or standardized.
- The seller's component represents a large portion of the total cost of the buyer's finished product. When the seller's product has a small cost share, buyers tend to be less price sensitive.
- Buyers are earning low profits and are thus more price sensitive than if they were highly profitable.
- The sellers' product is not critical in one way or another to the buyer. If it's critical to the quality, price, appeal, etc., of an industrial buyer group's finished product, for example, then the sellers will have power over the buyers.
- There is a threat that buyers can integrate backward to make the suppliers' product.

An industry's commercial buyers (retailers) have, in some cases, an additional source of bargaining power over their manufacturing vendors. They can influence customers' purchase decisions.

This capability allows retailers to gain price, delivery time, order quantity, and other concessions from their suppliers that other classes of buyers might not receive.

Suppliers

Providers of goods and services to an industry have power over their customers through their ability to set price and control quality, delivery time, and order quantity.

If these customers cannot successfully play off one supplier against another to protect themselves, then the industry's profits can be drained off by suppliers.

- The power of suppliers is high in the following situations:
- There are few suppliers who are more concentrated than their customers
- Suppliers' product is differentiated
- Customers' switching costs are high
- There is little pressure on suppliers to protect themselves from substitutes or replacements for their product
- When suppliers have the capability to integrate forward. A supplier of engines to a manufacturer of lawnmowers would have a strong bargaining position if the mower company realized the engine supplier's ability to make the whole lawnmower.
- The industry is not one of the major customers of the supplier. Important customers would be protected from aggressive moves by the supplier because of their mutual interests; unimportant customers would not enjoy this position.

An interesting example of the power of suppliers is the unusual relationship between the growers of seed shrimp and the growers of mature shrimp in the shrimp mariculture industry in the country of Ecuador.

The preferred seed stock (baby shrimp placed in growth ponds to grow to a marketable size) are wild post- larval shrimp (called "PLs") netted in the country's estuarine areas by fishermen. These PL shrimp are much hardier than their hatchery-grown substitutes—as many as 80 per cent of the hatchery-grown PLs die before reaching maturity compared with a mortality rate of about 20 per cent for the wild ones.

The problem is that the supply of wild PLs fluctuates dramatically from year-to-year with climatic conditions. In some years there are not enough wild PLs to stock all the growth farms. In other years there is an oversupply of wild PLs. During the years of wild PL undersupply, the price of hatchery-grown PLs skyrockets and the PL hatchery operators thrive. Indeed, they have the power during these years to control the profitability of the much larger (in terms of revenue) mature shrimp mariculture industry.

But during the wild PL oversupply years, they may receive no revenue at all. For Ecuadorian shrimp hatchery operators, periods of extremely high bargaining power and virtually no bargaining power may be separated by only a few months.

Substitute Products

The shrimp industry example above also demonstrates the plight of an industry facing a substitute for its product. Although it is an extreme case, seed shrimp hatchery operators really only have an industry at all during the years when their product's substitute, wild seed shrimp, are in short supply. Hatchery operators are spending heavily on research to increase the survival rate of their product.

If they are successful in this endeavor, then they may be able to displace the wild seed shrimp industry altogether.

During years when there are not quite enough wild seed shrimp to go around, shrimp growers use some hatchery grown seed stock. Their availability limits the price that the wild PL fishermen can charge for their product. This price ceiling is typical of all industries facing substitutes.

Manufacturers of products and suppliers of services must constantly scan their environments for the potential emergence of substitutes.

The most dangerous substitutes are those that show potential for improving price-performance trade-offs and those made by firms or industries earning high profits. In these cases, strategies must be formulated to protect against displacement by the substitute product/service.

Potential Entrants

New entrants to an industry pose several threats to existing competitors. New competitors can reduce the market share of all participants by dividing the "pie" into more pieces. They also may bring new technology or greater resources not available to present competitors and achieve a high market share position quickly to the detriment of all existing participants.

Corporate parent firms that diversify into an industry by acquisition are especially dangerous to existing competitors both because of their "deep pockets" and potential management expertise.

A restaurant in the tourism-driven town of Newport, Rhode Island, rapidly gained market share from other restaurants in town when it was acquired by a large international corporation.

The parent made capital available to the restaurant and after a major facilities overhaul, hiring of professional management, and implementation of other profit oriented moves, the restaurant quickly became the "industry leader" in Newport.

Although corporate ownership does not guarantee success of a restaurant, this example points out the threat to current participants presented by corporate diversification into their industry.

The threat of new entrants to an industry is high when barriers to entry are low. Low entry barriers would apply in the following situations:

- *Low economies of scale*: That small independent pizza parlors exists side-by-side with the units of national chains of pizza stores indicates that there are few economies of scale in his industry. Thus, one finds and would expect frequent appearance of new pizza places in just about every town and neighborhood.
- Undifferentiated products in an industry leads to new entrants. Most Americans can't tell a good shrimp from a bad one. As a result, Ecuador's dominant market position in the lucrative U.S. shrimp market is under attack by shrimp growers from all over the world.
- Low capital requirements for start-up in an industry leads to new entrants. An extreme example is the house painting business where capital costs are minimal. Every community sees the appearance of a large number of new house painters every year.
- Low switching costs leads to new entrants because customers sense little incentive to stay with current suppliers. Homeowners frequently change rubbish pickup companies because there is little incentive to stay with current provider. Compare this situation with the costs of changing from an oil heating system to gas, or visa versa.
- Easy access to distribution channels
- Low familiarization costs—where "learning the ropes" in the industry is easy or inexpensive for new entrants.
- Conducting an industry analysis following Porter's model involves collecting data and developing explanations for the ways in which industry competition is affected by the five forces.

Strategic Group Mapping

The firms that make up an industry are not all alike. They have different products, market shares, life cycle stage, profitability, and so on. Indeed, each one has a different strategy, at least in its details.

But there are always some similarities. There may be several who are striving to be market leaders. Some may be pursuing low profit margin-high volume pricing. Others may have succeeded in lowering per unit costs, or creating a high-value-for-price image in the market. They may consist of several groups that represent different extents of geographical coverage or breadth of product line.

Depending on what similarities exist, industry participants can be organized by them into a set of strategic groups. For mapping strategic groups, the best bases for organizing participants are key dimensions of competition. By arraying competitors according to two key competitive factors on a two-dimensional chart (where each axis represents one of the factors), their relative positions on those factors can be analyzed.

Then conclusions about market openings and closed segments can be drawn so that the analyst can plan offensive or defensive moves. The following strategic group map of product price versus geographical coverage shows room for potential growth in the high price-wide coverage part of the market:

DEVELOPMENT AND GROWTH IN DERIVATIVE PRODUCTS

Exchange rates and interest rates remained highly volatile during the 1970s and the early 1980s and created a need for hedging instruments which in turn stimulated the search for new products and techniques to transform and reallocate financial risks. The environment of financial liberalization, market innovation and relaxation of controls in the industrial countries made this search easier. Consequently, the interest rate and currency fluctuation hedging instruments came into being and their use expanded rapidly. A significant development was the use of exchange-traded contracts as opposed to over the counter (OTC) contracts. These contracts had the advantage that their associated secondary markets were far more liquid. Since the exchange acted as counterparty in such contracts and the margin requirements had to be maintained on a daily basis, exchange-traded instruments had much less credit risk than the OTC instruments. On exchanges around the world, this trading activity continued to expand vigorously not only in terms of the variety of instruments offered but also in terms of trading volume.

The Euro-dollar interest rate future contracts began life on the Chicago Mercantile Exchange (CME) in 1981 and expanded rapidly. By 1987, the average monthly trading volume at the CME had risen by 88 per cent to 1.8 million contracts having a face value of $1.8 billion, and the expansion continued. Of late, the LIFFE and SIMEX also expanded their trading in the Euro-dollar interest rate futures but the volumes traded on these exchanges were modest compared with those on the CME. Likewise, trading in Euro-dollar options contracts, which began in 1985 at the CME and the LIFFE, also expanded sharply. The SIMEX Euro-dollar options, however, have shown limited growth because of excessive premia.

The interest rate futures and options contracts have also traded actively on the major exchanges. For instance, the volume of futures contracts on US Treasury bonds on the LIFFE recorded a dramatic increase from a monthly average of 23,628 contracts in 1984 to 127,360 contracts in 1987 and has continued to expand. In August 1987, the LIFFE also began futures contracts on Japanese government bonds which began strongly but the market stabilized thereafter at a moderate level of about 11,000 contracts a month. The volume of trading of futures contracts on ninety-day US Treasury bills has also been large at CME but the average volumes have contracted recently. The same trend has been observed in options contracts on US Treasury bills.

The trading activity in currency futures has been concentrated in the CME and other exchanges in the USA, as noted in the preceding paragraph, and has expanded considerably. Of late, trading in yen futures experienced the highest growth rate. Similarly, trading currency options began in 1982 on the Philadelphia Stock Exchange (PHLX) and it has remained the most active centre for currency options. The trading volumes in the yen and the deutsche mark have recorded the highest expansion rates.

Since the early 1980s, an important OTC hedging instrument has emerged and its use has grown in significance and volume. It is the medium-term swap which is used to arbitrage differences in borrowing costs across financial markets and to reallocate the interest rate and exchange rate risks contained in medium-term financial transactions. The access to swaps is limited by creditworthiness considerations. Borrowers in industrial countries use interest rate swap markets to convert their floating interest rate debt into the equivalent of fixed interest rate debts, both measured on the same notional principal amount and the same maturity. The interest rate and currency swaps have been among the fastest growing financial instruments of the 1980s.

By the end of 1987, the total amount of outstanding swap transactions reached the $1.1 trillion mark. Interest rate swaps account for 80 per cent of the total outstanding swap transactions while currency swaps account for the remaining 20 per cent. A large part of the latter involves the dollar and the yen swaps. A study of the International Swap Dealers Association (ISDA), New York, revealed a very low incidence of losses. Of the seventy-one major firms covered, only eleven had any losses to report, which reflects the general creditworthiness of counterparties engaged in swaps. The expansion of OTC markets for derivative products has continued and by the end of 1988 the market volume for interest rate and currency swaps reached $1.3 trillion. Of this, about $1.0 trillion were the interest rate swaps and $317 million were currency swaps. The annual report of the ISDA revealed that, at the end of 1988, 72 per cent of the interest rate swaps were in dollars and 8 per cent in yen.

For currency swaps, 86 per cent involved dollars and 42 per cent yen. It should be noted that the percentage of swaps denominated in all currencies total 200 per cent because each currency swap involves two currencies. Other OTC derivative products, namely interest rate caps, floors, collars and 'swaptions', accounted for $327 billion of notional principal at the end of 1988.

Developing Countries In The Capital Markets: When measured in terms of net or gross capital flows, the degree of integration of developing countries in the international financial system was less at the end of the 1980s than at the beginning. This was the result of the development of the debt crisis and the resultant reappraisal of the risks involved in the bank lending to the public sectors of the highly indebted LDCs.

The spontaneous flows have declined and remained limited to the developing countries that have not restructured their debt in the recent past. The bond markets experienced the same and the volume of bonds issued by LDCs declined dramatically. As opposed to this, foreign direct investment in these countries rose, which was partly a consequence of debt-equity conversion schemes. Interest in the LDC portfolio investment also rose and several investment funds were established. The Asian newly industrializing economies (ANIEs) expanded their links with the international financial markets as both users and suppliers of capital, and integrated themselves better than most other LDCs.

A clear polarization can be observed in recent trends in bank claims. LDCs without debt-servicing problems recorded increases in bank claims as well as bond issues, whereas the claims on fifteen heavily indebted countries witnessed a decline. According to the Fund's *International Banking Statistics* (IBS), the estimated cash flow from banks to the latter group of LDCs during 1985-8 was $14 billion compared with a net repayment of $15 billion, measured by the exchange-rate-adjusted change in stocks. During the first three quarters of 1988, despite minor increases in disbursements, bank claims on this group of LDCs declined by an estimated $11.3 billion. Total disbursements under the conceited lending arrangements during 1988 were $6.0 billion, marginally above the 1987 level of $5.7 billion. Attempts to resolve the LDC debt riddle continued and the terms of rescheduling were relatively more favourable to LDCs in 1988 when the average maturities extended up to eighteen years and the average spreads above the LIBOR contracted to 83 points. The use of exit bonds also increased substantially. The banks found them more acceptable in the case of Brazil than they had in the past for Argentina. More attractive pricing was the main reason behind it. Several Latin American debtors made special efforts to reduce their debt.

In their eagerness to bring down the exposure to debt-ridden LDCs, banks accelerated the rate of disposing of claims on them in 1988. The US banks' claims declined by $12.7 billion in 1988, which followed a decline of $10 billion the year before. The smaller and regional US banks accounted for a major part of this decline. Banks in other countries, except Germany and Japan, bent with the wind and reduced their LDC exposures as well. Coupled with the strengthening of bank capital bases, this trend improves the ratio of LDC debt to bank capital in all major banking systems. Likewise, the nine US money-centre banks strengthened their capital bases considerably, although it should be noted that their levels of exposure in relation to capital were generally among the highest in the world. The trend in making provisions against LDC exposure continued in 1988, but it was much smaller than in the past. Japan was a late starter in this respect and the Japanese banks were allowed to raise their provisioning levels from 5 per cent to 15 per cent only in early 1989. Canada also raised the mandatory provisioning standards. However, in the USA and Japan, the mandatory provisioning standards remained at the lowest level in the world.

The debt of LDCs with servicing problems tended to be traded at a discount to its face value and gradually a secondary market developed in LDC debt. The exact size of the secondary market is not known but the 1988 transactions were in the vicinity of $40 billion, far above the $5 billion mark reached in 1985.

Although there was a decline in turnover in the first two months of 1989 to about one-half of the 1988 level, the announcement of the Brady Plan in March 1989 by the US Treasury caused the turnover to recover strongly. The participating banks anticipated more debt-restructuring agreements and the resumption of a debt-equity programme. Two kinds of transactions dominate the secondary market:

- Debt swaps, which help banks restructure their LDC loan portfolios to their advantage, and
- Cash transactions, which include purchases by countries of their own debt at a discount and conversion of debt into equity. Such transactions have grown in importance with the increase in debt conversion schemes.

The secondary market prices of LDC debt had a declining trend in the latter half of the 1980s, and they fell further sharply between July 1988 and March 1989. The weighted average price for the debt of fifteen heavily indebted LDCs came down to 33 cents per dollar of the face value. The 1985 level was 70 per cent of the face value.

In 1986 and 1987 the declines were largely due to the combination of the introduction of a moratorium by Brazil and the provisioning decision by Citibank. The recent fall reflected the market's tendency to respond sharply to changes in perceptions of the general outlook of the debt strategy possibly a sign of a thin market. The short-term movements in the secondary market prices were fuelled essentially by opportunities for debt-equity transactions.

The non-bank financial institutions have not shown a great deal of interest in LDC debt and efforts to repackage LDC loans as marketable securities have so far met little success. According to the estimates of the IMF, the total volume of debt conversion under officially recognized schemes was as low as $4.6 billion in 1987 and $8.2 billion in 1988.

It took about five years after the eruption of the LDC debt crisis for the capital market to evolve its strategy towards the secondary LDC debt market. Since this market has increased considerably in volume, banks now recognize that the secondary market prices contain a certain amount of information and that at these prices some of their claims could be liquidated. They have also become more aware of the possibilities that the secondary market offers them for reorganizing and streamlining their portfolios. That the secondary debt market is the market-oriented solution of a long-festering debt crisis is more widely accepted in the international capital market and several large banks have reorganized their LDC debt operations to merge with their asset-trading operations. These banks are actively reducing their LDC debt exposures through the secondary market.

In order to integrate themselves better with the international capital markets, LDCs will need to ensure that their policies foster and encourage an attractive financial environment for investors. Besides, domestic savers and investors can benefit from a more global outlook and the investment opportunities abroad. We have seen that the international capital movements have become easier because of financial liberalization and technological developments; therefore, there is an all the more pressing need to improve the standards of the domestic financial markets in LDCs. If this does not happen, capital flight will increase. In addition, to attract capital from both residents and foreign investors, well-functioning domestic financial systems are indispensable. Since the rates of return on many investment projects in LDCs are high, if their financial markets are integrated with those in the rest of the world many LDCs stand a reasonably good chance of attracting the much needed capital. The only conditional clause here is that these LDCs have to see that their country risk factor does not offset the high return factor.

The emerging stock markets: The emerging stock markets in India, Indonesia, Korea, Malaysia, Taiwan, Thailand, Brazil, Chile and Mexico performed well over the 1980s, the bulk of gains coming since 1985. The stock markets in these LDCs have come to be known as the emerging stock markets. Low oil prices, the booming world trade and relatively successful economic policies in the key emerging market developing countries helped share prices rise strongly. With the exception of Brazil, where large devaluations against the US dollar more than eroded gains in the local market, other emerging markets did extraordinarily well over the 1985-9 period. In Taiwan, the market recorded outstanding growth and roughly doubled each year. The majority of the key emerging stock markets are in outward-oriented economies which prospered faster on the back of sustained export growth, particularly in manufacturing. In Asia, for instance, Taiwan, Korea, Thailand and Malaysia were highly successful on the export front throughout the 1980s. Indonesia saw no growth in the dollar value of its exports between 1980 and 1989 but this conceals a 40 per cent increase in exports since the halving of oil prices in 1986. The Latin American three, Brazil, Chile and Mexico, showed less impressive growth during the 1980s than those in Asia but could still be judged to be exporting successes. India is not considered to be an export success.

Two factors, namely higher rates of share price appreciation and prospects of gains from diversification, make a strong case for investing in the emerging markets. The IFC data suggest that a portfolio with a mix of emerging and developed market securities will show lower variability than one with only the latter. Some investors and fund managers see emerging markets as a growth area that cannot be ignored. An indicator of potential growth is that their market capitalization in aggregate is only about 5 per cent of world stock market capitalization, despite a 12 per cent share in the world GDP.

However, fund managers believe that they need to be cautious in buying because company valuations in the embryonic markets may not fairly reflect the best forecast on earnings growth. Their emphasis is not to be on buying the market as a whole but on picking the specific stocks.

After several good years, 1990 has been a difficult period for these markets and by October 1990 market capitalization was down by an average of 39 per cent on their end 1989 levels (weighted by market capitalization). The relatively poor performance is also visible in the market prices of traded country funds. With only a few exceptions, their quoted prices fell during 1992. Some of the declines can be explained as being market corrections after rapid rises over the past few years had taken prices to unsustainable levels.

Risk Management In The International Financial Institutions: Inasmuch as competitive pressure in the international financial markets has increased as a result of a dynamic growth in innovative products and the use of derivative instruments and the advancement in telecommunications technology, the general level of risk has *pari passu* soared. Apparently, it is necessary to control it and keep it within prudent limits. To be sure, increased competition and market liberalization have had a favourable effect on the market efficiency because competition is considered as value creating. However, along with that the financial markets should remain sound and supportive of growth in the real economy and confidence in them must not waiver. Therefore, supervisory authorities in a number of countries are reassessing the adequacy of prudential arrangements, at both national and international levels.

There are two principal kinds of risks: credit risk and liquidity risk. The former implies that a counterparty is not able to reimburse the bank when an obligation falls due. The general perception is that the credit risk in the international banking system has been increasing and that banks have stumbled into riskier areas in search of higher rates of return on assets so that stock prices and capital can be raised. Second, there is evidence that liquidity risk has also increased. It refers to the inability of the banks to have, or to be able to raise, enough liquid assets to meet current needs. Some of the innovative products have turned out to be less liquid than initially believed. Besides, banks have moved into securities business and changes in securities market conditions can suddenly transform short-term credits into illiquid assets. This tendency has forced banks to examine each other's credit rating a little more carefully and look for new mechanisms for limiting exposure. Third, due to a gradual elimination of interest rate controls and a reduction in the sources of low cost funding, banks could become more exposed to interest rate risk if their interest rate in liabilities is not matched with that in assets. Funding raised on floating rates and lending on a similar basis reduces interest risk to an extent but effectively converts it into increased credit risk. A mismatch of currency composition in assets and liabilities can create an additional risk which exposes banks to the possibility of adverse changes in exchange rates. Lastly, although the derivative products were designed to control risk through various hedging techniques, these new instruments as alluded to earlier are not without their own risk characteristics. It is difficult to know what they are until sufficient experience has been gained regarding how they function, and in particular how they function during an economic downturn. With so many banks and financial institutions using innovative products, it is felt that the risk involved is at times inadequately appreciated. It is partly due to the arcane nature of some of the new instruments and computerized strategies that often drive their use. The Basle capital adequacy standards have begun to take such multiple exposures into account. The newest standards for banks, in fact, have been designed to achieve three objectives:

- To harmonize the competitive conditions under which international banks operate,
- To bring indirect financial commitments within a general prudential framework, and
- To inject more capital into the banking system. We shall return to this issue a little later.

The securities houses are not being left out of supervision and relative responsibilities of the parent company and of branches are being defined. Having uniform standards for securities houses is difficult because there are considerable differences in the structures of securities businesses in different countries. In addition, the focuses and objectives of securities market regulations differ from country to country. With financial markets becoming more fully integrated, the need for an internationally consistent supervision approach is greater than it was in the past. Deliberations are under way in the International Organization of Securities Commissions (IOSCO), the OECD and other fora on these and related aspects. Attention is also being paid to the safety and efficiency of the securities transactions.

The work of the regulatory authorities has become increasingly difficult with the gradual breakdown of functional barriers within the financial services industry. While the most apparent trend is in the integration of banking and securities businesses, there is also a gradual trend towards the integration of banking, insurance and other financial services. Regulating and supervising diversified financial conglomerates is therefore onerous but necessary because a problem in one area can quickly spread from one financial sector to another. Therefore, functional rather than institutional supervision is becoming more relevant. This approach was taken by the Financial Services Act of the UK which regulates specific lines of business, ignoring the fact of whether it is a bank or a security house that is involved.

In the ultimate analysis, the supervisory authorities have to establish a level of regulation that maximizes market competition without jeopardizing safety and soundness. With deepening market integration, the problem of striking a balance between the two prime objectives is becoming more complex. The over-arching challenge for the supervisory authorities lies in finding the appropriate level of prudential supervision in a liberalized regulatory environment.

The latest measures taken by the BIS and endorsed by the G10 in July 1988 were rather significant. They fixed a minimum capital base for international banks at 8 per cent of risk-weighted assets and off-balance-sheet commitments. These are the minimum capital requirements but national authorities are free to impose more stringent requirements. The general reaction of the banks was (a) to raise more capital,(b) to shed or restructure assets and (c) to endeavour to generate higher returns by improvising margins. The first measure has already led banks all over the world to increase their primary and secondary capital. The shedding of LDC debt or reducing their LDC exposure has been favourably received by the financial market. The pressure for higher capital ratios has led many banks either to securitize their claims or to sell to non-bank financial institutions and investors. It has also led some banks to rein in the growth of their assets. Many international banks have adjusted their balance sheets to switch the relative weight of capital-absorbing assets in favour of those with low-risk weights. The need to raise returns on assets and generate more funds has encouraged banks to move towards earning more fee income. This movement has been necessitated by a squeeze in margins in regular banking business due to an excess capacity in the industry.

Feldstein and Horioka upset conventional wisdom in 1980 when they concluded that changes in countries' rates of national saving had a very large effect on their rates of investment, and interpreted this finding as evidence of low capital mobility. Although their regressions have been subject to a great variety of criticisms, their basic finding seems to hold up. But does it imply imperfect capital mobility?

Let us begin by asking why we would ever expect a shortfall in one country's national saving *not* to reduce the overall availability of funds and thereby crowd out investment projects that might otherwise be undertaken in that country. After all, national saving and investment are linked through an identity. (The variable that completes the identity is, of course, the current account balance.)

The aggregation together of all forms of 'capital' has caused more than the usual amount of confusion in the literature on international capital mobility. Nobody ever claimed that international flows of foreign direct investment were large enough that a typical investment project in the domestic country would costlessly be undertaken directly by a foreign company when there was a shortfall in domestic saving. Rather, the argument was that the typical American corporation could borrow at the going interest rate in order to finance its investment projects and, if the degree of capital mobility were sufficiently high, the going interest rate would be tied down to the world interest rate by international flows of *portfolio* capital. If portfolio capital were a perfect substitute for physical capital, then the difference would be immaterial; but the two types of capital are probably not in fact perfect substitutes.

A number of alternative ways of quantifying the degree of international capital mobility are examined. One conclusion is that the barriers to cross-border flows are low enough that, by 1989, financial markets can be said to be virtually completely integrated among the large industrial countries (and among some smaller countries as well). But this is a different proposition from saying that real interest rates are equalized across countries, which is still different from saying that investment projects in a country are unaffected by a shortfall in national saving. We shall see that there are several crucial links that can, and probably do, fail to hold.

In many cases, notably the UK and Japan (and perhaps now Italy and France as well), the finding of high integration with world financial markets is a relatively new one, attributable to liberalization programmes over the last ten years. Even in the case of financial markets in the USA, integration with the Euromarkets appears to have been incomplete as recently as 1982. The USA is that the current account deficits of the 1980s have been large enough, and by now have lasted long enough, to reduce estimates of the correlation between saving and investment significantly. The increased degree of world-wide financial integration since 1979 is identified as one likely factor that has allowed such large capital flows to take place over the past decade. But even if US interest rates are now viewed as tied to world interest rates, there are still other weak links in the chain. The implication is that crowding out of domestic investment can still take place.

6

Marketing Research Management

INTRODUCTION

Managers need information in order to introduce products and services that create value in the mind of the customer. But the perception of value is a subjective one, and what customers value this year may be quite different from what they value next year. As such, the attributes that create value cannot simply be deduced from common knowledge. Rather, data must be collected and analysed. The goal of marketing research is to provide the facts and direction that managers need to make their more important marketing decisions.

To maximize the benefit of marketing research, those who use it need to understand the research process and its limitations.

MARKETING RESEARCH

These terms often are used interchangeably, but technically there is a difference.

Market research deals specifically with the gathering of information about a market's size and trends. *Marketing research* covers a wider range of activities. While it may involve market research, marketing research is a more general systematic process that can be applied to a variety of marketing

PROBLEMS IN VALUE OF INFORMATION

Information can be useful, but what determines its real value to the organization?

In general, the value of information is determined by:

- The ability and willingness to performance on the information.
- The accuracy of the information.
- The level of indecisiveness that would exist without the information.
- The amount of variation in the possible results.
- The level of risk aversion.
- The reaction of competitors to any decision improved by the information.
- The cost of the information in terms of time and money.

IMPORTANCE OF MARKETING RESEARCH

Research, as a general concept, is the process of gathering information to learn about something that is not fully known. Nearly everyone engages in some form of research. From the highly trained geologist investigating newly discovered earthquake faults, to the author of best selling spy novels gaining insight into new surveillance techniques, to the model train hobbyist spending hours hunting down the manufacturer of an old electric engine, each is driven by the quest for information.

For marketers, research is not only used for the purpose of learning, it is also a critical component needed to make good decisions. Market research does this by giving marketers a picture of what is occurring (or likely to occur) and, when done well, offers alternative choices that can be made. For instance, good research may suggest multiple options for introducing new products or entering new markets. In most cases marketing decisions prove less risky (though they are never risk free) when the marketer can select from more than one option.

Using an analogy of a house foundation, marketing research can be viewed as the foundation of marketing. Just as a well-built house requires a strong foundation to remain sturdy, marketing decisions need the support of research in order to be viewed favorably by customers and to stand up to competition and other external pressures. Consequently, all areas of marketing and all marketing decisions should be supported with some level of research.

While research is key to marketing decision making, it does not always need to be elaborate to be effective. Sometimes small efforts, such as doing a quick search on the Internet, will provide the needed information. However, for most marketers there are times when more elaborate research work is needed and understanding the right way to conduct research, whether performing the work themselves or hiring someone else to handle it, can increase the effectiveness of these projects.

DOING RESEARCH RIGHT

Marketing research is a process that investigates both organizations and people. Of course, organizations are made up of people so when it comes down to it, marketing research is a branch of the social sciences. Social science studies people and their relationships and includes such areas as economics, sociology and psychology.

To gain understanding into their fields, researchers in the social sciences use scientific methods that have been tested and refined over hundreds of years. Many of these methods require the institution of tight controls on research projects. For instance, many companies survey (i.e., ask questions) a small percentage of their customers (called a sample) to see how satisfied they are with the company's efforts. For the information obtained from a small group of customers to be useful when evaluating how all customers feel, certain controls must be in place including controls on who should be included in the sample.

Thus, doing research right means the necessary controls are in place to insure it is done correctly and increase the chance the results are relevant. Relying on results of research conducted incorrectly to make decisions could prove problematic if not disastrous. Thousands of examples exist of firms using faulty research to make decisions, including many dot-com companies that failed between 1999 and 2002.

As one might expect, the trade-off for doing research right is the increase in cost and time needed to conduct the research. So a big decision for marketers, when it comes to doing research, is to determine the balance between the need for obtaining relevant information and the costs involved in carrying out the research.

RESEARCH VALIDITY AND RELIABILITY

As we discussed, not all research requires undertaking an elaborate study. But even marketers conducting small, informal research should know that any type of research performed poorly will not yield relevant results. In fact, all research, no matter how well controlled, carries the potential to be wrong. There are many reasons why research may not yield good results (a full discussion being beyond the scope of this tutorial), however, most errors can be traced to problems with how data is gathered. In particular, many research mistakes occur due to problems associated with research validity and research reliability.

Research Validity

This problem with data gathering represents several concepts that to the non-researcher may be quite complex. But basically validity boils down to whether the research is really measuring what it claims to be measuring. For instance, if a marketer is purchasing a research report from a company claiming to measure how people prefer the marketer's products over competitors' products, the marketer should understand how the data was gathered to help determine if the research really captures the information the way the research company says it does.

While research validity is measured in several ways, those evaluating research results should keep asking this simple question: Is the research measuring what it is supposed to measure? If the marketer has doubts about the answer to this question then it is possible the results should also be questioned.

Research Reliability

This problem relates to whether research results can be applied to a wider group than those who took part in a study. In other words, would similar results be obtained if another group containing different respondents or a different set of data points were used? For example, if 40 salespeople out of 2,000-person corporate sales force participate in a research study focusing on company policy, is the information obtained from these 40 people sufficient to conclude how the entire sales forces feels about company policies? What if the same study was done again with 40 different salespeople, would the responses be similar?

Reliability is chiefly concerned with making sure the method of data gathering leads to consistent results. For some types of research this can be measured by having different researchers follow the same methods to see if results can be duplicated. If results are similar then it is likely the method of data gathering is reliable. Assuring research can be replicated and can produce similar results is an important element of the scientific research method.

RISK IN MARKETING RESEARCH

The discussion above regarding doing research right shows that good marketing research, especially when it involves formal research projects, requires strict controls in order to produce relevant information. Being relevant means the probability is high that the research results reflect what is happening now or might happen in the future. But following the right procedures to produce a relevant study does not insure the results of research will be 100% correct as there is always the potential that results are wrong.

Because of the risks associated with research, marketers are cautioned not to use the results of marketing research as the only input in making marketing decisions. Rather, smart marketing decisions require considering many factors, including management's own judgment of what is best. But being cautious with how research is used should not diminish the need to conduct research. While making decisions without research input may work sometimes, long-term success is not likely to happen without regular efforts to collect information.

Additionally, risk in research extends to research produced by others. The research process often includes using information initially gathered by other sources, such as market research firms. However, in many instances the methods for collecting this information is not be fully disclosed, thus questions exist regarding research validity and reliability. Marketers using research collected by third-party sources should do so with a reasonable level of skepticism. In fact, it is wise for marketers to always make an effort to locate multiple information sources that address the same issue (e.g., two or more sales forecasts reports). A good rule-of-thumb for all marketers is never to rely on one source for making definitive statements about a market.

MARKETING RESEARCH PROCESS

Once the need for marketing research has been established, most marketing research projects involve these steps:

- Define the problem
- Determine research design

- Identify data types and sources
- Design data collection forms and questionnaires
- Determine sample plan and size
- Collect the data
- Analyse and interpret the data
- Prepare the research report

PROBLEM DEFINITION

The decision problem faced by management must be translated into a market research problem in the form of questions that define the information that is required to make the decision and how this information can be obtained. Thus, the decision problem is translated into a research problem. For example, a decision problem may be whether to launch a new product. The corresponding research problem might be to assess whether the market would accept the new product. The objective of the research should be defined clearly. To ensure that the true decision problem is addressed, it is useful for the researcher to outline possible scenarios of the research results and then for the decision maker to formulate plans of action under each scenario. The use of such scenarios can ensure that the purpose of the research is agreed uponbefore it commences.

RESEARCH DESIGN

Marketing research can classified in one of three categories:

- Exploratory research
- Descriptive research
- Causal research

These classifications are made just as to the objective of the research. In some cases the research will fall into one of these categories, but in other cases different phases of the same research project will fall into different categories.

- *Exploratory research:* Has the goal of formulating problems more precisely, clarifying concepts, gathering explanations, gaining insight, eliminating impractical ideas, and forming hypotheses. Exploratory research can be performed using a literature search, surveying certain people about their experiences, focus groups, and case studies. When surveying people, exploratory research studies would not try to acquire a representative sample, but rather, seek to interview those who are knowledgeable and who might be able to provide insight concerning the relationship among variables. Case studies can include contrasting situations or benchmarking against an organization known for its excellence. Exploratory research may develop hypotheses, but it does not seek to test them. Exploratory research is characterized by its flexibility.

- *Descriptive research:* Is more rigid than exploratory research and seeks to describe users of a product, determine the proportion of the population that uses a product, or predict future demand for a product. As opposed to exploratory research, descriptive research should define questions, people surveyed, and the method of analysis prior to beginning data collection. In other words, the who, what, where, when, why, and how aspects of the research should be defined. Such preparation allows one the opportunity to make any required changes before the costly process of data collection has begun.

  There are two basic types of descriptive research: Longitudinal studies and cross-sectional studies. Longitudinal studies are time series analyses that make repeated measurements of the same individuals, thus allowing one to monitor behaviour such as brand-switching. However, longitudinal studies are not necessarily representative since many people may refuse to participate because of the commitment required. Cross-sectional studies sample the population to make measurements at a specific point in time. A special type of cross-sectional analysis is a cohort analysis, which tracks an aggregate of individuals who experience the same event within the same time interval over time. Cohort analyses are useful for long-term forecasting of product demand.
- *Causal research:* Seeks to find cause and effect relationships between variables. It accomplishes this goal through laboratory and field experiments.

DATA TYPES AND SOURCES

Secondary Data

Before going through the time and expense of collecting primary data, one should check for secondary data that previously may have been collected for other purposes but that can be used in the immediate study. Secondary data may be internal to the firm, such as sales invoices and warranty cards, or may be external to the firm such as published data or commercially available data. The government census is a valuable source of secondary data. Secondary data has the advantage of saving time and reducing data gathering costs. The disadvantages are that the data may not fit the problem perfectly and that the accuracy may be more difficult to verify for secondary data than for primary data. Some secondary data is republished by organizations other than the original source. Because errors can occur and important explanations may be missing in republished data, one should obtain secondary data directly from its source. One also should consider who the source is and whether the results may be biased.

There are several criteria that one should use to evaluate secondary data:

- Whether the data is useful in the research study.
- How current the data is and whether it applies to time period of interest.
- Errors and accuracy - whether the data is dependable and can be verified.
- Presence of bias in the data.
- Specifications and methodologies used, including data collection method, response rate, quality and analysis of the data, sample size and sampling technique, and questionnaire design.
- Objective of the original data collection.
- Nature of the data, including definition of variables, units of measure, categories used, and relationships examined.

Primary Data

Often, secondary data must be supplemented by primary data originated specifically for the study at hand.

Some common types of primary data are:

- Demographic and socioeconomic characteristics
- Psychological and lifestyle characteristics
- Attitudes and opinions
- Awareness and knowledge - for example, brand awareness
- *Antentions*: For example, purchase intentions. While useful, intentions are not a reliable indication of actual future behaviour.
- *Motivation*: A person's motives are more stable than his/her behaviour, so motive is a better predictor of future behaviour than is past behaviour.
- Behaviour

Primary data can be obtained by communication or by observation. Communication involves questioning respondents either verbally or in writing. This method is versatile, since one needs only to ask for the information; however, the response may not be accurate.

Communication usually is quicker and cheaper than observation. Observation involves the recording of actions and is performed by either a person or some mechanical or electronic device. Observation is less versatile than communication since some attributes of a person may not be readily observable, such as attitudes, awareness, knowledge, intentions, and motivation.

Observation also might take longer since observers may have to wait for appropriate events to occur, though observation using scanner data might be quicker and more cost effective.

Observation typically is more accurate than communication. Personal interviews have an interviewer bias that mail-in questionnaires do not have.

For example, in a personal interview the respondent's perception of the interviewer may affect the responses.

QUESTIONNAIRE DESIGN

The questionnaire is an important tool for gathering primary data. Poorly constructed questions can result in large errors and invalidate the research data, so significant effort should be put into the questionnaire design. The questionnaire should be tested thoroughly prior to conducting the survey.

MEASUREMENT SCALES

Attributes can be measured on nominal, ordinal, interval, and ratio scales:

- Nominal numbers are simply identifiers, with the only permissible mathematical use being for counting. *Example*: social security numbers.
- Ordinal scales are used for ranking. The interval between the numbers conveys no meaning. Median and mode calculations can be performed on ordinal numbers.

  Example: class ranking
- Interval scales maintain an equal interval between numbers. These scales can be used for ranking and for measuring the interval between two numbers. Since the zero point is arbitrary, ratios cannot be taken between numbers on an interval scale; however, mean, median, and mode are all valid. *Example*: temperature scale
- Ratio scales are referenced to an absolute zero values, so ratios between numbers on the scale are meaningful. In addition to mean, median, and mode, geometric averages also are valid.

  Example: weight.

ROLE OF MARKETING RESEARCH

The task of marketing research (MR) is to provide management with relevant, accurate, reliable, valid, and current information. Competitive marketing environment and the ever-increasing costs attributed to poor decision making require that marketing research provide sound information. Sound decisions are not based on gut feeling, intuition, or even pure judgment.

Marketing managers make numerous strategic and tactical decisions in the process of identifying and satisfying customer needs. They make decisions about potential opportunities, target market selection, market segmentation, planning and implementing marketing programs, marketing performance, and control. These decisions are complicated by interactions between the controllable marketing variables of product, pricing, promotion, and distribution.

Further complications are added by uncontrollable environmental factors such as general economic conditions, technology, public policies and laws, political environment, competition, and social and cultural changes. Another factor in this mix is the complexity of consumers. Marketing research helps the marketing manager link the marketing variables with the environment and the consumers. It helps remove some of the uncertainty by providing relevant information about the marketing variables, environment, and consumers. In the absence of relevant information, consumers' response to marketing programs cannot be predicted reliably or accurately. Ongoing marketing research programs provide information on controllable and non-controllable factors and consumers; this information enhances the effectiveness of decisions made by marketing managers.

Traditionally, marketing researchers were responsible for providing the relevant information and marketing decisions were made by the managers. However, the roles are changing and marketing researchers are becoming more involved in decision making, whereas marketing managers are becoming more involved with research. The role of marketing research in managerial decision making is explained further using the framework of the "DECIDE" model:

The DECIDE model conceptualizes managerial decision making as a series of six steps. The decision process begins by precisely defining the problem or opportunity, along with the objectives and constraints.[5] Next, the possible decision factors that make up the alternative courses of action (controllable factors) and uncertainties (uncontrollable factors) are enumerated. Then, relevant information on the alternatives and possible outcomes is collected. The next step is to identify and select the best alternative based on chosen criteria or measures of success. Then a detailed plan to develop and implement the alternative selected is developed and put into effect. Last, the outcome of the decision and the decision process itself are evaluated.

CLASSIFICATION OF MARKETING RESEARCH

Organizations engage in marketing research for two reasons: (1) to identify and (2) solve marketing problems. This distinction serves as a basis for classifying marketing research into problem identification research and problem solving research.

Problem identification research is undertaken to help identify problems which are, perhaps, not apparent on the surface and yet exist or are likely to company image, market characteristics, sales analysis, short-range forecasting, long range forecasting, and business trends research. Research of this type provides information about the marketing environment and helps diagnose a problem.

For example, The findings of problem solving research are used in making decisions which will solve specific marketing problems.

The Stanford Research Institute, on the other hand, conducts an annual survey of consumers that is used to classify persons into homogeneous groups for segmentation purposes. The National Purchase Diary panel (NPD) maintains the largest diary panel in the United States.

Standardized services are research studies conducted for different client firms but in a standard way. For example, procedures for measuring advertising effectiveness have been standardized so that the results can be compared across studies and evaluative norms can be established. The Starch Readership Survey is the most widely used service for evaluating print advertisements; another well-known service is the Gallup and Robinson Magazine Impact Studies. These services are also sold on a syndicated basis.

- Customized services offer a wide variety of marketing research services customized to suit a client's specific needs. Each marketing research project is treated uniquely.
- Limited-service suppliers specialize in one or a few phases of the marketing research project. Services offered by such suppliers are classified as field services, coding and data entry, data analysis, analytical services, and branded products. Field services collect data through mail, personal, or telephone interviewing, and firms that specialize in interviewing are called field service organizations. These organizations may range from small proprietary organizations which operate locally to large multinational organizations with WATS line interviewing facilities. Some organizations maintain extensive interviewing facilities across the country for interviewing shoppers in malls.
- Coding and data entry services include editing completed questionnaires, developing a coding scheme, and transcribing the data on to diskettes or magnetic tapes for input into the computer. NRC Data Systems provides such services.
- Analytical services include designing and pretesting questionnaires, determining the best means of collecting data, designing sampling plans, and other aspects of the research design. Some complex marketing research projects require knowledge of sophisticated procedures, including specialized experimental designs, and analytical techniques such as conjoint analysis and multidimensional scaling. This kind of expertise can be obtained from firms and consultants specializing in analytical services.
- Data analysis services are offered by firms, also known as tab houses, that specialize in computer analysis of quantitative data such as those obtained in large surveys. Initially most data analysis firms supplied only tabulations (frequency counts) and cross tabulations (frequency counts that describe two or more variables simultaneously). With the proliferation of software, many firms now have the capability to analyze their own data, but, data analysis firms are still in demand.
- Branded marketing research products and services are specialized data collection and analysis procedures developed to address specific

types of marketing research problems. These procedures are patented, given brand names, and marketed like any other branded product.

VALIDITY AND RELIABILITY

The validity of a test is the extent to which differences in scores reflect differences in the measured characteristic. Predictive validity is a measure of the usefulness of a measuring instrument as a predictor.

Proof of predictive validity is determined by the correlation between results and actual behaviour. Construct validity is the extent to which a measuring instrument measures what it intends to measure.

Reliability is the extent to which a measurement is repeatable with the same results. A measurement may be reliable and not valid. However, if a measurement is valid, then it also is reliable and if it is not reliable, then it cannot be valid. One way to show reliability is to show stability by repeating the test with the same results.

ATTITUDE MEASUREMENT

Many of the questions in a marketing research survey are designed to measure attitudes. Attitudes are a person's general evaluation of something.

Customer attitude is an important factor for the following reasons:

- Attitude helps to explain how ready one is to do something.
- Attitudes do not change much over time.
- Attitudes produce consistency in behaviour.
- Attitudes can be related to preferences.

Attitudes can be measured using the following procedures:

- *Self-reporting*: Subjects are asked directly about their attitudes. Self-reporting is the most common technique used to measure attitude.
- *Observation of behaviour*: Assuming that one's behaviour is a result of one's attitudes, attitudes can be inferred by observing behaviour. For example, one's attitude about an issue can be inferred by whether he/she signs a petition related to it.
- *Indirect techniques*: Use unstructured stimuli such as word association tests.
- *Performance of objective tasks*: Assumes that one's performance depends on attitude. For example, the subject can be asked to memorize the arguments of both sides of an issue. He/she is more likely to do a better job on the arguments that favour his/her stance.
- *Physiological reactions*: Subject's response to a stimuli is measured using electronic or mechanical means. While the intensity can be measured, it is difficult to know if the attitude is positive or negative.
- *Multiple measures*: A mixture of techniques can be used to validate the findings, especially worthwhile when self-reporting is used.

There are several types of attitude rating scales:

- *Equal-appearing interval scaling*: A set of statements are assembled. These statements are selected just as to their position on an interval scale of favourableness. Statements are chosen that has a small degree of dispersion. Respondents then are asked to indicate with which statements they agree.
- *Likert method of summated ratings*: A statement is made and the respondents indicate their degree of agreement or disagreement on a five point scale.
- *Semantic differential scale*: A scale is constructed using phrases describing attributes of the product to anchor each end. For example, the left end may state, "Hours are inconvenient" and the right end may state, "Hours are convenient". The respondent then marks one of the seven blanks between the statements to indicate his/her opinion about the attribute.
- *Stapel Scale*: Similar to the semantic differential scale except that
  - Points on the scale are identified by numbers,
  - Only one statement is used and if the respondent disagrees a negative number should marked, and
  - There are 10 positions instead of seven.

  This scale does not require that bipolar adjectives be developed and it can be administered by telephone.
- *Q-sort technique*: The respondent if forced to construct a normal distribution by placing a specified number of cards in one of 11 stacks just as to how desirable he/she finds the characteristics written on the cards.

SAMPLING PLAN

The sampling frame is the pool from which the interviewees are chosen. The telephone book often is used as a sampling frame, but have some shortcomings. Telephone books exclude those households that do not have telephones and those households with unlisted numbers. Since a certain percentage of the numbers listed in a phone book are out of service, there are many people who have just moved who are not sampled. Such sampling biases can be overcome by using random digit dialing. Mall intercepts represent another sampling frame, though there are many people who do not shop at malls and those who shop more often will be over-represented unless their answers are weighted in inverse proportion to their frequency of mall shopping.

In designing the research study, one should consider the potential errors. Two sources of errors are random sampling error and non-sampling error. Sampling errors are those due to the fact that there is a non-zero confidence interval of the results because of the sample size being less than the population being studied. Non-sampling errors are those caused by faulty coding, untruthful responses, respondent fatigue, etc.

There is a tradeoff between sample size and cost. The larger the sample size, the smaller the sampling error but the higher the cost. After a certain point the smaller sampling error cannot be justified by the additional cost.

While a larger sample size may reduce sampling error, it actually may increase the total error. There are two reasons for this effect. First, a larger sample size may reduce the ability to follow up on non-responses. Second, even if there is a sufficient number of interviewers for follow-ups, a larger number of interviewers may result in a less uniform interview process.

TRENDS IN MARKETING RESEARCH

Marketing research, as a specialized field of activity, is relatively new. As recently as 1920, firms actively engaged in specific marketing research activities, carried on in a department created for such a purpose, were rare indeed. The Curtis Publishing Company and the General Motors Corporation are outstanding early examples. Even by 1940 it was still the rather exceptional company that recognized marketing research as a specific function. Early marketing research activity tended to be narrowly restricted, in line with common business attitudes about the then prevailing concept of the job of marketing—namely, to dispose of the output of field and factory through selling effort. Hence, pioneering marketing research activity, as carried on within business firms, tended to emphasize the collection of information about markets and about the selling function of marketing. Since about 1950, the number of companies with specialized marketing research departments has greatly increased. It is now common to find persons with the title Director of Marketing Research among medium sized and large manufacturing companies, public utilities, publishing companies, advertising agencies, wholesaling corporations, retailing chains, financial institutions, transportation companies, and many other kinds of enterprises.

Not only has the number of marketing research practitioners increased greatly, but also the scope of their interests and activities has enlarged and become diversified. Whereas early marketing research tended to be confined to market characteristics and to analyses of selling effort, it is now commonplace for it to deal with buying policies, merchandise handling, location of facilities, transportation costs and methods, inventory levels and controls, order processing methods, risk management, credit and financial management, product development and testing, and general marketing administration.

The widening and enlarging scope of marketing research activities reflects an increasing acceptance of a broad and customer-oriented conception of marketing, compared with earlier and rather provincial attitudes that tended to equate marketing with selling effort. As the conception of marketing by business leaders broadens to coincide with that held by academicians, the scope of marketing research in business will correspondingly expand.

The nature of contemporary marketing research activity has also been influenced considerably by various trends relating to approaches, techniques, methods, and sources. First, there has been growing awareness that every business firm generates a great deal of internal information that can be utilized in solving marketing problems. Second, external sources of published and readily available marketing information have multiplied manifold and have been characterized by substantial improvement in quality of data. It is no small task for a research practitioner merely to keep informed about such information. Third, many of the crude survey methods that were a common attribute of early marketing research have been supplanted by more advanced techniques borrowed from other areas in the social sciences. A fourth trend has been the greater use of mathematical models that involve sophisticated techniques of quantitative analysis and which require modern electronic data processing equipment to handle vast quantities of numerical information that could not practically be processed in any other way.

SOCIAL AND PUBLIC ASPECTS

While marketing research is commonly and properly regarded as one of the most significant marketing functions within progressive business firms, certain of its broader implications and applications must not be overlooked. First, as will be conspicuously evident, various governmental agencies are actively engaged in the marketing research function, as providers of a vast stream of highly valued marketing information which could never be collected and processed by any individual enterprise. Second, marketing research often provides the factual basis for certain types of public policy. Illustrative is information collected for the purpose of anticipating effects of proposed antitrust or trade regulation legislation.

Other examples include data gathered by public agencies in regard to credit controls, price controls in periods of emergency, agricultural production control or price support programmes, public aids to business recovery in periods of recession, and so on. Such activities are not confined to the federal government but are also common at the state and local levels, especially in connection with programmes to stimulate industrial development, modify taxation, regulate trade, or forecast revenues which may be dependent upon future market conditions. Third, activities of a marketing research nature are often carried on in connection with solving operating problems of public agencies. One example is extensive research conducted within the armed forces on the problem of logistics of supply, which is similar in many respects to the management of physical distribution functions in industry. Another example would be demand analysis for purposes of deciding upon the desirability of proposed price changes in certain state-owned liquor stores.

DATA COLLECTION

In addition to the intrinsic sampling error, the actual data collection process will introduce additional errors. These errors are called non-sampling errors. Some non-sampling errors may be intentional on the part of the interviewer, who may introduce a bias by leading the respondent to provide a certain response. The interviewer also may introduce unintentional errors, for example, due to not having a clear understanding of the interview process or due to fatigue.

Respondents also may introduce errors. A respondent may introduce intentional errors by lying or simply by not responding to a question. A respondent may introduce unintentional errors by not understanding the question, guessing, not paying close attention, and being fatigued or distracted.

Such non-sampling errors can be reduced through quality control techniques.

DATA ANALYSIS-PRELIMINARY STEPS

Before analysis can be performed, raw data must be transformed into the right format. First, it must be edited so that errors can be corrected or omitted. The data must then be coded; this procedure converts the edited raw data into numbers or symbols. A codebook is created to document how the data was coded. Finally, the data is tabulated to count the number of samples falling into various categories. Simple tabulations count the occurrences of each variable independently of the other variables.

Cross tabulations, also known as cross tabs, treats two or more variables simultaneously. However, since the variables are in a two-dimensional table, cross tabbing more than two variables is difficult to visualize since more than two dimensions would be required.

Cross tabulation can be performed for nominal and ordinal variables. Cross tabulation is the most commonly utilized data analysis method in marketing research. Many studies take the analysis no further than cross tabulation. This technique divides the sample into sub-groups to show how the dependent variable varies from one subgroup to another. A third variable can be introduced to uncover a relationship that initially was not evident.

CONJOINT ANALYSIS

The conjoint analysis is a powerful technique for determining consumer preferences for product attributes.

HYPOTHESIS TESTING

A basic fact about testing hypotheses is that a hypothesis may be rejected but that the hypothesis never can be unconditionally accepted until all possible evidence is evaluated. In the case of sampled data, the information set cannot be complete.

So if a test using such data does not reject a hypothesis, the conclusion is not necessarily that the hypothesis should be accepted. The null hypothesis in an experiment is the hypothesis that the independent variable has no effect on the dependent variable. The null hypothesis is expressed as H0. This hypothesis is assumed to be true unless proven otherwise. The alternative to the null hypothesis is the hypothesis that the independent variable does have an effect on the dependent variable. This hypothesis is known as the alternative, research, or experimental hypothesis and is expressed as H1. This alternative hypothesis states that the relationship observed between the variables cannot be explained by chance alone.

There are two types of errors in evaluating a hypotheses:

- *Type I error*: Occurs when one rejects the null hypothesis and accepts the alternative, when in fact the null hypothesis is true.
- *Type II error*: Occurs when one accepts the null hypothesis when in fact the null hypothesis is false.

Because their names are not very descriptive, these types of errors sometimes are confused. Some people jokingly define a Type III error to occur when one confuses Type I and Type II. To emphasise the difference, it is useful to consider a trial by jury in which the null hypothesis is that the defendant is innocent. If the jury convicts a truly innocent defendant, a Type I error has occurred. If, on the other hand, the jury declares a truly guilty defendant to be innocent, a Type II error has occurred.

Hypothesis testing involves the following steps:

- Formulate the null and alternative hypotheses.
- Choose the appropriate test.
- Choose a level of significance—determine the rejection region.
- Gather the data and calculate the test statistic.
- Determine the probability of the observed value of the test statistic under the null hypothesis given the sampling distribution that applies to the chosen test.
- Compare the value of the test statistic to the rejection threshold.
- Based on the comparison, reject or do not reject the null hypothesis.
- Make the marketing research conclusion.

In order to analyse whether research results are statistically significant or simply by chance, a test of statistical significance can be run.

TESTS OF STATISTICAL SIGNIFICANCE

The chi-square goodness-of-fit test is used to determine whether a set of proportions have specified numerical values. It often is used to analyse bivariate cross-tabulated data.

Some examples of situations that are well-suited for this test are:

- A manufacturer of packaged products test markets a new product and wants to know if sales of the new product will be in the same relative proportion of package sizes as sales of existing products.

- A company's sales revenue comes from Product A (50%), Product B (30%), and Product C (20%). The firm wants to know whether recent fluctuations in these proportions are random or whether they represent a real shift in sales.

ANOVA

Another test of significance is the Analysis of Variance (ANOVA) test. The primary purpose of ANOVA is to test for differences between multiple means. Whereas the t-test can be used to compare two means, ANOVA is needed to compare three or more means. If multiple t-tests were applied, the probability of a TYPE I error (rejecting a true null hypothesis) increases as the number of comparisons increases. One-way ANOVA examines whether multiple means differ. The test is called an F-test. ANOVA calculates the ratio of the variation between groups to the variation within groups (the F ratio). While ANOVA was designed for comparing several means, it also can be used to compare two means. Two-way ANOVA allows for a second independent variable and addresses interaction.

To run a one-way ANOVA, use the following steps:

- Identify the independent and dependent variables.
- Describe the variation by breaking it into three parts - the total variation, the portion that is within groups, and the portion that is between groups (or among groups for more than two groups). The total variation is the sum of the squares of the differences between each value and the grand mean of all the values in all the groups. The in-group variation is the sum of the squares of the differences in each element's value and the group mean. The variation between group means is the total variation minus the in-group variation.
- Measure the difference between each group's mean and the grand mean.
- Perform a significance test on the differences.
- Interpret the results.

This F-test assumes that the group variances are approximately equal and that the observations are independent. It also assumes normally distributed data; however, since this is a test on means the Central Limit Theorem holds as long as the sample size is not too small. ANOVA is efficient for analyzing data using relatively few observations and can be used with categorical variables. Note that regression can perform a similar analysis to that of ANOVA.

DISCRIMINANT ANALYSIS

Analysis of the difference in means between groups provides information about individual variables, it is not useful for determine their individual impacts when the variables are used in combination. Since some variables will not be independent from one another, one needs a test that can consider them simultaneously in order to take into account their interrelationship.

One such test is to construct a linear combination, essentially a weighted sum of the variables. To determine which variables discriminate between two or more naturally occurring groups, discriminant analysis is used. Discriminant analysis can determine which variables are the best predictors of group membership.

It determines which groups differ with respect to the mean of a variable, and then uses that variable to predict new cases of group membership. Essentially, the discriminant function problem is a one-way ANOVA problem in that one can determine whether multiple groups are significantly different from one another with respect to the mean of a particular variable.

A discriminant analysis consists of the following steps:

- Formulate the problem.
- Determine the discriminant function coefficients that result in the highest ratio of between-group variation to within-group variation.
- Test the significance of the discriminant function.
- Interpret the results.
- Determine the validity of the analysis.

Discriminant analysis analyses the dependency relationship, whereas factor analysis and cluster analysis address the interdependency among variables.

FACTOR ANALYSIS

Factor analysis is a very popular technique to analyse interdependence. Factor analysis studies the entire set of interrelationships without defining variables to be dependent or independent. Factor analysis combines variables to create a smaller set of factors. Mathematically, a factor is a linear combination of variables. A factor is not directly observable; it is inferred from the variables. The technique identifies underlying structure among the variables, reducing the number of variables to a more manageable set. Factor analysis groups variables just as to their correlation.

The factor loading can be defined as the correlations between the factors and their underlying variables. A factor loading matrix is a key output of the factor analysis. An example matrix is shown below.

	Factor 1	**Factor 2**	**Factor 3**
Variable 1			
Variable 2			
Variable 3			

Column's Sum of Squares: Each cell in the matrix represents correlation between the variable and the factor associated with that cell. The square of this correlation represents the proportion of the variation in the variable explained by the factor. The sum of the squares of the factor loadings in each column is called an eigenvalue. An eigenvalue represents the amount of variance in the original variables that is associated with that factor. The communality is the amount of the variable variance explained by common factors.

A rule of thumb for deciding on the number of factors is that each included factor must explain at least as much variance as does an average variable. In other words, only factors for which the eigenvalue is greater than one are used. Other criteria for determining the number of factors include the Scree plot criteria and the percentage of variance criteria. To facilitate interpretation, the axis can be rotated. Rotation of the axis is equivalent to forming linear combinations of the factors. A commonly used rotation strategy is the varimax rotation. Varimax attempts to force the column entries to be either close to zero or one.

CLUSTER ANALYSIS

Market segmentation usually is based not on one factor but on multiple factors. Initially, each variable represents its own cluster. The challenge is to find a way to combine variables so that relatively homogenous clusters can be formed. Such clusters should be internally homogenous and externally heterogeneous. Cluster analysis is one way to accomplish this goal. Rather than being a statistical test, it is more of a collection of algorithms for grouping objects, or in the case of marketing research, grouping people. Cluster analysis is useful in the exploratory phase of research when there are no a-priori hypotheses.

Cluster analysis steps:

- Formulate the problem, collecting data and choosing the variables to analyse.
- Choose a distance measure. The most common is the Euclidean distance. Other possibilities include the squared Euclidean distance, city-block distance, Chebychev distance, power distance, and per cent disagreement.
- Choose a clustering procedure.
- Determine the number of clusters. They should be well separated and ideally they should be distinct enough to give them descriptive names such as professionals, buffs, etc.
- Profile the clusters.
- Assess the validity of the clustering.

MARKETING RESEARCH REPORT

The format of the marketing research report varies with the needs of the organization.

The report often contains the following:

- Authorization letter for the research
- Table of Contents
- List of illustrations
- Executive summary
- Research objectives
- Methodology
- Results
- Limitations
- Conclusions and recommendations
- Appendices containing copies of the questionnaires, etc.

CONCLUDING THOUGHTS

Marketing research by itself does not arrive at marketing decisions, nor does it guarantee that the organization will be successful in marketing its products. However, when conducted in a systematic, analytical, and objective manner, marketing research can reduce the uncertainty in the decision-making process and increase the probability and magnitude of success.

TRENDS IN MARKETING RESEARCH

In recent years the evolution of marketing research has been dramatic with marketers getting access to a wide variety of tools and techniques to improve their hunt for information. Below we discuss a few important trends shaping the marketing research field.

Gaining an Information Advantage

In its role as the foundation of marketing, marketing research is arguably marketing's most important task. Today marketers not only view research as a key ingredient in making marketing decisions they also consider information to be a critical factor in gaining advantage over competitors. Because organizations recognize the power information has in helping create and maintain products that offer value, there is an insatiable appetite to gain even more insight into customers and markets. Marketers in nearly all industries are expected to direct more resources to gathering and analyzing information especially in highly competitive markets. Many of the trends discussed below are directly related to marketers' quest to acquire large amounts of customer, competitive and market information.

Internet Technologies

To address the need for more information, marketing companies are developing new methods for collecting data. This has led to the introduction of several new technologies to assist in the information gathering process.

Many of these developments are Internet-based technologies that include:

- *Enhanced Tracking*: The Internet offers an unparalleled ability to track and monitor customers. Each time a visitor accesses a website they provide marketers with extensive information including how they arrived at the website (e.g., via a search engine) and what they did when on the website (e.g., what products were investigated). In many ways the vast data available through Internet tracking has yet to be used by the majority of marketers. However, as tracking software becomes more sophisticated the use of tracking data will be a routinely used research tool.
- *Improved Communication*: Not only is the Internet enabling marketers to monitor customers' website activity, it also offers significant improvement in customer-to-company communication which is vital for marketing research. For instance, the ability to encourage customers to offer feedback on the company's products and service is easy using website popup notices and email reminders. The use of the Internet for conducting online focus group research is expanding.
- *Research Tools*: A large number of Internet services have added options for conducting research. These include the ubiquitous search engines, tools for conducting online surveys, and access to large databases containing previous research studies (i.e., secondary research).

Other Technologies

In addition to the Internet, marketing research has benefited from other technological improvements including:

- *Virtual Reality and Simulations*: Marketers can use computer developed virtual worlds to simulate real world customer activity such as store shopping. While this type of research is mostly performed in a controlled laboratory setting, there are emerging virtual worlds on the Internet where marketers can test concepts and communicate with customers.
- *Global Positioning Systems*: GPS enables marketers to track inventory and even track mobile sales and service personnel. Soon GPS will be a common feature of customers' communication devices, such as cell phones, offering marketers the potential to locate and track customers.
- *Data Analysis Software*: Research includes gathering information and it also involves analyzing what is collected. A number of software and statistical programs have been refined to give marketers greater insight into what the data really means.

Affordable Research

For many years formal research projects were considered something that only the largest marketers could afford due to the expense of carrying out relevant research. However, the technologies discussed above make it affordable for companies of all sizes to engage in research that were financially prohibitive just few years ago. For instance, surveying customers is quick and easy using one of the many online survey services which charge low fees to create, distribute and analyse results.

Merging of Data Sources

The wide range of technologies used to gather data has led to the creation of data centers where information is stored. Today many of these data centers are sharing information with other centers in a manner that offers the marketer a fuller picture of their customers.

Many companies have multiple contact points where customers can interact with the company (e.g., in-person, on the web, via phone call). In the past the information gathered at these points was often stored separately so if a customer contacted the company through one contact point they may not be recognized if they also contacted the company through a different point.

Companies now see the value in knowing what customers do across all contact points and work to integrate customer information. Additionally, some marketers are going outside their own data collection and seek information on their customers from other sources, such as information provided by credit card companies. This information is then merged with the company-owned information to get a fuller picture of customer activity.

Privacy Concerns

The continual demand for customer information, along with advances in technology and the merging of information sources, has lead marketing organizations to gather information in ways that raise concerns among privacy advocates. Many customers are unaware of the amount and nature of the data marketers collect. As new information gathering techniques and technologies emerge customer response to issues of privacy may determine whether these methods are feasible or forbidden.

Respondent Cooperation at Issue

The growing concern with privacy is leading many customers to limit their participation in a company's research activities. This includes customers choosing not to respond to company requests to take part in research studies that may come via telephone or email solicitation. Customers are also becoming more aware of how their Internet activities are tracked and are responding by using techniques to restrict marketers tracking efforts. For example, marketers can place small data files called cookies on customers' computer and then use this to track user activity. Many customers are learning to disable the cookies and, in doing so, limit the marketer's ability to track customer activity.

Research as a Promotional Tool

While most people do not equate marketing research with promotion, the fact is many companies are discovering research can also function as a major promotional tool. The practice of distributing company-produced research reports to potential customers and the news media has been used for a number of years in scientific and technology industries. In recent years the practice has expanded into many other fields, particularly among firms involved in consulting, healthcare and financial industries. Such reports often provide readers with information related to product features and benefits, comparisons with competitor's offerings and target market perceptions. These reports are produced using high quality graphs and charts backed up by carefully created narratives that proudly emphasize the company's strengths.

Unfortunately, many research reports produced for promotional reasons are not scientific and thus may not carry much value. While many companies claim the research supports their products, many of these claims may in fact be more fluff than substance since they are not grounded in good research methods.

7

Consumer Marketing and Behaviour

AN OVERVIEW

The study of consumers helps firms and organizations improve their marketing strategies by understanding issues such as how.

- The psychology of how consumers think, feel, reason, and select between different alternatives;
- The psychology of how the consumer is influenced by his or her environment;
- The behaviour of consumers while shopping or making other marketing decisions;
- Limitations in consumer knowledge or information processing abilities influence decisions and marketing outcome;
- How consumer motivation and decision strategies differ between products that differ in their level of importance or interest that they entail for the consumer; and
- How marketers can adapt and improve their marketing campaigns and marketing strategies to more effectively reach the consumer.

One "official" definition of consumer behaviour is "The study of individuals, groups, or organizations and the processes they use to select, secure, use, and dispose of products, services, experiences, or ideas to satisfy needs and the impacts that these processes have on the consumer and society."

Although it is not necessary to memorize this definition, it brings up some useful points:

- Behaviour occurs either for the individual, or in the context of a group or an organization.
- Consumer behaviour involves the use and disposal of products as well as the study of how they are purchased. Product use is often of great interest to the marketer, because this may influence how a product is best positioned or how we can encourage increased consumption. Since many environmental problems result from product disposal this is also an area of interest.

- Consumer behaviour involves services and ideas as well as tangible products.
- The impact of consumer behaviour on society is also of relevance. For example, aggressive marketing of high fat foods, or aggressive marketing of easy credit, may have serious repercussions for the national health and economy.

There are four main applications of consumer behaviour:

- The most obvious is for *marketing strategy*—i.e., for making better marketing campaigns. For example, by understanding that consumers are more receptive to food advertising when they are hungry, we learn to schedule snack advertisements late in the afternoon. By understanding that new products are usually initially adopted by a few consumers and only spread later, and then only gradually, to the rest of the population, we learn that
  - Companies that introduce new products must be well financed so that they can stay afloat until their products become a commercial success and
  - It is important to please initial customers, since they will in turn influence many subsequent customers' brand choices.
- A second application is *public policy*. In the 1980s, Accutane, a near miracle cure for acne, was introduced. Unfortunately, Accutane resulted in severe birth defects if taken by pregnant women. Although physicians were instructed to warn their female patients of this, a number still became pregnant while taking the drug. To get consumers' attention, the Federal Drug Administration took the step of requiring that very graphic pictures of deformed babies be shown on the medicine containers.
- *Social marketing* involves getting ideas across to consumers rather than selling something. Marty Fishbein went on sabbatical to work for the Centres for Disease Control trying to reduce the incidence of transmission of diseases through illegal drug use. The best solution, obviously, would be if we could get illegal drug users to stop. This, however, was deemed to be infeasible. It was also determined that the practice of sharing needles was too ingrained in the drug culture to be stopped. As a result, using knowledge of consumer attitudes, Dr. Fishbein created a campaign that encouraged the cleaning of needles in bleach before sharing them, a goal that was believed to be more realistic.
- As a final benefit, studying consumer behaviour should make us better consumers. Common sense suggests, for example, that if you buy a 64 liquid ounce bottle of laundry detergent, you should pay less per ounce than if you bought two 32 ounce bottles. In practice, however, you often pay a size *premium* by buying the larger

quantity. In other words, in this case, knowing this fact will sensitize you to the need to check the unit cost labels to determine if you are *really* getting a bargain.

There are several units in the market that can be analysed. Our main thrust in this course is the *consumer*. However, as suggested, also need to analyse our own firm's strengths and weaknesses and those of *competing firms*. Suppose, for example, that we make a product aimed at older consumers, a growing segment. A competing firm that targets babies, a shrinking market, is likely to consider repositioning toward our market. To assess a competing firm's potential threat, we need to examine its assets against pressures it faces from the market. Finally, we need to assess conditions. For example, although we may have developed a product that offers great appeal for consumers, a recession may cut demand dramatically.

CUSTOMER VALUE

As it is used in the business world, customer value is the amount of benefit that a customer will get from a service or product relative to its cost. Some businesspeople explain customer value as "realization" compared to "sacrifice." Realization is a formal term for what customers get out of their purchases. Sacrifice is what they pay for the product or service.

Businesses of all sizes use customer value as part of a greater analysis to determine how well they are supplying their customer base. Detailed research might include what customers generally do with the products they receive, or how they use services to increase the value of assets like real estate. Businesses also look at the prices of their products in order to price them competitively.

Businesses that identify the value of their wares to customers might go a step further and consider other similar ideas. In order to generate more thought about customer value, and to reach out to a customer base, a business might promote a customer value proposition. The customer value proposition is basically a promise of benefits from a vendor to customers.

We see examples of customer value propositions all the time in advertising. Companies pinpoint the benefits that they believe a customer will realise, and display them in advertising to attract more customers. The question is whether these propositions are made in good faith, or whether they may not be entirely true. When business leaders and others are talking about customer value, it is important that everyone at the table understands that customer value does not relate to the value of customers, but to the value that customers receive from the business. Those who are talking about how valuable customers are to a business might use terms like customer retention, or refer to the customer base as "valued customers," or VIPs. Since customer service is also a critical element for many businesses, it's possible that these two ideas might sometimes get confused.

Along with the basic idea of customer value, other terms help further define that value precisely. Relative performance identifies how the product or service gives customer value relative to what competitors offer. Access cost is something that business analysts add into the mix as an estimated cost of the effort involved in purchase. Value propositions often include these levels of detail to help leaders look at how well a business is serving its intended audience.

SATISFACTION

Customer satisfaction, a business term, is a measure of how products and services supplied by a company meet or surpass customer expectation. It is seen as a key performance indicator within business and is part of the four of a Balanced Scorecard. In a competitive marketplace where businesses compete for customers, customer satisfaction is seen as a key differentiator and increasingly has become a key element of business strategy. There is a substantial body of empirical literature that establishes the benefits of customer satisfaction for firms.

Measuring Customer Satisfaction

Organizations need to retain existing customers while targeting non-customers;. Measuring customer satisfaction provides an indication of how successful the organization is at providing products and/or services to the marketplace.

Customer satisfaction is an abstract concept and the actual manifestation of the state of satisfaction will vary from person to person and product/service to product/service. The state of satisfaction depends on a number of both psychological and physical variables which correlate with satisfaction behaviours such as return and recommend rate. The level of satisfaction can also vary depending on other factors the customer, such as other products against which the customer can compare the organization's products.

Work done by Parasuraman, Zeithaml and Berry between 1985 and 1988 delivered SERVQUAL which provides the basis for the measurement of customer satisfaction with a service by using the gap between the customer's expectation of performance and their perceived experience of performance. This provides the researcher with a satisfaction "gap" which is semi-quantitative in nature. Cronin and Taylor extended the disconfirmation theory by combining the "gap" described by Parasuraman, Zeithaml and Berry as two different measures into a single measurement of performance relative to expectation.

The usual measures of customer satisfaction involve a survey with a set of statements using a Likert Technique or scale. The customer is asked to evaluate each statement in terms of their perception and expectation of performance of the service being measured.

Improving Customer Satisfaction

Published standards exist to help organizations develop their current levels of customer satisfaction. The International Customer Service Institute has released The International Customer Service Standard. TICSS enables organizations to focus their attention on delivering excellence in the management of customer service, whilst at the same time providing recognition of success through a 3rd Party registration plan. TICSS focuses an organization's attention on delivering increased customer satisfaction by helping the organization through a Service Quality Model.

TICSS Service Quality Model uses the 5 P's - Policy, Processes, People, Premises, Product/Services, as well as performance measurement. The implementation of a customer service standard should lead to higher levels of customer satisfaction, which in turn influences customer retention and customer loyalty.

CONSUMER BUYING BEHAVIOUR

Possibly the most challenging concept in marketing deals with understanding why buyers do what they do (or don't do). But such knowledge is critical for marketers since having a strong understanding of buyer behaviour will help shed light on what is important to the customer and also suggest the important influences on customer decision-making. Using this information, marketers can create marketing programs that they believe will be of interest to customers.

As you might guess, factors affecting how customers make decisions are extremely complex. Buyer behaviour is deeply rooted in psychology with dashes of sociology thrown in just to make things more interesting. Since every person in the world is different, it is impossible to have simple rules that explain how buying decisions are made. But those who have spent many years analyzing customer activity have presented us with useful "guidelines" in how someone decides whether or not to make a purchase. In fact, pick up any textbook that examines customer behaviour and each seems to approach it from a different angle. The perspective we take is to touch on just the basic concepts that appear to be commonly accepted as influencing customer behaviour.

CONTINUOUS CONSUMER PANELS

The process of obtaining information about the behaviour of consumers throughout a prolonged time period involves a research approach known as the continuous consumer panel. This is different from making a number of surveys at intervals in the sense that a relatively static group of consumers provides information about their individual behaviour on a continuing, day-to-day basis. Consumer panels are used for a variety of purposes, including the testing of new products, measurement of broadcast media audiences, and determining purchase behaviour. The method of obtaining information is by a self-administering form which is usually referred to as a diary. Consumers daily record all purchases made by family members, often supplemented by information about price, place of purchase, and so on. Reports are sent periodically to the research organization, where specific items of information are transferred to tabulating cards for sorting and analysis. Consumers are usually compensated in cash or premium merchandise for their cooperation.

As compared with store audits, purchase panels provide a wider range of data, including characteristics of consumers making or not making purchases of certain types or specific brands of products. One of the main advantages is the ability to measure both gross and net changes in consumer purchases of a particular product during a time period. This can be illustrated as follows: During one six-month period, consumers purchased 1 million units of product X. Purchases in the next period dropped to 800,000 units, indicating a *net* change of 200,000 units. If 200,000 of the 800,000 units were purchased by people who did not make any purchases during the first period, the *gross* change would be 400,000 units. Since the research organization has complete information on the socioeconomic characteristics of all households in the sample, elaborate analyses can be made of purchase diary information in relation to such characteristics.

Warranty Card Analysis

Store audit and consumer panel procedures are widely used in the case of convenience goods but have not been widely applied to shopping or specialty goods where sales are much more infrequent at the retail level or involve significant seasonal variations. To determine the movement of such commodities to consumers, manufacturers of many forms of appliances make detailed statistical analyses of warranty cards. Such cards are usually given to the consumer at the time the product is delivered or installed, and must be filled out and mailed to the manufacturer in order to register the beginning of the warranty period. Customers must furnish their name and address, model and serial number of the unit, place of purchase, date of delivery or installation, and, often, other information of marketing significance.

In the Automatic Blanket and Fan Department of the General Electric Company, for example, about 1 million returned warranty cards are processed annually. A postal-size card is used, which is designed with holes around the edges that can be notched for machine sorting.

The card is so designed that the consumer can provide a variety of information merely by placing check-marks in boxes and by filling in certain data, such as name, address, and date and place of purchase. From the flow of these cards, the department can accurately estimate its sales at the retail level for current periods, determine the average store-shelf life of products, and ascertain other consumer information, such as sex of buyer, reason for purchase (own use, gift, etc.), and advertising media that prompted the sale.

By periodically checking the total production of a given model during a long time period, and later comparing this with the total number of warranty cards eventually returned, and how many at different intervals after purchase, the department establishes formulas which enable it to estimate sales on a current basis, depending upon the number of warranty cards returned during a given week or month. Through this type of analysis, the manufacturer knows the rate of consumer sales from week to week and can judge whether consumer sales are up to expectations and, consequently, whether to maintain production at expected levels or to increase or curtail manufacturing activity, revise prices, or enter into different types of promotional activity.

Obtaining Marketing Information from the Consumer

It often happens that the marketing information needed to solve a particular problem cannot be obtained from published sources, cannot be developed from analyses of a firm's internal records, and cannot be supplied by agencies in the channel of distribution. In such cases it is often necessary to resort to surveys of consumer opinion. Various applications of the findings of consumer research, in connection with the study of consumer motivation. Little attention was given, however, to the complexity of planning and administering a comprehensive consumer survey. An operational chart indicating the sequence of activities in a well planned consumer investigation is provided. Such an investigation begins with a statement of the marketing organization's problem, which may be of the form, "What can we do to increase the share of the market now enjoyed by our frozen orange juice?" Through discussions with the client, the research organization attempts to obtain pertinent data on the product, its position in the market, and the client's aims and philosophy of doing business. This is ordinarily supplemented by information from available research studies on related problems and a study of the position of competitive products in the markets. After a review of such information, research personnel develops ideas or hunches by observations of their own behaviour or attitudes in relation to the problem at hand, perhaps by inquiring why they do or do not like or use orange juice or the particular client's brand of orange juice. On the basis of such hunches, information is obtained about other people's behaviour or motivations. This may be done by conducting long and detailed interviews with a variety of consumers to ascertain their feelings, by using various kinds of direct or projective techniques developed in psychology or psychiatry to test consumer reactions to ideas relevant to the investigation, or by employing some form of statistically sound surveys to ascertain the relative significance of different buying motives. From the information gleaned from such preliminary study, the researchers can proceed to develop the experimental design for a complete investigation of the problem. This usually involves the formulation of some hypotheses, of the following illustrative character: "Consumers would like to buy frozen orange juice in larger cans." It is then necessary to determine just what types of analyses are required in order to confirm or refute such hypotheses, to determine interviewing and sampling procedures, and to formulate the pattern of tabulations for the data to be collected.

At this point, the research organization is ready to undertake a field survey. A questionnaire is developed and usually pretested on a small group of consumers to determine whether the wording is clear and whether the questions are understood by respondents as intended by the research objectives. Decisions must be made about the type of sample to be surveyed, including such matters as the number of respondents, kind of respondents (*e.g.*, only housewives), how the sample is to be distributed geographically, and when consumers are to be reached (season of year, day of week, time of day). Interviewers must then be obtained and instructed in their work. When the questionnaires are completed by the interviewing staff, they are edited for legibility and meaning and the responses are grouped into categories for coding and tabulation.

When tabulations are completed, researchers analyse the data to ascertain their meaning in relation to the hypotheses. After interpretation of the results, specific conclusions are formulated in terms of various courses of action that might be taken by the client. Recommendations are statements of the course of action that the research organization thinks the client should take and the results that are to be expected if such courses of action are followed. From the foregoing, it is apparent that consumer research is a complicated undertaking. It is not the mere collection and analysis of facts, but it involves also the attempt to predict the results of a recommended course of action.

TYPES OF CONSUMER PURCHASE DECISIONS

Consumers are faced with purchase decisions nearly every day. But not all decisions are treated the same. Some decisions are more complex than others and thus require more effort by the consumer. Other decisions are fairly routine and require little effort. In general, consumers face four types of purchase decisions:

- *Minor New Purchase*: These purchases represent something new to a consumer but in the customer's mind is not a very important purchase in terms of need, money or other reason (e.g., status within a group).
- *Minor Re-Purchase*: These are the most routine of all purchases and often the consumer returns to purchase the same product without giving much thought to other product options (i.e., consumer is brand loyalty).
- *Major New Purchase*: These purchases are the most difficult of all purchases because the product being purchased is important to the consumer but the consumer has little or no previous experience making these decisions. The consumer's lack of confidence in making this type of decision often (but not always) requires the consumer to engage in an extensive decision-making process..
- *Major Re-Purchase*: These purchase decisions are also important to the consumer but the consumer feels confident in making these decisions since they have previous experience purchasing the product.

For marketers it is important to understand how consumers treat the purchase decisions they face. If a company is targeting customers who feel a purchase decision is difficult (i.e., Major New Purchase), their marketing strategy may vary greatly from a company targeting customers who view the purchase decision as routine. In fact, the same company may face both situations at the same time; for some the product is new, while other customers see the purchase as routine. The implication of buying behaviour for marketers is that different buying situations require different marketing efforts.

WHY CONSUMERS BUY

Customers make purchases in order to satisfy needs. Some of these needs are basic and must be filled by everyone on the planet (e.g., food, shelter) while others are not required for basic survival and vary depending on the person. It probably makes more sense to classify needs that are not a necessity as wants or desires. In fact, in many countries where the standard of living is very high, a large portion of the population's income is spent on wants and desires rather than on basic needs. In this tutorial when we mention the consumer we are referring to the actual buyer, the person spending the money. But is should also be pointed out that the one who does the buying is not necessarily the user of what is bought and that others may be involved in the buying decision in addition to the actual buyer. While the purchasing process in the consumer market is not as complex as the business market, having multiple people involved in a purchase decision is not unusual. For example, in planning for a family vacation the mother may make the hotel reservations but others in the family may have input on the hotel choice. Similarly, a father may purchase snacks at the grocery store but his young child may be the one who selected it from the store shelf.

So understanding consumer purchase behaviour involves not only understanding how decisions are made but also understanding the dynamics that influence purchases.

WHAT INFLUENCES PURCHASING

As we discussed the decision-making process for consumers is anything but straight forward. There are many factors that can affect this process as a person works through the purchase decision. The number of potential influences on consumer behaviour is limitless. However, marketers are well served to understand the KEY influences. By doing so they may be in a position to tailor their marketing efforts to take advantage of these influences in a way that will satisfy the consumer and the marketer (remember this is a key part of the definition of marketing).

For the purposes of this tutorial we will break these influences down into three main categories: Internal, External and Marketing. However, those interested in learning more about customer buying activity may want to consult one or more consumer behaviour books where they will find additional methods for explaining consumer buying behaviour. For the most part the influences are not mutually exclusive. Instead, they are all interconnected and, as we will see, work together to form who we are and how we behave. For each of the influences that are discussed we will provide a basic description and also suggest its implication to marketers. Bear in mind we only provide a few marketing implications for each influence; clearly there are many more.

INTERNAL INFLUENCES

We start our examination of the influences on consumer purchase decisions by first looking inside ourselves to see which are the most important internal factors that affect how we make choices.

Perceptual Filter

Perception is how we see ourselves and the world we live in. However, what ends up being stored inside us doesn't always get there in a direct manner. Often our mental makeup results from information that has been consciously or subconsciously filtered as we experience it, a process we refer to as a perceptual filter. To us this is our reality, though it does not mean it is an accurate reflection on what is real. Thus, perception is the way we filter stimuli (e.g., someone talking to us, reading a newspaper story) and then make sense out of it.

Perception has several steps:

- *Exposure*: Sensing a stimuli (e.g. seeing an ad)
- *Attention*: An effort to recognize the nature of a stimuli (e.g. recognizing it is an ad)
- *Awareness*: Assigning meaning to a stimuli (e.g., humorous ad for particular product)
- *Retention*: Adding the meaning to one's internal makeup (i.e., product has fun ads)

How these steps are eventually carried out depends on a person's approach to learning. By learning we mean how someone changes what they know, which in turn may affect how they act. There are many theories of learning, a discussion of which is beyond the scope of this tutorial, however, suffice to say that people are likely to learn in different ways.

For instance, one person may be able to focus very strongly on a certain advertisement and be able to retain the information after being exposed only one time while another person may need to be exposed to the same advertisement many times before he/she even recognizes what it is.

Consumers are also more likely to retain information if a person has a strong interest in the stimuli. If a person is in need of new car they are more likely to pay attention to a new advertisement for a car while someone who does not need a car may need to see the advertisement many times before they recognize the brand of automobile.

Marketing Implications

Marketers spend large sums of money in an attempt to get customers to have a positive impression of their products. But clearly the existence of a perceptual filter suggests that getting to this stage is not easy. Exposing consumers to a product can be very challenging considering the amount of competing product messages (ads) that are also trying to accomplish the same objective (i.e., advertising clutter). So marketers must be creative and use various means to deliver their message. Once the message reaches consumer it must be interesting enough to capture their attention (e.g., talk about the product's benefits). But attending to the message is not enough. For marketers the most critical step is the one that occurs with awareness. Here marketers must continually monitor and respond if their message becomes distorted in ways that will negatively shape its meaning. This can often happen due in part to competitive activity (e.g., comparison advertisements). Finally, getting the consumer to give positive meaning to the message they have retained requires the marketer make sure that consumers accurately interpret the facts about the product.

Knowledge

Knowledge is the sum of all information known by a person. It is the facts of the world as he/she knows it and the depth of knowledge is a function of the breadth of worldly experiences and the strength of an individual's long-term memory. Obviously what exists as knowledge to an individual depends on how an individual's perceptual filter makes sense of the information it is exposed to.

Marketing Implications

Marketers may conduct research that will gauge consumers' level of knowledge regarding their product. As we will see below, it is likely that other factors influencing consumer behaviour are in large part shaped by what is known about a product. Thus, developing methods (e.g., incentives) to encourage consumers to accept more information (or correct information) may affect other influencing factors.

Attitude

In simple terms attitude refers to what a person feels or believes about something. Additionally, attitude may be reflected in how an individual acts based on his or her beliefs. Once formed, attitudes can be very difficult to change. Thus, if a consumer has a negative attitude toward a particular issue it will take considerable effort to change what they believe to be true.

Marketing Implications

Marketers facing consumers who have a negative attitude toward their product must work to identify the key issues shaping a consumer's attitude then adjust marketing decisions (e.g., advertising) in an effort to change the attitude. For companies competing against strong rivals to whom loyal consumers exhibit a positive attitude, an important strategy is to work to see why consumers feel positive toward the competitor and then try to meet or beat the competitor on these issues. Alternatively, a company can try to locate customers who feel negatively toward the competitor and then increase awareness among this group.

Personality

An individual's personality relates to perceived personal characteristics that are consistently exhibited, especially when one acts in the presence of others. In most, but not all, cases the behaviors one projects in a situation is similar to the behaviors a person exhibits in another situation. In this way personality is the sum of sensory experiences others get from experiencing a person (i.e., how one talks, reacts). While one's personality is often interpreted by those we interact with, the person has their own vision of their personality, called Self Concept, which may or may not be the same has how others view us.

Marketing Implications

For marketers it is important to know that consumers make purchase decisions to support their self concept. Using research techniques to identify how customers view themselves may give marketers insight into products and promotion options that are not readily apparent. For example, when examining consumers a marketer may initially build marketing strategy around more obvious clues to consumption behaviour, such as consumer's demographic indicators (e.g., age, occupation, income). However, in-depth research may yield information that shows consumers are purchasing products to fulfill self-concept objectives that have little to do with the demographic category they fall into (e.g., senior citizen may be making purchases that make them feel younger). Appealing to the consumer's self concept needs could expand the market to which the product is targeted.

Lifestyle

This influencing factor relates to the way we live through the activities we engage in and interests we express. In simple terms it is what we value out of life. Lifestyle is often determined by how we spend our time and money.

Marketing Implications

Products and services are purchased to support consumers' lifestyles. Marketers have worked hard researching how consumers in their target markets live their lives since this information is key to developing products, suggesting promotional strategies and even determining how best to distribute products. The fact that lifestyle is so directly tied to marketing activity will be further examined as we discuss developing target market strategies.

Roles

Roles represent the position we feel we hold or others feel we should hold when dealing in a group environment. These positions carry certain responsibilities yet it is important to understand that some of these responsibilities may, in fact, be perceived and not spelled out or even accepted by others. In support of their roles, consumers will make product choices that may vary depending on which role they are assuming. As illustration, a person who is responsible for selecting snack food for an office party his boss will attend may choose higher quality products than he would choose when selecting snacks for his family.

Marketing Implications

Advertisers often show how the benefits of their products aid consumers as they perform certain roles. Typically the underlying message of this promotional approach is to suggest that using the advertiser's product will help raise one's status in the eyes of others while using a competitor's product may have a negative effect on status.

Motivation

Motivation relates to our desire to achieve a certain outcome. Many internal factors we have already discussed can affect a customer's desire to achieve a certain outcome but there are others. For instance, when it comes to making purchase decisions customers' motivation could be affected by such issues as financial position (e.g., *Can I afford the purchase?*), time constraints (e.g., *Do I need to make the purchase quickly?*), overall value (e.g., *Am I getting my money's worth?*), and perceived risk (e.g., *What happens if I make a bad decision?*).

Marketing Implications

Motivation is also closely tied to the concept of Involvement, which relates to how much effort the consumer will exert in making a decision. Highly motivated consumers will want to get mentally and physically involved in the purchase process. Not all products have a high percentage of highly involved customers (e.g., milk) but marketers who market products and services that may lead to high level of consumer involvement should prepare options that will be attractive to this group. For instance, marketers should make it easy for consumers to learn about their product (e.g., information on website, free video preview) and, for some products, allow customers to experience the product (e.g., free trial) before committing to the purchase.

EXTERNAL INFLUENCES

Consumer purchasing decisions are often affected by factors that are outside of their control but have direct or indirect impact on how we live and what we consume.

Culture

Culture represents the behaviour, beliefs and, in many cases, the way we act learned by interacting or observing other members of society. In this way much of what we do is shared behaviour, passed along from one member of society to another. Yet culture is a broad concept that, while of interest to marketers, is not nearly as important as understanding what occurs within smaller groups or Sub-Cultures to which we may also belong. Sub-cultures also have shared values but this occurs within smaller groups. For instance, sub-cultures exist where groups share similar values in terms of ethnicity, religious beliefs, geographic location, special interests and many others.

Marketing Implications

As part of their efforts to convince customers to purchase their products, marketers often use cultural representations, especially in promotional appeals. The objective is to connect to consumers using cultural references that are easily understood and often embraced by the consumer. By doing so the marketer hopes the consumer feels more comfortable with or can relate better to the product since it corresponds with their cultural values. Additionally, smart marketers use strong research efforts in an attempt to identify differences in how sub-culture behaves. These efforts help pave the way for spotting trends within a sub-culture, which the marketer can capitalize on through new marketing tactics (e.g., new products, new sales channels, added value, etc.).

Other Group Membership

In addition to cultural influences, consumers belong to many other groups with which they share certain characteristics and which may influence purchase decisions. Often these groups contain Opinion Leaders or others who have major influence on what the customer purchases. Some of the basic groups we may belong to include:

- *Social Class*: Represents the social standing one has within a society based on such factors as income level, education, occupation
- *Family*: One's family situation can have a strong effect on how purchase decisions are made
- *Reference groups*: Most consumers simultaneously belong to many other groups with which they associate or, in some cases, feel the need to disassociate

Marketing Implications

Identifying and understanding the groups consumers belong to is a key strategy for marketers. Doing so helps identify target markets, develop new products, and create appealing marketing promotions to which consumers can relate. In particular, marketers seek to locate group leaders and others to whom members of the group look for advice or direction. These opinion leaders, if well respected by the group, can be used to gain insight into group behaviour and if these opinion leaders accept promotional opportunities could act as effective spokespeople for the marketer's products.

Purchase Situation

A purchase decision can be strongly affected by the situation in which people find themselves. In general, a situation is the circumstances a person faces when making a purchase decision, such as the nature of their physical environment, their emotional state, or time constraints. Not all situations are controllable, in which case a consumer may not follow their normal process for making a purchase decision. For instance, if a person needs a product quickly and a store does not carry the brand they normally purchase, the customer may choose a competitor's product.

Marketing Implications

Marketers can take advantage of decisions made in uncontrollable situations in at least two ways. First, marketers can use promotional methods to reinforce a specific selection of products when the consumer is confronted with a particular situation. For example, automotive services can be purchased that promise to service vehicles if the user runs into problems anywhere and at anytime.

Second, marketers can use marketing methods that attempt to convince consumers that a situation is less likely to occur if the marketer's product is used. This can also be seen with auto products, where marketers explain that using their product will prevent unexpected damage to their vehicles.

CONSUMER MARKET

The consumer market is composed of individuals who buy a specific good or service. Rarely does one product interest the entire population. This statement applies even to staples, such as sugar, flour, and salt. A small percentage of households do not eat these products, so even if a company did target the entire population, not everyone would be a potential consumer. The same statistical truth applies to cultural products. However, because of the extremely fragmented nature of the cultural sector, some distinctions are in order. For example, looking at this sector as a whole, it can be said that nearly 100% of the population consumes one type of cultural product or another. Indeed, in its broadest sense, the cultural sector encompasses everything from the performing arts to heritage, compact disks, movies, book and magazine publishing, and radio and television, with each of these disciplines appropriating a more or less important share of global demand.

In Canada, for example, statistics1 show that 37.0% of families attend a performing arts event at least once a year: movies 62.2%, museums and art galleries 32.9%. In the United States the figures for cultural consumption are: classical music 15.6%, opera 4.7%, musicals 24.5%, plays 15.8%, ballet 5.8%, art museums 34.5%, and historical parks 46.9%.2 In Australia3 the figures are: musical theatre 19.3%, classical music 7.7%, festivals 21.9%, concerts 23%, and museums 27.8%. Of course, within each of these sectors, consumers cluster just as to specific poles of interest.

This leads to sharper market segmentation. The consumer makes a discriminating choice among various cultural products to acquire or consume the type of product desired. The distribution of consumers just as to various market segments differs in both time and space. Markets undergo and reflect the influence of opinion leaders, trends, tastes, and societal characteristics.

Markets also vary from country to country just as to different social structures. Over the past 40 years, various surveys focusing on the sociodemographic profile of consumers of cultural products have been carried out in nearly every European country as well as in Canada, the United States, Australia, and Japan.4 It is fascinating to note that, regardless of whether the surveys were conducted in the 1970s, 1980s, or 1990s, they all obtained the same attendance rates and the same sociodemographic profiles.

Differences in the measuring tools used can sometimes make it difficult to compare countries; nonetheless, these studies have consistently and systematically revealed strong polarization of audiences between high art and popular culture across all countries over the past four decades. They show, for example, that cultural products catering to high art attract educated consumers, whereas those catering to popular culture draw on all segments of the population, in accordance with the relative weight of each.

The proportion of university graduates making up Canadian audiences, for example, ranges between 50% and 70% for high art, compared with 10% to 25% for popular culture. By way of comparison, the overall percentage of university graduates in Canada is 25%. Similar results have been found in other countries, most notably in France5 but also in Russia, where university graduates make up 50% of performing arts audiences but only 7% of the general population. Other sociodemographic variables are also linked to attendance, including average income and type of occupation. It should be pointed out once again that this profile is based on averages. Less-educated individuals with lower income may be great consumers of culture, as is the case for students and those specialized or working in the cultural milieu.

Indeed, it is well known that, as a rule many people active in the arts are highly educated yet so ill paid that they struggle to stay above the poverty line. On the other hand, there are people with both very high salaries and very high educational levels who are not interested in the arts and gladly keep their distance. Four factors are known to influence an individual's penchant for complex cultural products: family values that encourage or discourage high art; the educational milieu and the value it places on high art; the fact of having attended performances or visited museums as a child; and amateur art practice.

A more detailed analysis of the typical cultural consumer's traits reveals other nuances based on the different disciplines. For example, dance audiences are relatively younger and even more female in composition than those of the other performing arts; similarly, more women than men read novels, although a larger proportion of men read daily newspapers. In the film sector, there are two very different segments of avid cinema-goers; one of these segments is dominated by a young clientele, while the other is made up of educated people. The majority of consumers in the film sector belong to one or the other of these two segments.

CONSUMER BOYCOTTS AND CERTIFICATION SCHEMES

Consumer markets also offer opportunities to punish and/or reward corporate behavior. Product boycotts and product certification schemes represent contrasting mechanisms used by civil society groups, occasionally with governmental involvement or support, to influence MNE activities. Organized consumer boycotts usually target individual companies, either because the specific firm's actions are deemed particularly offensive or the company plays a prominent and influential role within an industry whose common practices generate opposition.

Boycott mechanisms do not work equally well in all situations. Boycotts enjoy greatest success when directed against recognizable consumer goods whose market position relies on brand-name image and reputation and where substitute products of satisfactory quality and price are readily available. In addition, the issue motivating the boycott must be conveyed in an easily understandable fashion that will evoke broad sympathy in the general consuming public. By contrast, companies that engage in minimal advertising and produce intermediate products for sale to other businesses are less vulnerable to a consumer boycott mechanism.

The use of consumer boycotts to protest MNE actions developed from the same general time period and set of issues that produced the capital market mechanisms. Anti-apartheid campaigns included product boycotts, including the adoption by many US state and city governments of selective procurement regulations that restricted purchases from companies maintaining investments in South Africa. The loss of large sales contracts to state and municipal agencies may have provided more measurable effective leverage against MNEs than stock divestment actions by activist pension funds. Another high-profile campaign urged a boycott of Nestlé's numerous consumer products to protest the corporation's methods of promoting its infant formula in developing counties.

Similar to shareholder activism, the potential effects of consumer boycotts often surpass the actual financial loss in terms of immediate sales. In order to reach the broad consuming public, boycott organizers generally seek maximum publicity and may organize demonstrations, marches or even engage in acts of civil disobedience to draw media attention to their cause. The short-term demand on management response time and potential for longer-term damage to a company's reputation can add significantly to overall boycott costs. Opponents often assert that boycott campaigns unfairly single out one or a small number of companies to protest actions undertaken by many enterprises, including MNEs in countries where comparable consumer actions seldom occur. Sometimes boycott targets show only minimal or distant causal connections to wrong actions. Similar to secondary rather than primary boycotts, the targeted firm or product may simply be used as a means to exert leverage on a different offending actor.

For example, in 1990 a civil society group called Neighbour to Neighbour helped organize a boycott action against Folger's coffee, sold by Procter & Gamble. In this case, the boycott campaign stemmed from opposition to human rights violations by right-wing death squads in El Salvador, allegedly connected with that country's government. Although less than 2 percent of the beans in Folger's coffee reportedly came from El Salvador, those purchases represented an important share of the country's coffee exports which in turn provided significant revenue to the government.

To help publicize their cause, the boycotting groups sponsored a dramatic television advertisement attacking Folger's and showing blood running from an overturned coffee cup. The advertisement was characterized by a P&G spokesperson as "inaccurate, grossly misleading and offensive." The company responded with its own type of boycott action, suspending advertising on some television stations that aired the anti-Folger's commercial. US government officials offered clear statements supporting P&G's coffee bean purchases, calling the actions "in the best interest of the peace process and the people of El Salvador." The case illustrates how boycotts, even when motivated by laudable objectives, may become ethically problematic as causal and capability connections grow more distant between a targeted product or company and the offending actor and actions. Another case of a successful boycott describes a campaign organized by the Rainforest Action Network (RAN) against Scott Paper, aimed at stopping Scott's plans to use a rain forest concession on the Indonesian island of Irian Jaya to develop a eucalyptus plantation and sawmill to supply pulp for its various paper products.

An observer reports that, despite corporate efforts to work with local representatives to limit the project's environmental and social impact, "RAN convinced environmental groups from all over the world to boycott Scott products if the company did not withdraw from Irian Jaya. The campaign focused on a single thing: Scott's name, the company's most valuable, and most vulnerable, asset." The company announced its withdrawal from the project just before the boycott began, prompting RAN to take out newspaper advertisements "declaring victory" and "hailing the power of consumer boycotts."

Without necessarily disputing the impact of the boycott mechanism, some critics subsequently questioned the substance of the victory as a state-owned forestry company replaced Scott in the project and, not subject to similar consumer pressures, reportedly engaged in broad deforestation actions. This case points up the challenge of projecting a boycott's effects which may depend on when outcomes are measured and whether or not potential impacts on other boycott actions are considered.

Product certification schemes also depend on consumer choice to provide leverage for influencing corporate behavior. Contrasted with boycott mechanisms, certification schemes focus less on penalizing bad corporate conduct to induce change and more on rewarding good corporate operations by giving their products a market advantage over uncertified competitors. To be credible, groups using this mechanism must demonstrate that consumers are sufficiently aware and concerned about an issue to affect their purchasing decisions. In addition, consumers need enough knowledge and understanding about the certification process to recognize and favour certified products. These requirements place a premium on media coverage and the development of alliances and support networks among sympathetic civil society groups, particularly in major consumer market economies.

No clear consensus exists regarding either the breadth or the depth of probable consumer response to product certification schemes. Certainly participation will vary depending on the nature of the issue, the location of the consumer market and the effectiveness of a particular campaign. Other important variables include the cost, quality and convenience differential in choosing certified over uncertified products.

Some polling data suggests that a core of committed individuals will act on certification criteria while a larger portion of the general public is open to considering corporate actions and reputation in their purchasing decisions. For example, a Mori survey in Great Britain defined 15 percent of the population as corporate responsibility activists, reporting that ethical considerations led 17 percent of adults to boycott a product and 14 percent to purchase a company's product during 2003. The survey also reported that 38 percent of the public stated corporate social responsibility was very important in making their purchases. The head of Mori's CSR research speculated that more individuals from this broader group might follow through with concrete actions if provided with more effective information.

The proliferation of product certification schemes touches many of the issues. A broad government-backed mechanism emerged to certify that international trade would be free of "conflict diamonds" associated with human rights violations in Africa. Exports of soccer balls and rugs from South Asia feature certification processes to assure the goods were not produced using child labour. "Green" labels tout the environment-friendly record of many products, from recycled paper or plastic products to energy-saving devices to "dolphin-safe" tuna. Remarkable variety exists in the types of issues addressed and certification measures employed. The constellation of certifying and supporting organizations can also mix public agencies, business organizations and civil society groups. Fair Trade initiatives represent a particular application of product certification schemes, usually but not exclusively applied to products based on agricultural commodities. The basic concept seeks to establish a dependable, long-term relationship with commodity growers in developing countries, offering them a higher price for their products by eliminating middlemen traders.

Many schemes also provide an additional premium to growers for using environmentally friendly methods and/or for community social development projects. The general approach reportedly stems from efforts begun in 1986 by the Max Havelaar Foundation in the Netherlands to respond to desires for development projects that emphasize trade rather than aid. Starting with coffee and expanding to honey, bananas, tea and orange juice, the Foundation supported Fair Trade products sold primarily in Europe.

During the 1990s fourteen other Fair Trade organizations were established, reaching over $200 million in sales by the end of the decade, still largely concentrated in European markets. Some approaches expect consumers to pay a somewhat higher price for certified Fair Trade products while other efforts try to remain price-competitive, using cost savings in the distribution chain to redistribute profits towards developing country growers. An important extension of the Fair Trade mechanism to the US market occurred in 2000 when Starbucks announced the introduction of a blend of Fair Trade coffee certified by the non-profit TransFair organization that encourages farmer co-operatives in developing countries to sell direct to coffee roasters or retailers. The breakthrough with Starbucks came after some of its coffee houses were vandalized during anti-globalization protests at a World Trade Organization meeting hosted in the company's hometown of Seattle, Washington. This initiative complemented Starbucks' broader social responsibility programmes and helped expand Fair Trade coverage in the United States beyond craft shops and a few grocery stores. Subsequent discussions between Starbucks and Oxfam also led to cooperation on a project to aid coffee growers in poverty-stricken areas of Ethiopia. The Rainforest Alliance, which promotes another certification scheme covering several products, has forged agreements with major coffee MNEs that could broaden the Fair Trade mechanism beyond the market for specialty coffees that represents only about 2 percent of supply.

CUSTOMER MANAGEMENT SYSTEMS

Companies need a method for viewing all customer and marketing-related information in an integrated way. Often marketing organizations maintain multiple databases for each business and marketing activity with data that is not easily integrated for strategic or operational purposes. A new generation of software that is Internet based gathers information from customer service, Web sites, direct mail operations, telemarketing, field sales, customer service, distributors, retailers and suppliers for the purpose of managing marketing, sales and customer service activities.

The major applications families are commonly referred to as sales force automation (SFA) and customer relationship management (CRM) systems.

Some CRM systems are fully integrated with SFA applications and some are standalone. The worldwide market for such systems is projected to grow five times faster than the overall software market, from $5 billion in 1999 to more than $22 billion in 2003.

Sales Force Automation

SFA is a customer management tool that is one of the fastest growing elements of the MkIS. SFA applications are often integrated with the CRM system. SFA involves the application of information technology to the sales function or, more appropriately, to the activities leading to a sale. These activities include acquiring sales leads, managing the sales opportunity, closing the sale and managing the customer relationship. The historic role of personal selling has been to move the product—to generate transactions.

As selling has become increasingly more professional, sales people emphasize building relationships with customers that will generate loyalty-based repeat transactions over time. Relationship building often necessitates that the sales person has consultative and advisory skills in addition to product knowledge and sales abilities. Team-based selling places emphasis on role specialization, collaboration and coordination. Customers have become more sophisticated as well.

Requirements for customised solutions, rapid response times and the need for concurrent and post-sale service have greatly increased the need for information technology in the sales process. The goals of SFA are to increase the effectiveness of the sales organization, improve its efficiency and to create superior value for the customer. Sales effectiveness focuses on getting the sale by improving lead generation, qualifying prospects, coordinating sales efforts, and tracking commitments.

Effectiveness is a function of improving the sales process. Sales efficiency is evaluated by measuring the return on sales efforts. SFA can improve sales efficiency by reducing sales cycle time, by managing workflow, and tracking the current status of critical activities related to the sale.

Proposal generation, opportunity management, fulfillment, and follow up are facilitated by SFA. Superior customer value is achieved when the customer expectations are exceeded. It is a primary determinant of customer satisfaction. SFA enables better understanding of customer expectations and management of the customer account.

The Sales Process

The typical field sales process consists of a series of steps that are designed to lead to a sale. The typical role of the MkIS is to support the sales process steps of lead generation, sales process management, and account management.

- *Lead generation*: Leads represent potential customers. The identification of a lead is the beginning of the sales cycle. After leads are identified, they must be qualified. This process involves gathering information about the lead and comparing the result against qualifying criteria. The lead generation process is becoming more automated with regard to obtaining more pre-qualifying information directly from the lead and augmenting it from commercial and other databases such as credit bureaus. The advent of Web-based technologies is driving this trend. Qualified leads are then distributed to the sales force.
- *Sales Process Management*: This process starts when the sales person receives the lead information. The primary information system need is for a convenient method to track the process and store data the data generated at each stage. There are a number of sub-steps to this stage of the process.
  - *Verification of the opportunity*: The sales person usually contacts the lead and attempts to verify the existence and nature of an opportunity including its size, timing, and appropriateness of the products and services of the selling company. Sales people will also desire to verify the lead's ability to purchase, identify the names of key decision-makers and influencers, and the level of budget authority. This information is entered into the sales database.
  - *The Sales Call*: If the lead is amenable and the opportunity justifies it, a sales call is scheduled. Information may be sent to the prospect and a custom presentation may be created. The SFA system is used to provide a single point of interface for the sales person to coordinate the activities leading up to the sales call. After the call, the SFA system is updated with customer requirements, new information and commitments made by the sales person.
  - *Opportunity Management*: If the sales person is successful, the next step is typically the receipt of a request for proposal

(RFP) from the prospective customer. The RFP will generally state the customer's requirements and the date for the final submission. Follow-on visits may be necessary to clear up or identify new requirements. The prospect may want to visit the seller's manufacturing site. The final product of this stage is the creation of a proposal and price quote to be presented to the prospect. This document should build a sound economic case for the purchase. All these interactions, requirements, commitments, and competitor information are tracked by the SFA system that provides the database, tools and templates to generate the proposal.

 - *Closing the Sale*: The presentation of the proposal and the price quote is the start of the closing process. Even if the sales person has done a good job of presenting the business case, further negotiations may be necessary to close the sale. If all objections are met and the proposal is accepted the close is successful. If not, the sales team will need to debrief the sessions learned to determine why the proposal was not accepted. The outcomes are recorded in the SFA system.

- *Account Management*: The automation of the sales process may result in a standalone system that is not integrated with other management systems. However, SFA is increasingly being integrated with the overall CRM system. This is especially true of the account management function. Since the primary goal of the CRM system is to manage the customer relationship in order to generate repeat sales, a good sales person will want to keep track of the status of a new account and how well the customer is being served. This is especially true if the account is to become "referenceable" to other prospects. The account management function of the CRM system enables the sales person to track order entry, order processing, shipment, and installation. The sales person may need to ensure that post-sales service is delivered or monitor the results of and installation and track the customer's satisfaction. The ability to track outcomes and interact with the customer in order to reassess needs and create new opportunities is a major benefit that flows from effective account management.

Sales Force Automation Tools

SFA tools consist of software applications that enable the salesperson to better target sales opportunities and manage the sales cycle. The tools are increasingly available bundled as integrated suites that are Internet enabled, accessible through a browser and linked to the CRM system.

The software applications may be categorized as:

- *Document management tools*: These tools support all stages of the sales process. They include word processors, graphics programmes, spreadsheets, e-mail, expense reports, proposal generators, and "product configurators." A Web-accessible sales library or encyclopedia of previously developed product information, brochures, product demonstrations, presentations, financial information, price lists, white documents, and public relations materials is a key resource for sales force productivity.
- *Personal management tools*: These tools focus on increasing the efficiency and effectiveness of the sales teams efforts. They typically include calendar and scheduling programmes, contact management systems, and call reporting capabilities.
- *Process management tools:* These tools are used to keep track of customer requirements and sales commitments. They include opportunity management systems, project management systems, account management systems, order-entry systems, telemarketing systems, team-selling systems.

Increasingly, with the rise of Web-based hosting and the application service provider (ASP) industry, SFA applications and databases are being hosted by third-party specialists and accessed remotely on the Internet. With the ASP model, client companies are essentially outsourcing all or part of there IS function. Remote hosting raises issues of security and scalability. The advantages of an ASP approach are its browser-based simplicity, rapid implementation, and lower cost of deployment. Most ASP applications use a subscription-based pricing model. Some vendors are proposing that renting the application or paying by the transaction may become the pricing model of the future.

Customer Relationship Management

The Internet has facilitated a fundamental shift in market power from sellers to buyers. Customers, newly endowed with the power of market information, have much different expectations than before. Customers can easily move their business to another vendor with the click of a mouse. They have access to the same cost data as their suppliers and they demand 24x7 customer service.

Customers now have almost unlimited ability for interactions with organizations through the Web in addition to the traditional phone and mail methods. Company web sites facilitate information search, shopping and customer support. E-mail communication can target specific offers on a one-to-one basis. Understanding and meeting demanding expectations has placed a renewed emphasis on managing customer relationships. The primary goal of CRM systems is to increase the return on marketing expenditures by enabling the understanding of the complete history of a firm's interactions with its customers.

CRM applications can deliver targeted solutions that promote customer loyalty as measured by increased response to promotions, purchase frequencies and volume, and minimizes the time between orders. CRM systems are able to target marketing communications to likely buyers, facilitate sales efforts and deliver customer service. CRM systems increase revenue, lower costs and optimize customer lifetime value.

Customer Relationship Management Design Principles

The CRM field is rapidly evolving into an integrated discipline that manages all of a company's touches with the customer.

Accordingly, several design principles have evolved as the foundation for CRM development:

- The CRM system should offer the customer multiple channels for communication such as the telephone, e-mail, fax, on-line or some combination. Each channel should lead to an interaction that satisfies customer expectations. Customers must be able to choose the method that best meets their needs on each occasion.
- Each CRM interaction should deliver value to the customer. The CRM system must be able to determine what value is required and deliver it quickly whether it is a product or service transaction or a customer service request.
- The CRM system integrates the customer throughout the firm's value chain. Customers should be able to reach into all necessary functions of the organization not just to the sales organization, or customer service, but to manufacturing and even the CEO. Better integration of the customer into the process can lead to higher levels of trust, loyalty and repeat purchases. The cost of acquiring a new customer often far exceeds that of retaining existing ones.
- Knowledge is captured during each CRM interaction. The CRM system should capture knowledge about the customer and the customer's relationship with the company over time. Sales and customer support histories should be analysed for indications of how well the vendor is doing in meeting customers' needs and how valuable the customer is to the marketer.

Customer Relationship Management Functions

CRM applications provide the customer-related information that is necessary to drive a firm's ebusiness activities. Better customer information enables more effective demand forecasting, product launches and marketing campaigns. CRM functions are sometimes referred to as the company's "front office."

CRM functionality includes:

- E-commerce support
- Sales force automation
- Telesales and call centre automation
- Direct mail and catalog sales
- E-mail and e-newsletter response
- Web sales and personalization
- Analysis of Web generated data
- Traditional customer support and service
- On-line support and customer service
- Mobile support through laptops, handheld devices.
- Training

Modern CRM systems are fully integrated with the "back office" elements of the enterprise resource planning (ERP) system such as accounting, manufacturing, project management, and human resources. This integration enables the sharing of customer information that can impact the operations of the enterprise and vice versa. Common customer definitions, price lists, employee definitions, service requests, call histories, order histories, contracts, service level agreements are accessible by all who need them. Correspondingly, marketing can access information on items such as new product development, product costs, order status, delivery dates and backorders.

TYPES OF BUSINESS PURCHASE DECISIONS

While it would appear business customers face the same four purchase situations faced by consumers (Minor New Purchase, Minor Re-Purchase, Major New Purchase, Major Re-Purchase), the nature of the business market noted above has led many marketing academics to group business purchase situations into only three categories. The reason is that the idea of a minor order may not hold as well in the business market, where buyers tend to place larger orders and where suppliers' marketing efforts are directed toward the most profitable buyers.

- *Straight Re-Purchase*: These purchase situations involve routine ordering. In most cases buyers simply reorder the same products or services that were previously purchased. In fact, many larger companies have programmed re-purchases into an automated ordering system that initiates electronic orders when inventory falls below a certain pre-determined level. For the supplier benefiting from the re-purchase this situation is ideal since the purchaser is not looking to evaluate other products. For competitors who are not getting the order it may require extensive marketing efforts to persuade the buyer to consider other product or service options.

- *Modified Re-Purchase*: These purchases occur when products or services previously considered a straight re-purchase are for some reason now under a re-evaluation process. There are many reasons why a product is moved to the status of a modified re-purchase. Some of these reasons include: end of purchase contract period, change in who is involved in making the purchase, supplier is removed from an approved suppliers list, mandate from top level of organization to re-evaluate all purchasing, or strong marketing effort by competitors. In this circumstance the incumbent supplier faces the same challenges they may have faced when they initially convinced the buyer to make the purchase. For competitors the door is now open and they must work hard to make sure their message is heard by those in charge of the purchase decision.
- *New Task Purchase*: As the name suggests, these purchases are ones the buyer has never or rarely made before. In some ways new task purchases can be considered as either minor or major depending on the total cost or overall importance of the purchase. In either case the buyer will spend considerably more time evaluating alternatives. For example, if faced with a major new task purchase, which often involves complex items, such as computer systems, buildings, robotic assembly lines, etc., the purchase cycle from first recognizing the need to placement of the order may be months or even years. The business market we now look at how purchasing decisions are made. Business purchasing follows the same five-step buying process faced by consumers:
  - Need Recognition
  - Search:
  - Evaluate Options
  - Purchase
  - After-Purchase Evaluation.

While the steps are the same as consumer purchasing, the activities occurring within each step are quite different as we discuss below.

NEED RECOGNITION

In a business environment needs arise from just about anywhere within the organization. The Buying Centre concept shows that Initiators are the first organizational members to recognize a need. In most situations the Initiator is also the User or Buyer. Users are inclined to identify the need for new solutions (i.e., new products) while Buyers are more likely to identify the need to re-purchase products.

But marketers should also understand that more companies are replacing human involvement in re-purchase decisions with automated methods, thus making it more challenging for competitors to replace currently purchased products. In straight re-purchase situations, whether there is human intervention or not, the purchasing process often jumps from Need Recognition to Purchase and little search activity is performed. As part of this step, a specifications document may be generated that lays out the requirements of the product or service to be purchased. Several members of the Buying Centre may be involved in creation of the specifications. For the marketer, establishing close contact with those who draw up the specifications may help position the marketer's product for inclusion in the search phase.

SEARCH

The search for alternatives to consider as potential solutions to recognized needs is one of the most significant differences between consumer and business purchasing. Much of this has to do with an organization's motive to reduce costs. While a consumer will probably not search hard to save two cents a gallon on gas, a company that has a large fleet of cars or trucks certainly will. In fact, this step in the purchase process is where professional buyers make their mark.

The primary intention of their search efforts is to identify multiple suppliers who meet product specifications and then, through a screening process, offer a selected group the opportunity to present their products to members of the Buying Centre. Although in some industries, such as chemicals, online marketplaces and auction sites offer buyers another option for selecting suppliers that may not include supplier presentations. For suppliers, the key to this step of the purchase process is to make sure they are included within the search activities of the Buyer or others in the Buying Centre. In some instances this may require that a supplier work to be included within an approved suppliers list. In the case of online marketplaces and auction sites, suppliers should work to be included within relevant sites.

EVALUATE OPTION

Once the search has produced options, members of the Buying Centre may then choose among the alternatives. In more advanced purchase situations, members of the Buying Centre may evaluate each option using a checklist of features and benefits sought by the buyer. Each feature/benefit is assigned a weight that corresponds to its importance to the purchase decision. In many cases, especially when dealing with Government and Not-For-Profit markets, suppliers must submit bids with the lowest bidder often being awarded the order, assuming products or services meet specifications.

PURCHASE

To actually place the order may require the completion of paperwork (or electronic documents) such as a purchase order. Acquiring the necessary approvals can delay the order for an extended period of time. And for very large purchases, such as buildings or large equipment, financing options may need to be explored.

AFTER-PURCHASE EVALUATION

After the order is received the purchasing company may spend time reviewing the results of the purchase. This may involve the Buyer discussing product performance issues with Users. If the product is well received it may end up moving to a straight re-purchase status thus eliminating much of the evaluation process on future purchases.

MEANING AND CONCEPT OF CONSUMER BEHAVIOUR

Through the application of sociology, psychology and demographics, marketers can begin to understand why consumers form attitudes and make decisions to purchase. Consumer-behaviour studies inform marketers, advertisers and public agencies how product and service selection is influenced by personality, perception, values and beliefs. For marketing, these influences are studied in the context of demographics, which includes ethnicity, age, marital status, size of family, income, education and employment.

PERCEPTION

Perception is how information is collected and categorized. Perception is affected by the amount of exposure to a stimulus and by individual interpretation. For example, a consumer who hears—once—that dairy herds contribute to greenhouse gas would not take the statement seriously. If the same consumer encountered that information often and from many sources, then the consumer's attitude towards dairy products might change enough to influence how often the consumer chose yogurt as a breakfast food.

PERSONALITY

Personality is a weak component of consumer behaviour. Personality means a pattern of behaviour founded on an individual's outlook and internal traits. In this use, outlook means point-of-view and traits mean the consumer's usual manner of responding to the environment. An example of outlook is the effect of a recessionary economy on consumer confidence. Examples of traits are introversion or extroversion, ambition or complacency, aggressiveness or timidity and compulsiveness or pragmatism. A consumer whose decision to purchase is influenced by extroversion or compulsiveness, might choose to be less innovative during an economic downturn because confidence is lower.

VALUES

Values are the consumer's set of standards about conduct that arise from learned culture. A "terminal value" is a long-term goal or role model, as when a consumer strives for a particular lifestyle, such as healthful diet and exercise. An "instrumental" value is a flexible and negotiable action that is exercised daily, such as when a consumer makes a decision to purchase either organic or nonorganic products.

BELIEFS

In consumer behaviour study, "beliefs" are specific beliefs about products in the marketplace. Consumer belief is a combination of knowledge, emotions and actual actions to purchase or not purchase. For example, if a consumer has a negative or prejudiced set of beliefs about Yugoslavia, then marketing an automobile manufactured in Yugoslavia would have to focus on changing those beliefs.

ATTITUDE

Consumer attitude is a combination of perceptions, values and beliefs. The consumer must first perceive the product and then focus values and beliefs onto the product and make a decision to purchase or not to purchase.

Beliefs are more vulnerable to marketing than values are, because beliefs are subject to knowledge and emotion. For example, positive facts can inform a consumer's knowledge about automobile manufacturing in Yugoslavia. A marketer might decide what demographic group can best afford a Yugoslavian automobile and then generate positive emotion by associating the automobile with music towards which that demographic group feels positive.

BUSINESS VS CONSUMER MARKETS

For marketers, the selling environment of business markets present uniquely different circumstances when compared to selling to consumers.

At the beginning of this tutorial we saw two ways in which consumer and business markets differ:

- Business markets are more likely to be price driven than brand driven, and
- Demand in business markets tends to be more volatile than consumer markets.

However, the two markets are dissimilar in other ways requiring marketers to take a different approach when selling to business customers than to consumers.

These differences include:

- How Decisions Are Made
- Existence of Experienced Purchasers
- Time Needed to Make Buying Decision
- Size of Purchases
- Number of Buyers
- Type of Promotional Effort Needed to Reach Buyer

BUYING DIFFERENCES

Buying Centre Decisions

In the consumer market a very large percentage of purchase decisions are made by a single person. As we discussed in the Consumer Buying Behaviour tutorial, there are situations in which multiple people may be involved in a consumer purchase decision, such as a child influencing a parent to choose a certain brand of cereal or a husband and wife deciding together to buy a house, but most of the time purchases are individual decisions. The business market is significantly different. While single person purchasing is not unusual, especially within a small company, a significant percentage of business buying, especially within larger organizations, requires the input of many.

In the marketing literature those associated with the purchase decision are known to be part of a Buying Centre, which consists of individuals within an organization that perform one or more of the following roles:

- *Buyer*: Responsible for dealing with suppliers and placing orders
- *Decider*: Has the power to make the final purchase decision
- *Influencer*: Has the ability to affect what is ordered such as setting order specifications
- *User*: Those who will actually use the product when it is received
- *Initiator*: Any Buying Centre member who is the first to determine that a need exists
- *Gatekeeper*: Anyone who controls access to other Buying Centre members

For marketers confronting a Buying Centre it is important to first identify who plays what role. Once identified the marketer must address the needs of each member, which may differ significantly. For instance, the Decider, who may be the company president wants to make sure the purchase will not negatively affect the company's bottom line while the Buyer wants to be assured the product will be delivered on time. Thus, the way each Buying Centre member is approached and marketed to requires careful planning in order to address the unique needs of each member.

Experienced Purchasers

As noted in the discussion of the Buying Centre, organizations often employ purchasing agents or professional buyers whose job is to negotiate the best deals for their company. Unlike consumers, who often lack information when making purchase decisions, professional buyers are generally as knowledgeable about the product and the industry as the marketer who is selling to them.

Decision Making Time

Depending on the product, business purchase decisions can drag on for an extensive period. Unlike consumer markets where impulse purchasing is rampant, the number of people involved in business purchase decisions results in decisions taking weeks, months or even years.

Size of Purchases

For products that are regularly used and frequently purchased, businesses will often buy a larger volume at one time compared to consumer purchases. Because of this business purchasers often demand price breaks for higher order levels.

Type of Promotions

Companies who primarily target consumers often use mass advertising methods to reach an often widely dispersed market. For business-to-business marketers the size of individual orders, along with a smaller number of buyers, makes person-to-person contact by sales representatives a more effective means of promotion.

BUYING MOTIVES AND CONSUMER BEHAVIOUR

Buying Behaviour is the decision processes and acts of people involved in buying and using products.

Need to understand:

- Why consumers make the purchases that they make?
- What factors influence consumer purchases?
- The changing factors in our society.

Consumer Buying Behaviour refers to the buying behaviour of the ultimate consumer.

A firm needs to analyse buying behaviour for:

- Buyers reactions to a firms marketing strategy has a great impact on the firms success.
- The marketing concept stresses that a firm should create a Marketing Mix that satisfies customers, therefore need to analyse the what, where, when and how consumers buy.
- Marketers can better predict how consumers will respond to marketing strategies.

STAGES OF THE CONSUMER BUYING PROCESS

Six Stages to the Consumer Buying Decision Process. Actual purchasing is only one stage of the process. Not all decision processes lead to a purchase. All consumer decisions do not always include all 6 stages, determined by the degree of complexity...discussed next.

The 6 stages are:

1. *Problem Recognition*: Difference between the desired state and the actual condition. Deficit in assortment of products. Hunger—Food. Hunger stimulates your need to eat.

2. Can be stimulated by the marketer through product information—did not know you were deficient? I.E., see a commercial for a new pair of shoes, stimulates your recognition that you need a new pair of shoes.
3. *Information search*:
   - Internal search, memory.
   - External search if you need more information. Friends and relatives. Marketer dominated sources; comparison shopping; public sources etc.

     A successful information search leaves a buyer with possible alternatives, the evoked set. Hungry, want to go out and eat, evoked set is:
   - Chinese food
   - Indian food
   - Burger king
   - Klondike kates etc
4. *Evaluation of Alternatives*: Need to establish criteria for evaluation, features the buyer wants or does not want. Rank/weight alternatives or resume search. May decide that you want to eat something spicy, indian gets highest rank etc.
5. If not satisfied with your choice then return to the search phase. Can you think of another restaurant? Look in the yellow pages etc. Information from different sources may be treated differently. Marketers try to influence by "framing" alternatives.
6. *Purchase decision*: Choose buying alternative, includes product, package, store, method of purchase etc.
7. *Purchase*: May differ from decision, time lapse between 4 and 5, product availability.
8. *Post-Purchase Evaluation*: Outcome: Satisfaction or Dissatisfaction. Cognitive Dissonance, have you made the right decision. This can be reduced by warranties, after sales communication etc. After eating an indian meal, may think that really you wanted a chinese meal instead.

TYPES OF CONSUMER BUYING BEHAVIOUR

Types of consumer buying behaviour are determined by:

- Level of Involvement in purchase decision. Importance and intensity of interest in a product in a particular situation.
- Buyers level of involvement determines why he/she is motivated to seek information about a certain products and brands but virtually ignores others.

High involvement purchases—Honda Motorbike, high priced goods, products visible to others, and the higher the risk the higher the involvement.

Types of risk:

- Personal risk
- Social risk
- Economic risk

The four type of consumer buying behaviour are:

1. *Routine Response/Programmed Behaviour*: Buying low involvement frequently purchased low cost items; need very little search and decision effort; purchased almost automatically. Examples include soft drinks, snack foods, milk etc.
2. *Limited Decision Making*: Buying product occasionally. When you need to obtain information about unfamiliar brand in a familiar product category, perhaps. Requires a moderate amount of time for information gathering. Examples include Clothes—know product class but not the brand.
3. Extensive Decision Making/Complex high involvement, unfamiliar, expensive and/or infrequently bought products. High degree of economic/performance/psychological risk. Examples include cars, homes, computers, education. Spend alot of time seeking information and deciding. Information from the companies MM; friends and relatives, store personnel etc. Go through all six stages of the buying process.
4. Impulse buying, no conscious planning.

The purchase of the same product does not always elicit the same Buying Behaviour. Product can shift from one category to the next.

For example:

- Going out for dinner for one person may be extensive decision making but limited decision making for someone else. The reason for the dinner, whether it is an anniversary celebration, or a meal with a couple of friends will also determine the extent of the decision making.

THE EXTENT IN POLICY DECISION-MAKING

Today's market is characterized by highly competitive organizations which are all vying for consumer's loyalty. Profit-oriented firms are faced with the challenge to maintain their own competitive edge in order to survive and be successful. Strategies are carefully planned and executed to gain the ultimate goal of all: company growth. However, internal factors are not the only elements which influence growth. There are also external factors and components working within the organization which shape the direction of the organization. Among this is the consumer - the fuel of the organization.

The dynamics of contemporary living define most of the aspects of human life today. From traditional ways to technologically driven mechanisms, life indeed is no longer the same decades and centuries ago. The recent developments and revolutionary processes resulting to increased convenience of people in various applications contributed to the topical standards of living. Along with the changing business world, customers change as well, becoming more demanding, knowledgeable and highly sophisticated. Before, it is enough if they have purchased a product or service the best way and condition possible. Now, the process of commercial interaction does not end that way. There are more complex steps to be completed to be able to achieve satisfactory results. In turn, company management had shifted their focus on their clients or customers so as to stay successfully in business. This transition meant that organizations have to completely reformulate their conventional business aims and purposes from being process-focused to customer-centred.

In the business, the consumers eventually developed as a result of the radical emergence and amalgamation of innovative and manipulative processes in the global marketplace. Established characteristics in terms of their behaviour and identity are important aspects to consider in studying the significant role they play in any economic endeavor. Furthermore, the subject of consumerism in given societies is becoming popular and a sought-after area of research. In connection, the presence of consumer policies and laws in the global market serve as controlling mechanisms to regulate the diversity of the international economic battlefield. This makes the buying experience even more multifaceted and interactive.

Advertising is the common playground where consumers ensnare themselves with products/services available in the market. The adverse effects of advertising are perceived to be reinforcing elements in the development of consumerist behaviour and culture. This is where the aspect of policy decision making is applicable. The creation of regulating policies in connection to advertising and its effects to consumerism and consumer behaviour is quantified.

This document aims to critically analyse the extent of the relationship of consumerism, consumer behaviour and identity with respect to policy decision-making of the state and business organizations predominantly in terms of the advertising medium. Specifically, it opts to qualify the extent of consumerism in relation to consumer behaviour and culture. Guidelines in advertising are the parametres to be used in policy decision-making. Additionally, it will provide several conceptual backgrounds about the said areas of the general consumer. To fully substantiate the arguments and findings in this research, information taken from vast sources of literature is used as supporting documents. There are also specific examples to be used to show the claims.

Initially, the understanding buyer behaviour is one of the more perplexing tasks confronting every manager. The difficulty arises from the heterogeneity of buyers, from their being groups of individuals who differ from one another. But differences notwithstanding, consumers do share attitudes, opinions, reactions, and desires at various times. Business experience, marketing research, theoretical constructs and models, and trial-and-error methods help to find some of the common denominators.

Believing on the idea that the consumers are the fuel of every profit and/or non-profit organization, studying their behaviour and identity remains parallel and important in every decision-making activity. Consumers have always been regarded as vital factors in relation to different organizational operations and functioning. They live and act in a constantly changing cultural, social, technological, legal, and economic environment. Shaped by the environment, marketing institutions, and activities in return have a major/minor impact on it. Their behaviour and identity, on the other hand, significantly determine the business future in a particular part of country and given culture. As we all know, as region varies on its own, so does the consumer behaviour and identity of such group of people in a region. Through observations of the consumer behaviour, the category in competition, organization, and the marketing strategies of businesses are well evaluated. Consumer behaviour is influenced by different aspects in its environment. It can be viewed with different factors such as the cultural, personal, psychological and social factors of the consumers.

The study of consumer behaviour is one of the most interesting and challenging as well as important aspects in marketing management. Practically, essential decisions that are taken in developing an effective marketing mix for specific product/service are based in the systematic knowledge of the consumers that make up its permanent target market. Believes that understanding the behaviour of the consumer is the most basic step in helping marketing authorities to visualize and predict future trends, reactions, and changes in the marketing mix. It may also serve as a reference in determining the potentials of new products and its adoption. Consumer behaviour is said to be closely associated to marketing research – another important field that deserves further comprehensive investigation.

Each organization provides some products/services that are used by consumers, even though they may not always recognize as products/ services by the consumers as such. For example, it seems fairly obvious that the college students who drink a cola produced by a specific beverage company are the consumers of that beverage product. In a general sense, we can all think of public high school students as the consumers of a state's educational product; voters can be thought of as consumers of a political candidate's leadership and administration product; and, the members of a religious group might be viewed as consumers of a church's spiritual product. Thus, the study of the behaviour of consumers involves an examination of a wide range record of everyday human buying behaviour.

Consumer behaviour as defined by is "the activities that people engage in when selecting, purchasing, and using products and services so as to satisfy needs and desires". continued: "...such activities involve mental and emotional processes, in addition to physical actions". In general perspective, consumer behaviour studies individuals, groups or organizations with regards to obtaining, using and disposing of products and services. It also accounts the decision processes that lead and follow these behaviours. Consumer behaviour investigates consumers' actions, as well as the reasons for those behaviours. In order to fully understand the broad spectrum of consumer behaviour, identified its macroscopic and microscopic perspectives.

Consumer behaviour in a macro level categorizes marketers to look for demographic shifts as well as the general public's values, beliefs and practices which affect their interaction with the economic marketplace. Meanwhile, the micro level indicates consumer behaviour focused on human behaviour and the motivations underlying these behaviours. These concepts are drawn out from sociological and psychological perspectives as proven results of studies in the said aspect.

There are many factors that determine these activities, and the product/ service is just one of them. There are some frameworks that helps explain customer behaviours. Among these are brand orientation model and integrated framework for cross-cultural consumer behaviour. Others, on the other hand, are expressed through demographic research, such as the relationship of culture on consumer behaviour. These models and studies are applicable to consumer behaviour in general products/services. But delving into such topic discussion will make this report technical and might astray away from its real objectives.

In the recent years, the study of consumer behaviour and consumer decision-making has become a sought-after research field. Topics in the various fields of consumer science are considered hot stuffs in scholastic as well as marketing management sectors. Theoretically, consumer science includes the former discipline of home economics – the foundation of basic consumption. The consumer science discipline also evolves around consumer behaviour and decision making concerning the necessities of live and survival. Among these are foods and nutrition, clothing and textiles, housing and interior merchandise in everyday living. Believe that the providence of the aforementioned goods will result to physical, psychological, socio-psychological and financial satisfaction in a complex micro and macro environment. Of specific importance, observed that buying and consumer decision-making are complicated as based on the result of external influences that have to be handled within an internal frame of reference that has come about through consumer socialization.

The complex phenomenon of consumer behaviour is dependent to some considerable factors in the working environment of people. It is somewhat innate or even cultural in its foundation, external or internal in nature, or just a by-product of the common circumstances in the purchasing experience.

Advertising is among the external factors that plays a great role in the buying experience of people. For the record, an average American household exposure to television advertising is about an estimated 7 hours per day times 9 to 16 minutes of nonprogram material per hour. Additionally, advertising traditions hold that the average consumer is exposed to over 1,500 radio, television, newspaper, magazine, and/or billboard advertisements per day. As a result, it could be said that advertising and its component influence the behaviour of consumers. The promises of advertised products/ services are subject to trial and materialization by the consumer. Thus, purchasing the said product/service is the sole way to prove its claims.

The daily exposure of people to all the different kinds of media makes it accessible and convenient for them to recognize the presence of the latest product/service in the market. With the assistance of ads, consumers are engaged in buying experience. As a part of their consumer behaviour stimulation, there are internal assessments that are occurring within the limits of the human nature. In Taiwan, and colleagues studied the behaviour of consumers in relation to the medium. They indicated that the elements of advertising, the manner of presentation, or a certain ad for instance, greatly affect the culture, concept and emotions, and other human attributes of a certain setting. More often than not, advertising contributes to the development of changes in connection to the existing behaviour and identity of the consumer. It may also lead to the practice of consumerism.

According to, most advertising agencies keep on striking into insights on how to gain a deeper understanding on the reason why consumers behave the way they do. Further, advertising practitioners found assessment in probing the thoughts of every individual by using focus groups as variables in eliciting ideas for new products and promotional campaigns to be established. In advertising, I believe that people who are only exposed to recurring ads focus and elaborate on tangential cues such as the credibility of the source. For instance, a controversial political figure endorsing a product/ service will simply be viewed as trash among its critics. Thus, the purchase of the product/service is almost impossible. This certain example is related in the process of forming brand attitude among the ordinary consumer that falls under the capacity of the advertising medium.

Largely, researchers linked consumer decision making in the study of perception. The study of perception is largely bounded on what humans consciously or subconsciously add to or subtract from their raw sensory inputs to produce a private and selective picture of the world. In general term, it is the process that involves the individual's decision in selecting, interpreting, and organizing stimuli into a meaningful and coherent picture of the world. A stimulus is any unit of input to the senses – may it be products, packages, brand names, advertisements, and commercials. In studies of consumerism, it has become almost a cliché to claim that the purchase, use and display of goods in some way expresses social identities and is rooted to the persuasive effects of advertising. The relationship of consumerism and customer behaviour plus advertising has been long overdue. Its interconnection opened up various horizons for academic marketing and management probing.

Consumerism is already deep-rooted part of every given culture. It has become so disturbing on a global scale. Defining consumerism is always equated into a negative image. However, with this report, consumerism will be tackled in connection to the rights of consumers as well as its association to consumer behaviour and identity towards policy decision-making. Traditionally, consumerism is known as the purchasing of products beyond the basic requirement of consumption.

Indicates:

- "In a Buddhist view of mutual co-arising and radical interrelatedness the cause of consumerism is boundlessly plural—a virtual infinity of conditions affecting and being affected by countless other conditions. The desires of individuals have been conditioned by the way parents raised them, by the historical conditions... by the use of media, and so on."

Furthermore, consumerism is related to environmental conditions that are persuasive. These conditions are contributory factors along with politics, economics, social institutions, industrial technology, and ideological tendency. Take for example, the consumerist behaviour of Filipino people during the holiday season perfectly show the factors affecting the practice.

With the various criticisms in consumerism, it has been connected with media applications such as advertising. In advertising, consumerism is a powerful mechanism that is driven by considerable sums spent on advertising. These are designed to generate both a desire to follow trends and the consequential personal self-reward scheme based on personal procurement. The basic idea of materialism and consumerism is one of the by-products of overt advertising.

The presence of consumerism in various cultures is studied in relation to policy decision making. The regulations made by the state are directed to the welfare and being of every buying individual. Laws on consumer rights are created to protect people against abuses in the economic marketplace. There are given considerations that are taken at hand when passing and eventually implementing such laws. The extent of consumer behaviour and identity as well as the relationship of culture are fully considered in realizing its intended purpose. For instance, the advertising medium proliferate consumerism. Every advertisement is produced with the aims to procure interest among the buyer and persuade him/her to have the product/service. The aesthetics of advertising easily provoke a culture of consumerism. Paradoxically, quaintness in advertising shows consumerism correcting itself, disassociating itself from its own conceited techniques, hiding consumerism from the consumer and ostensibly rejecting the commercialism on which it is based. Thus, animated or unrealistic presentation of some advertisements could easily attain its goal - persuasion.

In reference to my personal experiences, advertising materials that are too-good-to-be-true are appealing to me. The tendency is that I am persuaded to try on the product/service being advertise. My buying behaviour was stimulated by the ad. Therefore, it creates an identity that can lead to addiction and constant purchase beyond my normal consumption. As a result, I am practicing a culture of consumerism.

As of the moment, there are government policies that control media like advertising standards. Countries like UK, Canada, and some developing nations maintain protocol in using the said medium. It is always subject to regulation and continuous assessment. The measurement of its extent of applicability in connection to the personal characteristics of consumers is strictly implemented. Its degree of interdependency to consumer behaviour and the present existing culture is not fully taken into considerable contemplation. This is the reason why the extent of policies must be measured in connection to consumer behaviour as well as identity.

The emphasis on consumerism and an increasing awareness of environmental and ethical issues all have their implications for marketing strategists. Many firms are blending communications activities with public purpose policy decision making. Of course, innovation and the production of the new are intrinsic to consumerism and tend to structure the conceptual field of the study of consumerism. The connection of creating advertising policies to the release of new products/services is undeniable. Thus, advertising is among the medium where policies must be evaluated.

New connections between the cultural and the political, the visual and the material, advertising and personal belonging, consumerism and the rights of citizenship has been premeditated issues tackled by each government worldwide. Within European nation-states, individuals' access to citizenship rights has increasingly been framed through discourses of consumerism. The presence of communal and societal awareness and battle against consumerism is another turning point for legislative undertakings of the state's authorities. People in various countries individually contribute to the cessation of consumerist behaviours or practices. The sense of national belonging and citizenship to consumerism and focus on choice as a prime mechanism in the production of consumer-citizenship identities linked the idea of individual behaviour and culture. Thus, the fight against consumerist attitudes is unyielding.

With the present realities, the intervention of state policies in the subject of consumerism is appropriate. State policies must deal with the basics of consumer behaviour. Considering the various factors affecting the decision making of consumers, the government is expected to regulate advertising processes in all sorts of medium – print or broadcast. While advertising is a recognizable media to proliferate economic activity, policies created must deal with the common protection of consumers. However, the degree of effect to consumerism is boundless due to the fact that consumers possess the freedom to choose.

This is aside from the truth that every consumer differs in behaviour and identity. In advertising standards created, implemented, and promoted by authority, it is highly needed that every advertisement must present only what is real and substantial to consumers. The ethics of advertising is necessary for every media regulating system. Advertising policies and standards posed by authorities must be in accordance to the general moral discretion of the society and organizations. Thus, advertisements of organizations must maintain its commitment to corporate social responsibility. Prior to its public release, every advertisement must be taken into legal scrutiny in order to identify its effect in establishing the culture of consumerism. The protection of consumers' rights and welfare is the main concern of the state as well as the business organization.

Furthermore, the measurement of the extent of consumerism, consumer behaviour and identity in policy decision making of government is rooted on the natural laws of what is acceptable and not. As previously stated, ethics in advertising is the name of the game.

For instance,:

- "... The Federal Trade Commission should become concerned with regulating... type of potentially unfair advertising.... the FTC prohibits a company from stating that its product will cure an illness when such is not the case, the FTC might begin prohibiting a company from stating that its product will encourage sexual satisfaction, make one more masculine/feminine, or promote a happier homelife when such is not the case".

There are more concerns that the government and lawmakers need to qualify in relation to advertising regulation. But then again, the dynamic state in every given situation of human life is a significant factor in determining the extent in policy decision making and taking.

Materialism in modern life is rooted in the innate freedom and quest for satisfaction of people. In the U.S., personal freedoms and life satisfaction or the need to optimize on life's happenings are both integral elements in lifestyles. By this fact, the tendency to acquire a consumerist behaviour is ubiquitous. It is indeed true. There are internal processes that occur during a buying experience. This is simply apparent due to the personal characteristics of certain consumers especially to the environment. and colleagues stated that "the standards and values that stem from the environment greatly influence consumer behaviour, affecting purchasing and consumption activities, and the business organizations concerned."

The cultural context of consumer behaviour can be defined as "the totality of the customs, arts, sciences, religions, politics, and economics that distinguishes one society from another, and that influences the individual consumer's behaviour". The presence of subculture among the main culture makes the difference. Subculture is usually defined as a category of people who share a sense of identification that is distinguishable from that of the culture as a whole. This shared sense of identification may result from a shared set of values, from a common history, or from similarity in socio-demographic attributes. Social class is perhaps the type of subculture that is most often used by consumer psychologists. The attribute that distinguishes between levels of social class is the relative level of social benefits. In connection to principles of consumerism, it could be assumed that this process is now a subculture.

All in all, the premise on economic interpretation of consumerism as the belief in the freedom to choose among consumers should indicate the economic structure of a society. This must be the basis of evaluating the extent of policy decision making of the states as well as business organizations. The relationship of consumerism, consumer behaviour and identity in connection to activities, policies, and actions taken by the state and business organization must be based and dependent on the consumer's behaviour and identity.

The practice of consumerism, consumer behaviour and identity will always be pertinent to the buying experience of consumers. Thus, proper regulation of such laws implemented must be strictly determined and observed. This will eventually serve the welfare of the ultimate beneficiaries – the consumers.

CONSUMER SALES PROMOTION

Consumer sales promotions encompass a variety of short-term promotional techniques designed to induce customers to respond in some way. The most popular consumer sales promotions are directly associated with product purchasing. These promotions are intended to enhance the value of a product purchase by either reducing the overall cost of the product (i.e., get same product but for less money) or by adding more benefit to the regular purchase price (i.e., get more for the money).

While tying a promotion to an immediate purchase is a major use of consumer sales promotion, it is not the only one. As we noted above, promotion techniques can be used to achieve other objectives such as building brand loyalty or creating product awareness. Consequently, a marketer's promotional toolbox contains a large variety of consumer promotions.

The following 11 types of consumer sales promotions:

1. Coupons
2. Rebates
3. Promotional Pricing
4. Trade-In
5. Loyalty Programs
6. Sampling and Free Trials

7. Free Product
8. Premiums
9. Contests and Sweepstakes
10. Demonstrations
11. Personal Appearances

Coupons

Most consumers are quite familiar with this form of sales promotion, which offers purchasers price savings or other incentives when the coupon is redeemed at the time of purchase. Coupons are short-term in nature since most (but not all) carry an expiration date after which the value may not be received. Also, coupons require consumer involvement in order for value to be realized. In most cases involvement consists of the consumer making an effort to obtain the coupon (e.g., clip from newspaper) and then presenting it at the time of purchase.

Coupons are used widely by marketers across many retail industries and reach consumers in a number of different delivery formats including:

- *Free-Standing Inserts (FSI)*: Here coupon placement occurs loosely (i.e., inserted) within media, such as newspapers and direct mail, and may or may not require the customer to cut away from other material in order to use.
- *Cross-Product:* These consist of coupons placed within or on other products. Often a marketer will use this method to promote one product by placing the coupon inside another major selling product. For example, a pharmaceutical company may imprint a coupon for a cough remedy on the box of a pain medication. Also, this delivery approach is used when two marketers have struck a cross promotion arrangement where each agrees to undertake certain marketing activity for the other.
- *Printout:* A delivery method that is common in many food stores is to present coupons to a customer at the conclusion of the purchasing process. These coupons, which are often printed on the spot, are intended to be used for a future purchase and not for the current purchase which triggered the printing.
- *Product Display:* Some coupons are nearly impossible for customers to miss as they are located in close proximity to the product. In some instances coupons may be contained within a coupon dispenser fastened to the shelf holding the product while in other cases coupons may be attached to a special display where customers can remove them (e.g., tear off).
- *Internet:* Several specialized websites, such as HotCoupons.com, and even some manufacturer's sites, allow customers to print out coupons.

These coupons are often the same ones appearing in other media, such as newspapers or direct mail. In other cases, coupons may be sent via email, though to be effective the customer's email programme must be able to receive HTML email (and not text only) in order to maintain required design elements (e.g., bar code).

- *Electronic:* The Internet is also seeing the emergence of new non-printable coupons redeemable through website purchases. These electronic coupons are redeemed when the customer enters a designated coupon code during the purchase process.

Rebates

Rebates, like coupons, offer value to purchasers typically by lowering the customer's final cost for acquiring the product. While rebates share some similarities with coupons, they differ in several keys aspects. First, rebates are generally handed or offered (e.g., accessible on the Internet) to customers after a purchase is made and cannot be used to obtain immediate savings in the way coupons are used. (So called "instant rebates", where customers receive price reductions at the time of purchase, have elements of both coupons and rebates, but for our purposes we will classify these as coupons due to the timing of the reward to the customer.)

Second, rebates often request the purchaser to submit personal data in order to obtain the rebate. For instance, customer identification, including name, address and contact information, is generally required to obtain a rebate. Also, the marketer may ask those seeking a rebate to provide additional data such as indicating the reason for making the purchase.

Third, unlike coupons that always offer value when used in a purchase (assuming it is accepted by the retailer), receiving a rebate only guarantees value if the customer takes actions. Marketers know that not all customers will respond to a rebate. Some will misplace or forget to submit the rebate while others may submit after a required deadline.

Marketers factor in the non-redemption rate as they attempt to calculate the cost of the rebate promotion. Finally, rebates tend to be used as a value enhancement in higher priced products compared to coupons. For instance, rebates are a popular promotion for automobiles and computer software where large amounts of money may be returned to the customer.

Promotional Pricing

One of the most powerful sales promotion techniques is the short-term price reduction or, as known in some areas, "on sale" pricing. Lowering a product's selling price can have an immediate impact on demand, though marketers must exercise caution since the frequent use of this technique can lead customers to anticipate the reduction and, consequently, withhold purchase until the price reduction occurs again. Promotional pricing is also considered within the framework of the Price marketing mix component.

Trade-In

Trade-in promotions allow consumers to obtain lower prices by exchanging something the customer possess, such as an older product that the new purchase will replace. While the idea of gaining price breaks for trading in another product is most frequently seen with automobile sales, such promotions are used in other industries, such as computers and golf equipment, where the customer's exchanged product can be resold by the marketer in order to extract value.

Loyalty Programs

Promotions that offer customers a reward, such as price discounts and free products, for frequent purchasing or other activity are called loyalty programs. These promotions have been around for many years but grew rapidly in popularity when introduced in the airline industry as part of frequent-filer programs. Loyalty programs are also found in numerous other industries, including grocery, pizza purchasing and online book purchases, where they may also be known as club card programs since members often must use a verification card as evidence of enrollment in the programme.

Many loyalty programs have become ingrained as part of the value offered by a marketer. That is, a retailer or marketing organization may offer loyalty programs as general business practice. Under this condition loyalty programme does not qualify as a sales promotion since it does not fit the requirement of offering a short-term value (i.e., it is always offered). However, even within a loyalty programme that is part of a general business practice, a sales promotion can be offered such as special short-term offer that lowers the number of points needed to acquire a free product.

Samples and Free Trials

Enticing members of a target market to try a product is often easy when the trial comes at little or no cost to the customer. The use of samples and free trials may be the oldest of all sales promotion techniques dating back to when society advanced from a culture of self-subsistence to a culture of trade.

Sampling and free trials give customers the opportunity to experience products, often in small quantities or for a short duration, without purchasing the product. Today, these methods are used in almost all industries and are especially useful for getting customers to try a product for the first time.

Free Product

Some promotional methods offer free products but with the condition that a purchase be made. The free product may be in the form of additional quantities of the same purchased product (e.g., buy one, get one free) or specialty packages (e.g., value pack) that offer more quantity for the same price as regular packaging.

Premiums

Another form of sales promotion involving free merchandise is premium or "give-away" items. Premiums differ from samples and free product in that these often do not consist of the actual product, though there is often some connection. For example, a cellphone manufacturer may offer access to free downloadable ringtones for those purchasing a cellphone.

Contests and Sweepstakes

Consumers are often attracted to promotions where the potential value obtained is very high. In these promotions only a few lucky consumers receive the value offered in the promotion. Two types of promotions that offer high value are contests and sweepstakes.

Contests are special promotions awarding value to winners based on skills they demonstrate compared to others. For instance, a baking company may offer free vacations to winners of a baking contest. Contest award winners are often determined by a panel of judges.

Sweepstakes or drawings are not skill based but rather based on luck. Winners are determined by random selection. In some cases the chances of winning may be higher for those who make a purchase if entry into the sweepstake occurs automatically when a purchase is made. But in most cases, anyone is free to enter without the requirement to make a purchase.

A sub-set of both contests and sweepstakes are games, which come in a variety of formats such as scratch-off cards and collection of game pieces. Unlike contests and sweepstakes, which may not require purchase, to participate in a game customers may be required to make a purchase. In the United States and other countries, where eligibility is based on purchase, games may be subjected to rigid legal controls and may actually fall under that category of lotteries, which are tightly controlled.

Demonstrations

Many products benefit from customers being shown how products are used through a demonstration. Whether the demonstration is experienced in-person or via video form, such as over the Internet, this promotional technique can produce highly effective results. Unfortunately, demonstrations are very expensive to produce. Costs involved in demonstrations include paying for the expense of the demonstrator, which can be high if the demonstrator is well-known (e.g., nationally known chef), and also paying for the space where the demonstration is given.

Personal Appearances

An in-person appearance by someone of interest to the target market, such as an author, sports figure or celebrity, is another form of sales promotion capable of generating customer traffic to a physical location.

However, as with demonstrations, personal appearance promotion can be expensive since the marketer normally must pay a fee for the person to appear.

TRADE SALES PROMOTIONS

A trade promotion aimed at retailers may encourage retailers to instruct their employees to promote a marketer's brand over competitors' offerings. With thousands of products competing for limited shelf space, spending on trade promotion is nearly equal that spent on consumer promotions.

Many sales promotions aimed at building relationships with channel partners follow similar designs as those directed to consumers including promotional pricing, contests and free product. In addition to these, several other promotional approaches are specifically designed to appeal to trade partners. These approaches include:

- Point-of-Purchase Displays
- Advertising Support Programs
- Short Term Allowances
- Sales Incentives or Push Money
- Promotional Products
- Trade Shows

Point-of-Purchase Displays

Point of purchase (POP) displays are specially designed materials intended for placement in retail stores. These displays allow products to be prominently presented, often in high traffic areas, and thereby increase the probability the product will standout. POP displays come in many styles, though the most popular are ones allowing a product to stand alone, such as in the middle of a store aisle or sit at the end of an aisle (i.e., end-cap) where it will be exposed to heavy customer traffic.

For channel partners, POP displays can result in significant sales increases compared to sales levels in a normal shelf position. Also, many marketers will lower the per-unit cost of products in the POP display as an incentive for retailers to agree to include the display in their stores.

Advertising Support Programs

In addition to offering promotional support in the form of physical displays, marketers can attract channel members' interest by offering financial assistance in the form of advertising money. These funds are often directed to retailers who then include the company's products in their advertising. In certain cases the marketer will offer to pay the entire cost of advertising, but more often, the marketer offers partial support known as co-op advertising funds.

Short Term Trade Allowances

This promotion offers channel partners price breaks for agreeing to stock the product. In most cases the allowance is not only given as encouragement to purchase the product but also as an inducement to promote the product in other ways such as by offering attractive shelf space or store location, highlighting the product in company-produced advertising or website display, or by agreeing to have the retailer's sales personnel "talk-up" the product to customers.

Allowances can be in the form price reductions (a.k.a. off-invoice promotion) and buy-back guarantees if the product does not sell in certain period of time.

Sales Incentives or Push Money

Since sales promotions are intended to stimulate activity that leads to meeting promotional objectives, it makes sense that these can also apply to those in a channel member's organization who also affect sales. Thus, a marketer may offer sales promotions to their reseller's sales force and customer service staff where they are used as incentives to help sell more of the marketer's product. Sometimes called push money, these promotions typically offer employees cash or prizes, such as trips, for those that meet sales requirements.

Promotional Products

Among the most widely used methods of sales promotions is the promotional product; products labeled with the brand or company name that serve as reminders of the actual product. For instance, companies often hand out free calendars, coffee cups and pens that contain the product logo.

Trade Shows

One final type of trade promotion is the industry trade show (a.k.a. exhibitions, conventions). Trade shows are organized events that bring both industry buyers and sellers together in one central location. Spending on trade shows is one of the highest of all sales promotions. In fact, the Promotion Marketing Association estimates that over (US) $20 billion is spent annually by marketers to participate in trade shows.

Marketers are attracted to trade shows since these offer the opportunity to reach a large number of potential buyers in one convenient setting. At these events most sellers attempt to capture the attention of buyers by setting up a display area to present their product offerings and meet with potential customers. These displays can range from a single table covering a small area to erecting specially built display booths that dominate the trade show floor.

8

Brand Management

INTRODUCTION

Brand management is the application of marketing techniques to a specific product, product line, or brand. It seeks to increase a product's perceived value to the customer and thereby increase brand franchise and brand equity. Marketers see a brand as an implied promise that the level of quality people have come to expect from a brand will continue with future purchases of the same product. This may increase sales by making a comparison with competing products more favourable. It may also enable the manufacturer to charge more for the product. The value of the brand is determined by the amount of profit it generates for the manufacturer. This can result from a combination of increased sales and increased price, and/or reduced COGS, and/or reduced or more efficient marketing investment. All of these enhancements may improve the profitability of a brand, and thus,"Brand Managers" often carry line-management accountability for a brand's P&L profitability, in contrast to marketing staff manager roles to manage and execute. In this regard, Brand Management is often viewed in organizations as a broader and more strategic role than Marketing alone.

The annual list of the world's most valuable brands, published by Interbrand and Business Week, indicates that the market value of companies often consists largely of brand equity. Research by McKinsey and Company, a global consulting firm, in 2000 suggested that strong, well-leveraged brands produce higher returns to shareholders than weaker, narrower brands. Taken together, this means that brands seriously impact shareholder value, which ultimately makes branding a CEO responsibility.

PRINCIPLES OF BRAND MANAGEMENT

A good brand name should:

- Be protected under trademark law.
- Be easy to pronounce.
- Be easy to remember.
- Be easy to recognize.

- Be easy to translate into all languages in the markets where the brand will be used.
- Attract attention.
- Suggest product benefits or suggest usage
- Suggest the company or product image.
- Distinguish the product's positioning relative to the competition.
- Be attractive.
- Stand out among a group of other brands.

ONLINE BRAND MANAGEMENT

Companies are embracing brand reputation management as a strategic imperative and are increasingly turning to online monitoring in their efforts to prevent their public image from becoming tarnished. Online brand reputation protection can mean monitoring for the misappropriation of a brand trademark by fraudsters intent on confusing consumers for monetary gain. It can also mean monitoring for less malicious, although perhaps equally damaging, infractions, such as the unauthorized use of a brand logo or even for negative brand information from online consumers that appears in online communities and other social media platforms. The red flag can be something as benign as a blog rant about a bad hotel experience or an electronic gadget that functions expectations.

BRAND ARCHITECTURE

The different brands owned by a company are related to each other via brand architecture. In "product brand architecture", the company supports many different product brands with each having its own name and style of expression while the company itself remains invisible to consumers. Procter & Gamble, considered by many to have created product branding, is a choice example with its many unrelated consumer brands such as Tide, Pampers, Abunda, Ivory and Pantene.

With "endorsed brand architecture", a mother brand is tied to product brands, such as The Courtyard Hotels by Marriott. Endorsed brands benefit from the standing of their mother brand and thus save a company some marketing expense by virtue promoting all the linked brands whenever the mother brand is advertising. This is most commonly referred to as "corporate branding". The mother brand is used and all products carry this name and all advertising speaks with the same voice. A good example of this brand architecture is the UK-based conglomerate Virgin. Virgin brands all its businesses with its name.

TECHNIQUES

Companies sometimes want to reduce the number of brands that they market. This process is known as "Brand Rationalization." Some companies tend to create more brands and product variations within a brand than economies of scale would indicate. Sometimes, they will create a specific service or product brand for each market that they target. In the case of product branding, this may be to gain retail shelf space. A company may decide to rationalize their portfolio of brands from time to time to gain production and marketing efficiency, or to rationalize a brand portfolio as part of corporate restructuring. A recurring challenge for brand managers is to build a consistent brand while keeping its message fresh and relevant. An older brand identity may be misaligned to a redefined target market, a restated corporate vision statement, revisited mission statement or values of a company. Brand identities may also lose resonance with their target market through demographic evolution. Repositioning a brand may cost some brand equity, and can confuse the target market, but ideally, a brand can be repositioned while retaining existing brand equity for leverage.

Brand orientation is a deliberate approach to working with brands, both internally and externally. The most important driving force behind this increased interest in strong brands is the accelerating pace of globalization. This has resulted in an ever-tougher competitive situation on many markets. A product's superiority is in itself no longer sufficient to guarantee its success. The fast pace of technological development and the increased speed with which imitations turn up on the market have dramatically shortened product lifecycles. The consequence is that product-related competitive advantages soon risk being transformed into competitive prerequisites. For this reason, increasing numbers of companies are looking for other, more enduring, competitive tools – such as brands. Brand Orientation refers to "the degree to which the organization values brands and its practices are oriented towards building brand capabilities".

BRAND

A brand is the identity of a specific product, service, or business. A brand can take many forms, including a name, sign, symbol, colour combination or slogan. The word brand began simply as a way to tell one person's cattle from another by means of a hot iron stamp. A legally protected brand name is called a trademark. The word brand has continued to evolve to encompass identity - it affects the personality of a product, company or service.

A brand is the personality that identifies a product, service or company and how it relates to key constituencies: Customers, Staff, Partners, Investors etc.

Some people distinguish the psychological aspect, brand associations like thoughts, feelings, perceptions, images, experiences, beliefs, attitudes, and so on that become linked to the brand, of a brand from the experiential aspect.

The experiential aspect consists of the sum of all points of contact with the brand and is known as the brand experience. The psychological aspect, sometimes referred to as the brand image, is a symbolic construct created within the minds of people and consists of all the information and expectations associated with a product or service.

People engaged in branding seek to develop or align the expectations behind the brand experience, creating the impression that a brand associated with a product or service has certain qualities or characteristics that make it special or unique. A brand is therefore one of the most valuable elements in an advertising theme, as it demonstrates what the brand owner is able to offer in the marketplace. The art of creating and maintaining a brand is called brand management. Orientation of the whole organization towards its brand is called brand orientation.

Careful brand management seeks to make the product or services relevant to the target audience. Brands should be seen as more than the difference between the actual cost of a product and its selling price - they represent the sum of all valuable qualities of a product to the consumer.

There are many intangibles involved in business, intangibles left wholly from the income statement and balance sheet which determine how a business is perceived. The learned skill of a knowledge worker, the type of mental working, the type of stitch: all may be without an 'accounting cost' but for those who truly know the product, for it is these people the company should wish to find and keep, the difference is incomparable.

A brand which is widely known in the marketplace acquires brand recognition. When brand recognition builds up to a point where a brand enjoys a critical mass of positive sentiment in the marketplace, it is said to have achieved brand franchise. One goal in brand recognition is the identification of a brand without the name of the company present. For example, Disney has been successful at branding with their particular script font which it used in the logo for go.com.

Consumers may look on branding as an important value added aspect of products or services, as it often serves to denote a certain attractive quality or characteristic.

From the perspective of brand owners, branded products or services also command higher prices. Where two products resemble each other, but one of the products has no associated branding people may often select the more expensive branded product on the basis of the quality of the brand or the reputation of the brand owner.

BRAND AWARENESS

Brand awareness refers to customers' ability to recall and recognize the brand under different conditions and link to the brand name, logo, jingles and so on to certain associations in memory. It helps the customers to understand to which product or service category the particular brand belongs to and what products and services are sold under the brand name.

It also ensures that customers know which of their needs are satisfied by the brand through its products. 'Brand love', or love of a brand, is an emerging term encompassing the perceived value of the brand image. Brand love levels are measured through social media posts about a brand, or tweets of a brand on sites such as Twitter. Becoming a Facebook fan of a particular brand is also a measurement of the level of 'brand love'.

BRAND PROMISE

The marketer and owner of the brand has a vision of what the brand must be and do for the consumers.

GLOBAL BRAND

A global brand is one which is perceived to reflect the same set of values around the world. Global brands transcend their origins and creates strong, enduring relationships with consumers across countries and cultures.

Global brands are brands sold to international markets. Examples of global brands include Coca-Cola, McDonald's, Marlboro, Levi's, Shell etc.. These brands are used to sell the same product across multiple markets, and could be considered successful to the extent that the associated products are easily recognizable by the diverse set of consumers.

BENEFITS OF GLOBAL BRANDING

In addition to taking advantage of the outstanding growth opportunities, the following drives the increasing interest in taking brands global:

- Economies of scale
- Lower marketing costs
- Laying the groundwork for future extensions worldwide
- Maintaining consistent brand imagery
- Quicker identification and integration of innovations
- Preempting international competitors from entering domestic markets or locking you out of other geographic markets
- Increasing international media reach is an enabler
- Increases in international business and tourism are also enablers

GLOBAL BRAND VARIABLES

The following elements may differ from country to country:

- Corporate slogan
- Products and services
- Product names
- Product features
- Positionings
- Marketing mixes

These differences will depend upon:

- Language differences
- Different styles of communication
- Other cultural differences
- Differences in category and brand development
- Different consumption patterns
- Different competitive sets and marketplace conditions
- Different legal and regulatory environments
- Different national approaches to marketing

Local Brand

A brand that is sold and marketed in a relatively small and restricted geographical area. A local brand is a brand that can be found in only one country or region. It may be called a regional brand if the area encompasses more than one metropolitan market. It may also be a brand that is developed for a specific national market, however an interesting thing about local brand is that the local branding is mostly done by consumers then by the producers. Examples of Local Brands in Sweden are Stomatol, Mijerierna etc.

Ambient Brand

An Ambient Brand is a movement, where the brand is organized around values and social needs instead of promoting a specific product. It is a virtual space, defined by values and occupied by a community of like minded people. Whereas a traditional brand is entirely independent of products and their parent corporations, an ambient brand is an independent social movement that companies can participate in. They are not selling products, they are allowing their company to participate in a social movement and allow their brand to be identified with this.

It exists as a shared values space where consumers gather, converse and ultimately transact with organizations that are in alignment with the values associated with that community. Corporations do not create ambient brands. They must qualify for inclusion within them by demonstrating that they share the values and will service the interests of their associated communities. The brands develop organically as a result of emerging social and cultural codes and are materialized through peoples ability to organize around them through the use of mainly virtual communities on the web.

Brand Name

The brand name is quite often used interchangeably within "brand", although it is more correctly used to specifically denote written or spoken linguistic elements of any product. In this context a "brand name" constitutes a type of trademark, if the brand name exclusively identifies the brand owner as the commercial source of products or services. A brand owner may seek to protect proprietary rights in relation to a brand name through trademark registration. Advertising spokespersons have also become part of some brands, for example: Mr. Whipple of Charmin toilet tissue and Tony the Tiger of Kellogg's. Local Branding is usually done by the consumers rather than the producers.

Types of Brand Names

Brand names come in many styles.
A few include:

- *Acronym*: A name made of initials such as UPS or IBM
- *Descriptive*: Names that describe a product benefit or function like Whole Foods or Airbus
- *Alliteration and rhyme*: Names that are fun to say and stick in the mind like Reese's Pieces or Dunkin' Donuts
- *Evocative*: Names that evoke a relevant vivid image like Amazon or Crest
- *Neologisms*: Completely made-up words like Wii or Kodak
- *Foreign word*: Adoption of a word from another language like Volvo or Samsung
- *Founders' names*: Using the names of real people like Hewlett-Packard or Disney
- *Geography*: Many brands are named for regions and landmarks like Cisco and Fuji Film
- *Personification*: Many brands take their names from myth like Nike or from the minds of ad execs like Betty Crocker

The act of associating a product or service with a brand has become part of pop culture. Most products have some kind of brand identity, from common table salt to designer jeans. A brandnomer is a brand name that has colloquially become a generic term for a product or service, such as Band-Aid or Kleenex, which are often used to describe any kind of adhesive bandage or any kind of facial tissue respectively.

Brand Identity

A product identity, or brand image are typically the attributes one associates with a brand, how the brand owner wants the consumer to perceive the brand - and by extension the branded company, organization, product or service. The brand owner will seek to bridge the gap between the brand image and the brand identity. Effective brand names build a connection between the brand personality as it is perceived by the target audience and the actual product/service. The brand name should be conceptually on target with the product/service. Furthermore, the brand name should be on target with the brand demographic. Typically, sustainable brand names are easy to remember, transcend trends and have positive connotations. Brand identity is fundamental to consumer recognition and symbolizes the brand's differentiation from competitors.

Brand identity is what the owner wants to communicate to its potential consumers. However, over time, a product's brand identity may acquire gaining new attributes from consumer perspective but not necessarily from the marketing communications an owner percolates to targeted consumers. Therefore, brand associations become handy to check the consumer's perception of the brand.

Brand identity needs to focus on authentic qualities - real characteristics of the value and brand promise being provided and sustained by organisational and/or production characteristics.

Visual Brand Identity

The recognition and perception of a brand is highly influenced by its visual presentation. A brand's visual identity is the overall look of its communications. Effective visual brand identity is achieved by the consistent use of particular visual elements to create distinction, such as specific fonts, colours, and graphic elements. At the core of every brand identity is a brand mark, or logo. In the United States, brand identity and logo design naturally grew out of the Modernist movement in the 1950s and greatly drew on the principles of that movement – simplicity and geometric abstraction. These principles can be observed in the work of the pioneers of the practice of visual brand identity design, such as Paul Rand, Chermayeff & Geismar and Saul Bass.

TRADEMARK

Generally speaking, a trademark is a word, symbol, phrase or device which uniquely identifies a particular company or individual. There are many types of bottles used to contain soft drinks, for example, but only one with the distinctive logo and design of Coca-Cola. Each element of a Coca-Cola bottle- the shape, red imprint and name-could be considered a trademark of the Coca-Cola company. Because all of these elements have been legally registered with the United States Patent and Trademark Office, no other soft drink company can create a similar trademark.

This same philosophy holds true with distinctive slogans or brand names. A photocopying machine is not a trademark, but 'Xerox' is. Any product bearing the name Xerox implies the same level of quality as the original product.

Sometimes a trademark becomes so popular that it replaces the generic description of the product. Consumers shop for Q-Tips instead of cotton swabs, for instance, even though the name 'Q-Tip' is a registered trademark of the Johnson and Johnson company. Other trademarks which have become universal include Jacuzzi, Band-Aid and Crayola. A trademark should be registered with agencies such as the United States Patent and Trade Office for maximum legal protection.

Trademark laws work much like copyright laws in the sense of first rights. Once a company or individual successfully registers a trademark, a circled "R" or the abbreviation "Reg. TM" can be legally imprinted on the product or slogan. There is no such condition as 'trademark pending', unlike applications for patents which may take years to process through the USPTO. Sometimes the criteria for trademark registration can be challenging to understand. Companies and individuals cannot simply register ownership of common words or phrases, but they can turn a distinctive combination of words into a trademark. The Nike shoe company has a legal right to trademark the phrase 'Just Do It' because the words have become an identifiable slogan. The Nike swoosh, as simple as it may appear, is also a registered trademark. This doesn't mean, however, that another company can't use a stylized check mark, but it can't be readily confused with the swoosh logo owned by Nike.

Companies and individuals who have registered a trademark will pursue many legal avenues to protect it. Courts must decide if the unauthorized use of a trademarked slogan or product by others has caused actual damage in the marketplace. A local restaurant featuring fried chicken, for example, cannot use the image of an elderly man in a white suit as its official logo. This would create confusion with the registered trademark of Colonel Sanders owned by Kentucky Fried Chicken. But it would be legal for the local restaurant to say 'If Mr. Sanders ate here, he'd be a General.' Kentucky Fried Chicken's registered trademark does not protect individual words, just the entire phrase or symbol.

CORPORATE BRANDING

Corporate branding refers to a company applying its name to a product. The product and the company name become the brand name. The company can advertise several of its products under a single brand name in a practice referred to as *family branding* or *umbrella branding*.

By using corporate branding with a successfully marketed product, a company can familiarize consumers with its products and may create brand loyalty. If the public likes one product from this company, then they may seek out the brand name when buying other products. Corporate branding is usually only successful if the company is well known and sells reputable products with a positive image. One of the disadvantages of corporate branding is that the company can become identified with only one type of product.

To consumers, corporate branding represents a level of quality that they have come to expect from the company. They will expect every product with the same brand name to have the same level of quality that they are familiar with. The company can increase sales by comparing one of their more popular products with a similar product by another company. The value of the brand is determined by the profits the products have made. If profits are high, then the manufacturer is able to charge more for their product.

When applying corporate branding to a product or products, companies need to follow a few guidelines. A corporate brand should be easy to recognize and attract attention. It should also be legally protectable and suggest the company or product image.

Ideally, the brand should be easy to pronounce and easy to remember. A premier brand product typically costs more to purchase than an economy brand. Consumers are paying for the name and the quality of product that name guarantees.

There are a few extensions to corporate branding. One brand name may be used for a number of products in family branding, or all the products may be given different brand names in a practice called *individual branding*. When large retailers buy goods in bulk and then put their own brand name on them, this is called *store branding, label branding*, or *private branding*. *Co-branding* is when two or more manufactures combine to sell their products. When a company sells the right to use their brand name to another company for use in another location or for non-competitive purposes, this is called *brand licensing*.

Corporate branding has the ability to make a product very successful. If the brand name has a track record of a guarantee of quality, then there are huge amounts of money to be made by using the name. However, just one shoddy product under the brand name may cause bad word of mouth, affecting sales of all the other products under the same name and causing irreversible damage to the company.

IMPORTANCE OF BRAND AWARENESS

You may be asking yourself, is brand awareness really all that important? You may be saying to yourself, I have plenty of customers and sales are decent, why bother? The answer is: There are few things more worthwhile than investing time in your brand's awareness. It can play a major role in purchasing decisions. The reality is, the more aware consumers are of your product and your brand, the more likely they are to buy from you.

Among the challenges faced in selling pure maple products are:

- Do potential customers know you exist?
- Why pay more for Pure Maple vs. an artificial syrup?
- Isn't Vermont maple syrup better?
- Why pay more for your products rather than from a less expensive alternative?

In the future, and for the sake of your business, it is in your best interests to take action to increase awareness of your brand.

THE GOAL

Thus, it is a good idea to draw up a brand awareness strategy that you can continue to update throughout the development of your brand. To begin, for example, you can do preliminary research to determine how aware the consumers of your brand are prior to any changes. Then, decide what you think and perhaps what others suggest that you might do to increase awareness and public recognition. Next, compose a strategy for how you would like to go about this.

For example, perhaps your focus may be on your name, or perhaps the colours people associate with your brand, or even the way in which you promote and sell your products. Finally, decide upon how you would like to execute these changes and increase your brand awareness. Ultimately, you should be able to see a change in how consumers perceive your brand and the level of recognition your brand has acquired. For example, perhaps your consumer base expands to include of nearby towns or attract a different core consumer. Truly successful brand awareness often takes time to develop. First there is the time required to develop an effective awareness effort. Then there is the time required for your message to reach potential customers. A few customers will respond early, but most will take time to hear about your products, make a decision to try them, and even later return for more. Establishing customer loyalty takes the most time, as it requires extended experience with your business and products.

As a result of specific actions, positive brand awareness is promoted. Brand awareness is essentially the impression people have of your brand. Do they know your brand as reliable high quality? As well established and distinctive? As a bargain? How is it that they have formed these perceptions? Perhaps from your logo? Or maybe from the way your products are displayed or priced? These opportunities to make a good impression are what are influencing your consumers' awareness of your brand.

HOW TO BEGIN CREATING BRAND AWARENESS

How do you, over time, establish positive brand awareness that promotes the possibility of purchase of your product in the future? There is always the initial impression of your brand that is of utmost importance. Beyond this, however, are all of the future impressions that may be formed regarding your brand. In deciding how you will go about creating brand awareness, you need to consider and to be aware of how your product value becomes know to the consumer and the importance of consistency:

- The message of what a brand is offering to the consumer should be consistent. Wegmans, for example, offers fresh, high-quality foods for purchase and advertises the advantages, such as home-cooked meals, that their goods can provide for you. The layout of their perishable goods, the organization of complementary condiments and staple products, and the stands offering sample recipes to be cooked at home are all evidence of the company attempting to present a consistent message of what they are all about to the consumer. The presentation of Wegmans as a prominent player in providing quality foods for quality home-cooked meals is evident in each of the aforementioned examples.

The company does not, for example, attempt to convey quality in its store layout and offerings and then convey cheap alternative in the mailings sent out. The impressions you hope to make on consumers and potential consumers should be consistent across various mediums, situations, and promotional attempts.

- Images you present should also be consistent in order to increase brand awareness. It is important that you are consistent in your use of images so that you maximize recognition and positive impressions. Wegmans logo, for example, can be found on its storefront, on the products it produces itself, on the receipt consumers receive after purchase, on the bags customers carry out of the store, and in many of its distributed informational material.
- Slogans and taglines should also be consistent throughout mediums and material. Once again, consistency is important in conveying a message that promotes awareness of your brand in a organized, recognizable manner. Wegmans' tagline, "Helping you make great meals easy", is consistent throughout its promotional materials, website, and logo, to name a few.

Consistency cannot be emphasized enough. It presents the consumer with an image that in the future the consumer can continue to associate with your products. For example, if the materials you distribute, the set-up of your sale table, the packaging of your product, and the logo and tagline are not all relatively similar, regularly consistent, and repeatedly recognizable over time, it is likely you will get nowhere with your brand. Creating brand awareness, through a collaborative, well-developed overall image, is essential to developing a success brand that achieves maximum benefits.

MAINTAINING BRAND AWARENESS

It is important to keep working at the issues and activities identified. Pay attention to how customers are responding to products, packaging, displays, and messages. Look for ways to improve the image you are trying to get across. Ask your customers for suggestions. Work to maintain a consistent presence in the market place. This can mean a location and regular times where customers can reliably expect to find you. The NY Maple Producers booth at the State Fair has been in a prime location for many years.

They need to move to gain more sales space and will have to have a plan to help customers find their new location. If your business is wholesaling maple products to retail locations, you need to stay in regular and reliable contact with your customers. They should not have to come looking for you when they need to re-stock or they will turn to suppliers that make it easier for them to operate their businesses.

PURCHASING DECISION PROCESS

Understanding the decision-making process helps you to better understand how to structure your brand awareness process. What makes them buy your product? Do they decide, upon an impulse, to purchase your product? Do they need several hours to mull over the possibility of making the purchase? To what extent does product type, price, and environment affect the purchasing decision.

Marketing specialists recognize five stages to a purchasing decision. The first stage in making a purchase decision is to perceive a need. The range, complexity, and severity varies in regard to this need. It could range, for example, from a need to purchase a gift for a friend's birthday to a need to eat something sweet to a need to drink something refreshing. It is easy to see how different containers would appeal to someone thinking about a gift vs. buying syrup for personal use. Messages with your product display about possible uses can prompt a need-based decision.

The second stage in making purchasing decisions is to seek information. This may be simply reading an ingredient list to an internet search to an inquiring call. Providing information about your products and their value can be important to making a sale. Why is "pure" or "local" important? What flavour experience or possible uses await the purchaser? Might the history and tradition of maple products be important to some consumer decisions? The third stage is where the potential customer evaluates alternatives to your brand or product. This, obviously, is the stage in which your product is compared to those of competitors.

It may also include other products that you may have to offer or other products they remember from the past. Essentially the potential buyer is assessing the qualities of your product that might make it worth the purchase. If the signage, slogans, and literature does not address the more obvious questions, then you need to be ready to do so when asked. If you want to sell at the premium end of the price range then type of products, packaging, display, and product messages must be consistent with the price. The fourth stage involves an assessment of the buying value.

Is the product worth the price? Do the values it possesses make it a worthwhile purchase? This is the culmination of the prior stages and results in a decision to either buy or pass up on an offer. The fifth and final stage involves an assessment of the purchase decision. This can occur a day, a month, or a year or more after the sale. Essentially, the customer is either reaffirming or doubting their purchasing decision. For example, seeing other people enjoying the product reaffirms their decision or makes them wish they had bought more. Testimonials from satisfied customers may help to shape these after-purchase expectations. Or perhaps they discover an off-taste or crystallized sugar in the syrup, in which case it may be more likely that the person would doubt that they made the correct decision in making the purchase. If the consumer decided not to make the purchase, they may later regret such a decision if the value of that product to them, for example, were to increase.

Understanding that the stages of a purchasing decision vary both in time and whether the stages really are distinct, one can better assess where they might be able to have an influence on someone's decision to purchase. For example, it may help to offer the person more information or to tell them about all the other people that have been really impressed with your product.

ADVERTISING

Obviously advertising is an important way to have your brand and products become known to consumers. This topic is covered more in CMP Bulletin 106. Some of the topics covered in this bulletin may be valuable ingredients in external advertising. But the messages conveyed at the place of purchase are equally important and should leave your targeted customers with a consistent impression of your business and its products.

BRANDING DECISIONS

Branding involves decisions that establish an identity for a product with the goal of distinguishing it from competitors' offerings. In markets where competition is fierce and where customers may select from among many competitive products, creating an identity through branding is essential. It is particularly important in helping position the product in the minds of the product's target market. While consumer products companies have long recognized the value of branding, it has only been within the last 10-15 years that organizations selling component products in the business-to-business market have begun to focus on brand building strategies. The most well-known company to brand components is Intel with its now famous "Intel Inside" slogan. Intel's success has led many other b-to-b companies and even non-profits to incorporate branding within their overall marketing strategy.

BRAND NAMES AND BRAND MARKS

At a very basic level branding is achieved through the use of unique brand names and brand marks. The brand name, which may be either the individual product name or a name applied to a group or family of products, is important for many reasons including suggesting what the product is or does (e.g., Mop-and-Glow). The name is also what we utter when we discuss the product (i.e., word-of-mouth marketing). The brand mark is a design element, such as a symbol (e.g., Nike swoosh), logo (e.g., Yahoo! graphic), a character (e.g., Keebler elves) or even a sound (e.g., Intel inside sound), that provides visual or auditory recognition for the product.

ADVANTAGES OF BRANDS

A strong brand offers many advantages for marketers including:

- Brands provide multiple sensory stimuli to enhance customer recognition. For example, a brand can be visually recognizable from its packaging, logo, shape, etc. It can also be recognizable via sound, such as hearing the name on a radio advertisement or talking with someone who mentions the product.
- Customers who are frequent and enthusiastic purchasers of a particular brand are likely to become Brand Loyal. Cultivating brand loyalty among customers is the ultimate reward for successful marketers since these customers are far less likely to be enticed to switch to other brands compared to non-loyal customers.
- Well-developed and promoted brands make product positioning efforts more effective. The result is that upon exposure to a brand (e.g., hearing it, seeing it) customers conjure up mental images or feelings of the benefits they receive from using that brand. The reverse is even better. When customers associate benefits with a particular brand, the brand may have attained a significant competitive advantage. In these situations the customer who recognizes he needs a solution to a problem (e.g., needs to bleach clothes) may automatically think of one brand that offers the solution to the problem (e.g., Clorox). This "benefit = brand" association provides a significant advantage for the brand that the customer associates with the benefit sought.
- Firms that establish a successful brand can extend the brand by adding new products under the same "family" brand. Such branding may allow companies to introduce new products more easily since the brand is already recognized within the market.
- Strong brands can lead to financial advantages through the concept of Brand Equity in which the brand itself becomes valuable. Such gains can be realized through the out-right sale of a brand or through licensing arrangements. For example, Company A may have a well-recognized brand (Brand X) within a market but for some reason they are looking to concentrate their efforts in other markets. Company B is looking to enter the same market as Brand X.

If circumstances are right Company A could sell to Company B the rights to use the Brand X name without selling any other part of the company. That is, Company A simply sells the legal rights to the Brand X name but retains all other parts of Brand X, such as the production facilities and employees. In cases of well developed brands such a transaction may carry a very large price tag. Thus, through strong branding efforts Company A achieves a large financial gain by simply signing over the rights to the name. But why would Company B seek to purchase a brand for such a high price tag? Because by buying the brand Company B has already achieved an important marketing goal – building awareness within the target market. The fact the market is already be familiar with the brand allows the Company B to concentrate on other marketing decisions.

Packaging

Nearly all tangible products (i.e., goods) are sold to customers within a container or package that, as we will discuss, serves many purposes including protecting the product during shipment. In a few cases, such as with certain produce items, the final customer may purchase the product without a package but the produce marketer still faces packaging decisions when it comes to shipping to the store. Thus, for many products there are two packaging decisions – final customer and distribution.

BRANDING STRATEGY

Branding is an important decision designed to enhance the identity of the product through the use of unique brand names, symbols and other distinctive measures. With competition growing more intense in almost all industries, establishing a strong brand allows an organization's products to stand out and avoid potential pitfalls, such as price wars, that have befallen many products. Therefore, a clear understanding of branding strategy is essential in order to build solid products and product lines.

In particular, marketers should be aware of various branding approaches that can be pursued. By branding approach we are referring to different product identification strategies that can be deployed to establish a product within the market.

The purpose of these approaches is to build a brand that will exist for the long term. Making smart decisions up front is crucial since a company may have to live with the decision for a long time.

Branding approaches include the following:

- *Individual Product Branding*: Under this branding approach new products are assigned new names with no obvious connection to existing brands offered by the company. Under individual product branding the marketing organization must work hard to establish the brand in the market since it cannot ride the coattails of previously introduced brands. The chief advantage of this approach is it allows brands to stand on their own thus lessening threats that may occur to other brands marketed by the company. For instance, if another company brand receives negative publicity this news is less likely to rub off on the company's other brands that carry their own unique names. Brands can create financial gains through the concept known as brand equity. Under an individual branding approach, each brand builds its own separate equity which allows the company, if they choose, to sell off individual brands without impacting other brands owned by the company. The most famous marketing organization to follow this strategy is Procter and Gamble, which has historically introduced new brands without any link to other brands or even to the company name.

- *Family Branding:* Under this branding approach new products are placed under the umbrella of an existing brand. The principle advantage of this approach is that it enables the organization to rapidly build market awareness and acceptance since the brand is already established and known to the market. But the potential disadvantage is that the market has already established certain perceptions of the brand. For instance, a company that sells low-end, lower priced products may have a brand that is viewed as an economy brand. This brand image may create customer confusion and hinder the company if they attempt to introduce higher-end, higher priced products using the same brand name. Additionally, with family branding any negative publicity that may occur for one product within a brand could spread to all other products that share the same name.
- *Co-Branding:* This approach takes the idea of individual and family branding a step further. With co-branding a marketer seeks to partner with another firm, which has an established brand, in hopes synergy of two brands on a product is even more powerful than a single brand. The partnership often has both firms sharing costs but also sharing the gains. For instance, major credit card companies, such as Visa and MasterCard, offer co-branding options to companies and organizations. The cards carry the name of a co-branded organization (e.g., University name) along with the name of the issuing bank (e.g., Citibank) and the name of the credit card company. Besides tapping into awareness for multiple brands, the co-branding strategy is also designed to appeal to a larger target market, especially if each brand, when viewed separately, does not have extensive overlapping target markets with the other brand. Thus, co-branding allows both firms to tap into market segments where they did not previously have a strong position.
- *Private or Store Branding:* Some suppliers are in the business of producing products for other companies including placing another company's brand name on the product. This is most often seen in the retail industry where stores or online sellers contract with suppliers to manufacture the retailer's own branded products. In some cases the supplier not only produces product for the retailer's

brand but also markets their own brand so that store shelves will contain both brands.

- *No-Name or Generic Branding:* Certain suppliers supply products that are intentionally "brandless." These products are mostly basic commodity-type products that consumer or business customers purchase as low price alternatives to branded products. Basic household products such as paper products, over-the-counter medicines such as ibuprofen, and even dog food are available in a generic form.
- *Brand Licensing:* Under brand licensing a contractual arrangement is created in which a company owning a brand name allows others to produce and supply products carrying the brand name. This is often seen when a brand is not directly connected with a product category. For instance, several famous children's characters, such as Sesame Street's Elmo, have been licensed to toy and food manufacturers who market products using the branded character's name and image.

FUNDAMENTAL CHANGES IN MARKET TRENDS

The developments and changes that have taken place in financial markets in the recent past have been influenced by two fundamental processes: first, the strengthening of the linkages between the individual markets which tended to integrate national economies and provide a deeper market for instruments of different kinds; second, in so far as the market participants operate with increasing freedom in the various segments of the international financial system, the international financial markets are globalized-the decision-maker can increasingly think of them as an integrated whole.

MARKET INTEGRATION

An integration process between countries, between different market sectors, between institutions, between maturities and between instruments gained momentum during the 1980s. It brought the capital markets closer together and linked them, enabling the intermediation process between saving and investment to become more efficient and thereby reducing the cost of capital to firms and increasing returns to savers. Better integrated markets facilitate the reallocation of a broadening spectrum of risks, thus enhancing the scope and efficiency of international and intertemporal resource allocation. The flip-side of this coin is that this process may be creating new risks that are not fully understood as yet.

The integration of capital markets followed the policy initiatives to liberalize restrictions and deregulate the domestic markets in all the major industrialized economies. For instance, in the US financial markets the dividing line between banking and the securities business has become increasingly nebulous. Several restrictions have been eliminated between

Eurocurrency markets in Germany and the UK, encouraging the merging of domestic and offshore capital markets. The most recent steps in this direction were taken by the Japanese authorities who have freed interest rates through a reduction in the minimum size of deposits bearing full market rates. Steps to liberalize Euro-yen lending and encourage the development of domestic money markets are also under way. Dismantling of restrictions on the entry of foreign banks and financial institutions in domestic markets stimulated the market integration process. Since the foreign banks lack the base of retail business, they do most of their business with other customers and other banks, yet they do make the domestic markets more competitive. In this context, it should be noted that the OECD has a code regarding the freedom of capital movement and the industrial countries are party to this code. However, some industrial countries are still opposed to the idea of allowing the takeover of large domestic banks and securities houses by non-residents.

An economic integration process in the EC is at present under way and several dramatic strides have been made towards the integration of financial markets. Likewise, under the US-Canada Free Trade Agreement similar efforts are under way in North America. In the EC, the Second Banking Directive allows a Community bank to perform throughout the Community all the functions it is authorized to perform in its home country. Since several important measures have already been taken and there is a high degree of commitment to integrating financial services in the Community, the remaining restrictions will fizzle away gradually. In addition, the freedom of capital movements will pressurize the authorities to harmonize taxes and other regulations.

The blurring of distinctions between different instruments is another characteristic feature of the current capital markets. Although the distinction between syndicated loans and bonds exists, syndicate banks are becoming more like underwriters because they tend to sell off almost all the loan participation to other banks and financial institutions. The note issuing programmes adopted by corporate borrowers used to be a prerogative of banks in the past. The integration process in the financial markets has been assisted by growth and expansion of the derivative products. They have managed to increase the efficiency of the financial markets at both national and international levels. Integration of the international financial markets leads to globalization of investor and borrower behaviour. Let us look at that now.

Globalization

Over the 1980s, large institutional investors dominated the assets issued on international capital markets. A large proportion of assets were issued by insurance companies, pension funds, mutual funds and other investment trusts. The institutional investors have a markedly different behavioural pattern from that of individual investors which, in turn, has important implications for the development of capital markets. They are under intense competitive pressure and are better placed to use the derivative products to adjust their portfolios than individual investors are. They also respond more rapidly to market developments and their moves are well researched, which implies that the institutional investors have a shorter time horizon than the individual investors.

There has been a strong tendency among institutional investors to turn to foreign assets to reduce the volatility of their returns and steady their earnings. For instance, the share of foreign equities and bonds in the total portfolio of UK pension funds rose from 5 per cent in 1979 to 20 per cent in 1988. The foreign securities in total securities holdings of life insurance companies rose from 15 per cent in 1981 to 31 per cent in 1988. However, most countries for prudential reasons regulate and limit the amount of foreign assets that can be acquired, although these regulations are now dwindling.

The globalization trend in the financial markets was assisted by the advances in financial information and telecommunications technology and the emergence of the derivative products markets. Together they changed their roles of institutional investors and financial intermediaries. The large market power of these investors increased the scope and reduced the cost of financial engineering, *i.e.* the creation of customized products for both borrowers and investors. At present, in many markets large institutional investors can obtain tailor-made assets that are not available to the general public. The telecommunications technology now also allows these investors to circumvent the middleman function of the securities houses and have a direct real-time access to capital markets and bid on securities directly as they are issued. In fact, 'disintermediation' became a buzz word of the late 1980s.

BUILDING AND MANAGING BRAND EQUITY

In his 1989 document, Managing Brand Equity, Peter H. Farquhar outlined the following three stages that are required in order to build a strong brand:

1. *Introduction*: Introduce a quality product with the strategy of using the brand as a platform from which to launch future products. A positive evaluation by the consumer is important.
2. *Elaboration*: Make the brand easy to remember and develop repeat usage. There should be accessible brand attitude, that is, the consumer should easily remember his or her positive evaluation of the brand.
3. *Fortification*: The brand should carry a consistent image over time to reinforce its place in the consumer's mind and develop a special relationship with the consumer. Brand extensions can further fortify the brand, but only with related products having a perceived fit in the mind of the consumer.

ALTERNATIVE MEANS TO BRAND EQUITY

Building brand equity requires a significant effort, and some companies use alternative means of achieving the benefits of a strong brand. For example, brand equity can be borrowed by extending the brand name to a line of products in the same product category or even to other categories. In some cases, especially when there is a perceptual connection between the products, such extensions are successful. In other cases, the extensions are unsuccessful and can dilute the original brand equity.

Brand equity also can be "bought" by licensing the use of a strong brand for a new product. As in line extensions by the same company, the success of brand licensing is not guaranteed and must be analysed carefully for appropriateness.

MANAGING MULTIPLE BRANDS

Different companies have opted for different brand strategies for multiple products.

These strategies are:

- *Single brand identity*: A separate brand for each product. For example, in laundry detergents Procter & Gamble offers uniquely positioned brands such as Tide, Cheer, Bold, etc.
- *Umbrella*: All products under the same brand. For example, Sony offers many different product categories under its brand.
- *Multi-brand categories*: Different brands for different product categories. Campbell Soup Company uses Campbell's for soups, Pepperidge Farm for baked goods, and V8 for juices.
- *Family of names*: Different brands having a common name stem. Nestle uses Nescafe, Nesquik, and Nestea for beverages.

Brand equity is an important factor in multi-product branding strategies.

PROTECTING BRAND EQUITY

The marketing mix should focus on building and protecting brand equity. For example, if the brand is positioned as a premium product, the product quality should be consistent with what consumers expect of the brand, low sale prices should not be used compete, the distribution channels should be consistent with what is expected of a premium brand, and the promotional campaign should build consistent associations. Finally, potentially dilutive extensions that are inconsistent with the consumer's perception of the brand should be avoided. Extensions also should be avoided if the core brand is not yet sufficiently strong.

BRAND EQUITY

A brand is a name or symbol used to identify the source of a product. When developing a new product, branding is an important decision. The brand can add significant value when it is well recognized and has positive associations in the mind of the consumer. This concept is referred to as brand equity.

WHAT IS BRAND EQUITY

Brand equity is an intangible asset that depends on associations made by the consumer.

There are at least three perspectives from which to view brand equity:

- *Financial*: One way to measure brand equity is to determine the price premium that a brand commands over a generic product. For example, if consumers are willing to pay $100 more for a branded television over the same unbranded television, this premium provides important information about the value of the brand. However, expenses such as promotional costs must be taken into account when using this method to measure brand equity.
- *Brand extensions*: A successful brand can be used as a platform to launch related products. The benefits of brand extensions are the leveraging of existing brand awareness thus reducing advertising expenditures, and a lower risk from the perspective of the consumer. Furthermore, appropriate brand extensions can enhance the core brand. However, the value of brand extensions is more difficult to quantify than are direct financial measures of brand equity.
- *Consumer-based*: A strong brand increases the consumer's attitude strength towards the product associated with the brand. Attitude strength is built by experience with a product. This importance of actual experience by the customer implies that trial samples are more effective than advertising in the early stages of building a strong brand. The consumer's awareness and associations lead to perceived quality, inferred attributes, and eventually, brand loyalty.

Strong brand equity provides the following benefits:

- Facilitates a more predictable income stream.
- Increases cash flow by increasing market share, reducing promotional costs, and allowing premium pricing.
- Brand equity is an asset that can be sold or leased.

However, brand equity is not always positive in value. Some brands acquire a bad reputation that results in negative brand equity. Negative brand equity can be measured by surveys in which consumers indicate that a discount is needed to purchase the brand over a generic product.

MEASURING OUTCOMES OF BRAND EQUITY

The previous part described different approaches for marketers to gain a good understanding of consumer brand knowledge structures to be able to identify and quantify potential sources of brand equity. As a consequence of creating such knowledge structures, consumers should respond more favourably to the marketing activity for a brand than if the brand had not been identified to consumers.

Specifically, a product with positive brand equity can potentially enjoy the following seven important customer-related benefits:

1. Be perceived differently and produce different interpretations of product performance;
2. Enjoy greater loyalty and be less vulnerable to competitive marketing actions;
3. Command larger margins and have more inelastic responses to price increases and elastic responses to price decreases;
4. Receive greater trade cooperation and support;
5. Increase marketing communication effectiveness;
6. Yield licensing opportunities;
7. Support brand extensions.

These benefits, and thus the ultimate value of a brand, depends on the underlying components of brand knowledge and sources of brand equity. Via the indirect approach, individual components can be measured, but to provide more direct estimates, their resulting value still must be estimated in some way. The direct approach to measuring customer-based brand equity attempts to more explicitly assess the impact of brand knowledge on consumer response to different aspects of the marketing programme for the firm. The direct approach is useful in approximating the possible outcomes and benefits that arise from differential response to marketing activity due to the brand, either individually or in aggregate.

Comparative Methods

The main way to measure the outcomes and benefits of brand equity is with comparative methods. Comparative methods involve experiments that examine consumer attitudes and behaviour towards a brand to more directly estimate the benefits arising from having a high awareness and a positive brand image. There are two types of comparative methods. Brand-based comparative approaches use experiments in which one group of consumers respond to the marketing programme or some marketing activity when it is attributed to the target brand and another group responds to that same activity when it is attributed to a competitive or fictitiously named brand.

Marketing-based comparative approaches use experiments where consumers respond to changes in the marketing programme or marketing activity for the target brand or competitive brands. We describe each of these two approaches in turn. Conjoint analysis is then identified as a technique that, in effect, combines the two approaches.

Brand-based Comparative Approaches

As a means of measuring the outcomes of brand equity, brand-based comparative approaches hold the marketing activity under consideration fixed and examine consumer response based on changes in brand identification. These measurement approaches typically employ experiments where one group of consumers respond to questions about the product or some aspect of its marketing programme when it is attributed to the brand and one groups of consumers respond to the same product or aspect of the marketing programme when it is attributed to some other brand or brands, typically a fictitiously named or unnamed version of the product or service or one or more competitive brands.

Comparing the responses of the two groups provides some useful insights into the equity of the brand. Consumer responses may be on the basis of beliefs, attitudes, intentions, actual behaviour or even feelings. The classic example of the brand-based comparative approach is "blind testing" research studies where consumers examine or use a product with or without brand identification. These studies often reveal how dramatically consumer perceptions differ depending on the presence or absence of brand identification.

Brand-based comparative approaches are also especially useful to determine brand equity benefits related to price margins and premiums. Critique. The main advantage to a brand-based comparative approach is that — because it holds all aspects of the marketing programme fixed except for the brand — it isolates the value of a brand in a very real sense. Understanding exactly how knowledge of the brand affects consumer responses to prices, advertising, etc. is extremely useful in developing strategies in these different areas. At the same time, there is almost an infinite variety of marketing activities that potentially could be studied so that the totality of what is learned will depend on how many different applications are examined. A crucial consideration with the brand-based comparative approach is the experimental realism that can be achieved when some aspect of the marketing programme is attributed to a fictitiously named or unnamed version of the product or service.

Brand-based comparative methods are particularly applicable when the marketing activity under consideration represents a change from past marketing of the brand, e.g., a new sales or trade promotion, ad campaign, or proposed brand extension. If the marketing activity under consideration is already strongly identified with the brand, it may be difficult to attribute some aspect of the marketing programme to a fictitiously named or unnamed version of the product or service in a believable fashion.

There will necessarily be a tradeoff involving a sacrifice of some realism in order to gain sufficient control to be able to isolate the effects of brand knowledge. Detailed concept statements of the particular marketing activity under consideration can be employed in some situations when it may be otherwise difficult for consumers to examine or experience that element of the marketing programme without being aware of the brand. Nevertheless, a concern with brand-based comparative approaches is that the simulations and concept statements that are used may highlight those particular characteristics that are mentioned or featured and make them more salient than they would otherwise be, distorting the results.

Marketing-based Comparative Approaches

Marketing-based comparative approaches hold the brand fixed and examines consumer response based on changes in the marketing programme. For example, there is a long tradition exploring price premiums with these types of comparative approaches. In the mid-1950's, Pessemier developed a dollarmetric measure of brand commitment which involved a step-by-step increase of the price difference between the brand normally purchased and an alternative brand.

Variations of this approach have been adopted by a number of marketing research suppliers to derive similar types of demand curves, and many firms now try to assess price sensitivity and thresholds for different brands. For example, Intel has routinely surveyed computer shoppers to find out how much of a discount they would require before switching to a personal computer which did not have an Intel microprocessor in it or, conversely, what premium they would be willing to pay to buy a personal computer with an Intel microprocessor in it. Marketing-based comparative approaches can be applied in other ways. Consumer response to different advertising strategies, executions or media plans can be assessed through multiple test markets.

For example, IRI's electronic test markets and other such research methodologies can permit tests of different advertising weights or repetition schedules as well as ad copy tests. By controlling for other factors, the effects of the brand and product can be isolated. Potential brand extensions can also be explored in this fashion by collecting consumer evaluation to a range of concept statements describing brand extension candidates.

Critique. The main advantage with the marketing-based comparative approach is the ease of implementation. Virtually any proposed set of marketing actions can be compared for the brand. At the same time, the main drawback of the comparative approach is that it may be difficult to discern whether consumer response to changes in the marketing stimuli are being caused by brand knowledge or more generic product knowledge. In other words, it may be that for any brand in the product category, consumers would be willing or unwilling to pay certain prices, accept a particular brand extension, etc. One way to determine whether consumer response is specific to the brand or not is to conduct similar tests of consumer response with competitive brands, e.g., via conjoint analysis.

Conjoint Analysis

Conjoint analysis is a survey-based multivariate technique that enables marketers to profile the consumer buying decision process with respect to products and brands. Specifically, by asking consumers to express preferences or make choices among a number of carefully designed different product profiles, marketing researchers can determine the "trade-offs" consumers are making between various brand attributes and thus the importance that consumers are attaching to those attributes.

From a brand equity perspective, the main advantage of the conjoint approach is that it allows for both different brands and different aspects of the product or marketing programme to be simultaneously studied. Thus, information about consumers response to different marketing activities can be uncovered for both the focal and competing brands. One of the disadvantages of conjoint analysis is that marketing profiles may be presented to consumers that violate their expectations based on what they already know about brands. Thus, if conjoint analysis is employed, care must be taken that consumers do not evaluate unrealistic product profiles or scenarios. Additionally, it can be difficult to specify and interpret brand attribute levels, although some useful guidelines have been out forth to more effectively apply conjoint analysis to brand positioning problems.

Holistic Methods

Comparative methods attempt to approximate specific benefits of brand equity. Holistic methods attempt to place an overall value for the brand in either abstract utility terms or concrete financial terms. Thus, holistic methods attempt to "net out" various considerations to determine the unique contribution of the brand.

The residual approach attempts to examine the value of the brand by subtracting out consumers' preferences for the brand based on physical product attributes alone from their overall brand preferences. The valuation approach attempts to place a financial value on brand equity for accounting purposes, mergers and acquisitions, or other such reasons. We describe each of these two approaches in turn.

Residual Approaches

Several researchers have employed "residual approaches" to estimate brand equity. A basic tenet behind these approaches is that it is possible to infer the relative valuation of brands through the observation of consumer preferences and choices if as many sources of measured attribute values are taken into account as possible. According to these approaches brand equity is what remains of consumer preferences and choices after subtracting out objective characteristics of the physical product. Some researchers, e.g., Barwise et al., however, have challenged the separability assumption implicit in these approaches.

Dillon et al. present a model for decomposing ratings of a brand on an attribute into two components:

1. Brand-specific associations and
2. General brand impressions.

They empirically demonstrate their model properties in three product categories: Cars, toothpaste, and document towels. Critique. Residual approaches provide a useful benchmark to interpret brand equity. In particular, they may be useful for situations when approximations of brand equity are necessary and thus may also be valuable to researchers interested in a financially-oriented perspective on brand equity. The disadvantages with these approaches is that they are most appropriate for brands characterized with a predominance of product-related attribute associations because they are unable to distinguish between different types of non-product-related attribute associations. Consequently, its diagnostic value for strategic decision-making in other cases is much more limited. More generally, note also that residual approaches takes more of a "static" view of brand equity by attempting to identify sources of consumer preferences in order to uncover the contribution by the brand.

This approach contrasts sharply with a "process" view, as reflected by the brand-based and marketing-based comparative approaches, which stress looking at consumer response to the marketing of a brand and attempt to uncover the extent to which that consumer response is affected by brand knowledge. Consumer response is defined in terms of perceptions, preferences, and behaviours and, most importantly, with respect to a variety of marketing activities. That is, comparative approaches go beyond attempting to dissect overall consumer product preferences towards a brand to assess how consumers actually respond to the marketing of a brand and, especially, new marketing activity supporting it.

Valuation Approaches

The ability to evaluate and put a price tag on a brand's value may be useful for a number of reasons:

- *Mergers and acquisitions*: Both to evaluate possible purchases as well as to facilitate disposal;
- *Brand licensing*: Internally for tax reasons and to third parties;
- *fund raising*: As collateral on loans or for sale or leaseback arrangements; and
- *Brand management decisions*: To allocate resources, develop brand strategy, or prepare financial reports.

For example, many companies are attractive acquisition candidates because of the strong competitive positions of their brands and their reputation with consumers. Unfortunately, the value of the brand assets in many cases is largely excluded from the company's balance sheet and therefore of little use in determining the firm's value. It has been argued that adjusting the balance sheet to reflect the true value of a company's brands permits a more realistic view and allows assessment of the purchase premium to book value that might be earned from the brands after acquisition.

Such a calculation, however, would require estimates of capital required by brands and the expected after-acquisition return-on-investment of a company. Separating out the percentage of revenue or profits that is attributable to brand equity is a difficult task. In the U.S., there is no conventional accounting method for doing so, and marketbased estimates of value can differ dramatically from those based on U.S. accounting conventions.

In determining the value of a brand in an acquisition or merger, three main approaches are possible:

- *Cost approach*: This view maintains that brand equity is the amount of money that would be required to reproduce or replace the brand. One commonly noted criticism of approaches involving historic or replacement cost is that it rewards past performance in a way that may bear little relation to future profitability — e.g., many brands with expensive introductions have been unsuccessful. On the other hand, for brands such as Heinz, Kellogg's, and Chanel who have been around for decades, it would be virtually impossible to find out what was the investment in brand development – and largely irrelevant too. Finally, it obviously is easier to estimate costs of tangible assets than intangible assets but the latter often may lie at the heart of brand equity. Similar problems would exist with a replacement cost approach – e.g., the cost of replacing a brand would depend a great deal on how quickly the process were to take and what competitive, legal, logistical obstacles that might be encountered.
- *Market approach*: According to this view, brand equity can be thought of as the present value of the future economic benefits to be derived by the owner of the asset. In other words, the amount an active market would allow such that the asset would exchange between a willing buyer and willing seller. The main problem with this approach is the lack of open market transactions for brand name assets and the fact that the uniqueness of brands makes extrapolating from one market transaction to another problematic.
- *Income approach*: The third approach to determining the value of a brand argues that brand equity is the discounted future cash flow from the future earnings stream for the brand. Three such income approaches are:
  - Capitalizing royalty earnings from a brand name;
  - Capitalizing the premium profits which are earned by a branded product;
  - Capitalizing the actual profitability of a brand after allowing for the costs of maintaining it and the effects of taxation.

- *Interbrand methodology*: Interbrand follows a methodology that is largely based on an income approach. According to Interbrand, to capture the complex value creation of a brand, the following five valuation steps brand should be performed
  - *Market Segmentation*: Split the consumer market for the brand into nonoverlapping and homogenous groups of consumers according to applicable criteria such as product or service, distribution channels, consumption patterns, purchase sophistication, geography, existing and new customers, etc. The brand is valued in each segment and the sum of the segment valuations constitutes the total value of the brand.
  - *Financial Analysis*: Identify and forecast revenues and "earnings from intangibles' generated by the brand for each of the distinct segments determined in step 1. Intangible Earnings are defined as: Branded revenues less operating costs, applicable taxes and a charge for the capital employed. The concept is similar to the notion of economic profit.
  - *Demand Analysis*: Assess the role that the brand plays in driving demand for products and services in the markets in which it operates. The proportion of Intangible Earnings attributable to the brand is measured by an indicator referred to as the 'Role of Branding Index' by first identifying the various drivers of demand for the branded business, then determining the degree to which each driver is directly influenced by the brand. The Role of Branding represents the percentage of Intangible Earnings that are generated by the brand. Brand Earnings are derived by multiplying the Role of Branding by Intangible Earnings.
  - *Competitive Benchmarking*: Determine the competitive strengths and weaknesses of the brand. A specific Brand Discount Rate that reflects the risk profile of its expected future earnings is derived via a 'Brand Strength Score.' This measure comprises extensive competitive benchmarking and a structured evaluation of the brand's market, stability, leadership position, growth trend, support, geographic footprint and legal protectability.
  - *Brand Value Calculation*: Calculate the Brand Value as the net present value of the forecast Brand Earnings, discounted by the Brand Discount Rate. The NPV calculation comprises both the forecast period and the period beyond, reflecting the ability of brands to continue generating future earnings.

BRAND PERFORMANCE

Brand performance relates to the ways in which the product or service attempts to meet customers' more functional needs. Thus, brand performance refers to the intrinsic properties of the brand in terms of inherent product or service characteristics. How well does the brand rate on objective assessments of quality? To what extent does the brand satisfy utilitarian, aesthetic, and economic customer needs and wants in the product or service category? The specific performance attributes and benefits making up functionality will vary widely by category.

Nevertheless, there are five important types of attributes and benefits that often underlie brand performance and can be measured, as follows:

1. *Primary characteristics & supplementary features*: Customers often have beliefs about the levels at which the primary characteristics of the product operate. Additionally, they may also may have beliefs as to special, perhaps even patented, features or secondary elements of a product that complement these primary characteristics.
2. *Product reliability, durability, & serviceability*: Reliability refers to the consistency of performance over time and from purchase to purchase. Durability refers to the expected economic life of the product. Serviceability refers to the ease of servicing the product if it needs repair. Thus, measures of product performance can capture factors such as the speed, accuracy, and care of product delivery and installation; the promptness, courtesy, and helpfulness of customer service and training; the quality of repair service and the time involved; and so on.
3. *Service effectiveness, efficiency, and empathy*: Service effectiveness refers to how completely the brand satisfies customers' service requirements. Service efficiency refers to the manner by which these services are delivered in terms of speed, responsiveness, etc. Service empathy refers to the extent to which service providers are seen as trusting, caring, and with customer's interests in mind.
4. *Style and design*: Consumers may have associations to the product that go beyond its functional aspects to more aesthetic considerations such as its size, shape, materials, and colour involved. Thus, performance may also depend on sensory aspects as to how a product looks and feels and perhaps even what it sounds or smells like.
5. *Price*: Finally, the pricing policy for the brand can create associations in consumers' minds to the relevant price tier or level for the brand in the category, as well as to its corresponding price volatility or variance.

Brand Imagery

The other main type of brand meaning involves brand imagery. Brand imagery deals with the extrinsic properties of the product or service, including the ways in which the brand attempts to meet customers' more psychological or social needs. Brand imagery is how people think about a brand abstractly rather than what they think the brand actually does. Thus, imagery refers to more intangible aspects of the brand.

All different kinds of intangibles can be linked to a brand, but five categories can be highlighted:

1. *User profiles*: The type of person or organization who uses the brand. This imagery may result in a profile or mental image by customers of actual users or more aspirational, idealized users. Associations of a typical or idealized brand user may be based on descriptive demographic factors or more abstract psychographic factors. In a business-to-business setting, user imagery might relate to the size or type of organization.
2. *Purchase situations*: Under what conditions or situations the brand could or should be bought and used. Associations of a typical purchase situation may be based on a number of different considerations, such as:
   - Type of channel;
   - Specific store; and
   - Ease of purchase and associated rewards, if any.
3. Usage situations: Under what conditions or situations the brand could or should be used. Associations of a typical usage situation may be based on a number of different considerations, such as:
   - Particular time of the day, week, month, or year to use the brand;
   - Location to use the brand; and
   - Type of activity where the brand is used.
4. Personality and values. Brands may also take on personality traits and values similar to people. Brand personality is often related to the more descriptive usage imagery but involves much richer, more contextual information.
5. History, heritage, and experiences. Finally, brands may take on associations to their past and certain noteworthy events in the brand history. These types of associations may involve distinctly personal experiences and episodes or be related to past behaviours and experiences of friends, family, or others.

For example, take a brand with rich brand imagery, such as Nivea skin cream in Europe. Some of its more intangible associations include: family/

shared experiences/maternal; multpurpose; classic/timeless; and childhood memories.

General, Higher-order Brand Associations

The purpose of measuring higher-order brand associations is to find out how consumers combine all of the specific considerations about the brand in their minds to form different responses. Brand responses refer to how customers respond to the brand and all its marketing activity and other sources of information. Brand responses can be distinguished according to brand judgments and brand feelings, i.e., in terms of whether they arise more from the "head" or from the "heart." Scale questions can be developed to tap into each of these dimensions.

Brand Judgments

Brand judgments focus upon customers' own personal opinions and evaluations with regard to the brand. Brand judgments involve how customers put together all the different performance and imagery associations for the brand to form different kinds of opinions.

Although customers may make all types of judgments with respect to a brand, four types of summary brand judgments are particularly important:

1. *Brand quality*: Among the most important attitudes that customers may hold relates to the perceived quality of the brand. Other notable attitudes related to quality pertain to perceptions of value and satisfaction.
2. *Brand credibility*: Customers may form judgments that transcend more specific brand quality concerns. Brand credibility refers to the extent to which the company or organization making the product or providing the service as a whole is seen as being:
   - Competent, innovative, and a market leader;
   - Dependable and keeping customer interests in mind; and
   - Fun, interesting, and worth spending time with.
3. Brand consideration. Consideration deals with the likelihood that customers will actually include the brand in the set of possible options of brands they might buy or use. Consideration depends in part on how personally relevant customers find the brand, i.e., the extent to which customers view the brand as being appropriate and meaningful to themselves.
4. Brand superiority. Finally, superiority relates to the extent to which customers view the brand as unique and better than other brands. Do customers believe that the brand offers advantages that other brands cannot?

Brand Feelings

Brand feelings are customers' emotional responses and reactions with respect to the brand. Brand feelings also relate to the social currency evoked by the brand. What feelings are evoked by the marketing programme for the brand or by other means? How does the brand affect customers' feelings about themselves and their relationship with others? These feelings can be mild or intense and be positive or negative in nature.

Six important types of brand-building feelings are:

1. *Warmth*: Warmth refers to more soothing types of feelings – the extent to which the brand makes consumers feel a sense of calm or peacefulness. Consumers may feel sentimental, warmhearted, or affectionate about the brand. Hallmark is a brand typically associated with warmth.
2. *Fun*: Feelings of fun are also upbeat types of feelings when the brand makes consumers feel amused, light-hearted, joyous, playful, cheerful, and so on. Disney is a brand often associated with fun.
3. *Excitement*: Excitement relates to more upbeat types of feelings – the extent to which the brand makes consumers feel energized and a feeling that they are experiencing something special. Brands that evoke feelings of excitement may result in consumers feeling a sense of elation or "being alive" – cool, sexy, etc. MTV is a brand seen by many teens and young adults as exciting.
4. *Security*: Security feelings occur when the brand produces a feeling of safety, comfort, and self-assurance. Feelings of security are when consumers do not experience worry or concerns that they might have otherwise felt as a result of the brand. Allstate insurance is a brand that communicates security to many.
5. *Social approval*: Social approval is when the brand results in consumers having positive feelings about the reactions of others – i.e., when consumers feel others look favourably on their appearance, behaviour, and so on. This approval may be a result of direct acknowledgement of the consumer using the brand by others or less overt and a result of attribution of the product itself to consumers. Mercedes is a brand that may signal social approval to consumers.
6. *Self-respect*: Self-respect occurs when the brand makes consumers feel better about themselves, e.g., when consumers feel a sense of pride, accomplishment or fulfillment. A brand like Tide laundry detergent is able to link its brand to "doing the best things for the family" to many homemakers.

The first three are more experiential and immediate, increasing in level of intensity. The latter three are more private and enduring, increasing in level of gravity.

Key Success Criteria

Although all types of customer responses are possible – driven from both the "head and heart" – ultimately what matters is how positive and unique they are. Additionally, it is also important that they are also accessible and come to mind when consumers think of the brand. Brand performance, imagery, judgments, or feelings can only favourably impact consumer behaviour if it is the case that consumers internalize or think of positive meaning or responses in any of their encounters with the brand.

Index

A

Accomplishes 188
Acquisitions 279, 280
Aforementioned 264
Agreeableness 116, 118, 120
Algorithm 201
AMD 96
ANOVA 199, 200
ASP 235
Assessment 245, 266, 280, 283
Assumptions 77, 121

B

Bankruptcy 130
Brand Equity 268, 270
Branding Decisions 267
Branding Strategy 269, 270
Brochures 233
Brokerage 153
Business-level 167

C

Campaigns 52, 53, 54, 247, 261, 279, 282
Capabilities 130, 135, 234, 256
Competency 135
Compulsiveness 234
Conceptual 115, 118, 122
Conscientiousness 116, 117, 118, 120
Consumer Behaviour 72
Consumerism 240, 244, 245, 246, 247
Contemporary 115, 116, 240
Convenient Method 232
Corporate Branding 262, 263
Criteria 76, 77, 100, 189, 201, 262
CRM 230, 231, 233, 236, 237, 247
Cross Tabulations 197

D

Defensive 174
Dimensions 164, 166, 173
Diversification 76, 130, 142
Dramatically 68, 208

E

Elaboration 273
Elements 128, 129, 167
Emphasizes 134
Empowerment 113
Endorsement 151
Environmental Analysis 164, 167
Equilibrium 18
Exaggerated 21, 23
Expense 168, 169
Extroversion 234
Extroversion-introversion 116

F

Fictitiously 276, 277
Fluctuations 199

Formulation 128, 129
Fortification 273
FTC 246

G

Goals 127, 128, 129, 167

H

Hazardous 21
Heterogeneous 113, 201
Hierarchy 114, 123
Holistic Methods 279
Homogeneous 113

I

ICMA 115
Indebtedness 76
Industry Analysis 164, 165, 166, 167, 173
Inventory Management 54, 55

L

Lateral Linkages 129
Legislation 47

M

Managing Product Movement 54
Market Diversity 72
Marketing Environment 71
Marketing Strategy 55
Mission 128
MkIS 231, 232

N

Neuroticism 116, 117, 120, 121
NPV 144, 282

O

Occurrence 197
OCEAN Model 120
Offensive 168, 174

P

Portfolio 99
Potential Entrants 172
Power 164, 165, 167, 169, 170, 171, 172
Preliminary 197
Price 166, 168, 169, 170, 171, 172, 173, 174
Procurement 34, 156
Product Positioning 55, 268
Product Storage 54, 57
Profitability 21, 53, 130, 150, 153, 281
Protectability 282
Protection 57

Q

Quantifiable 78, 114

R

Repositioning 208, 256
Revenue 169, 171, 172
ROI 35

S

Solicitations 45, 46
Sophisticated 231, 240
Substantially 47
Substitute Products 172
Suppliers 164, 166, 167, 168, 170, 171, 172, 173
SWOT 32, 99, 100, 111

T

Tangible 2, 4, 77, 207
Taxonomy 117, 118, 120, 121
Testimonials 266

U

Unscrupulous 23, 134
Unsolicited 23, 45, 47, 48